GREAT SCHISMS
IN JEWISH HISTORY

GREAT SCHISMS
IN JEWISH HISTORY

Edited by
RAPHAEL JOSPE
and
STANLEY M. WAGNER

CENTER FOR JUDAIC STUDIES
UNIVERSITY OF DENVER
and
KTAV PUBLISHING HOUSE, INC.
NEW YORK
1981

Library of Congress Cataloging in Publication Data
Main entry under title:

Great schisms in Jewish history.

Includes bibliographies and index.
1. Jewish sects—History—Addresses, essays, lectures.
2. Faith and reason (Jewish theology)—History of
doctrines—Addresses, essays, lectures.   3. Hasidism—
History—Addresses, essays, lectures.   4. Haskalah—
History—Addresses, essays, lectures.   5. Judaism—
United States—History—Addresses, essays, lectures.
I. Jospe, Raphael.   II. Wagner, Stanley M.   III.   Den-
ver. University. Center for Judaic Studies.
BM175.A1G73   296.8   80-21041
ISBN 0-87068-711-5

Manufactured in the United States of America

This volume is dedicated
to the memory of
Benjamin Cohen
by his wife Anna,
his children, Shep, Dorothy and Leonard,
and by his grandchildren
Matthew, Ruth, Benjamin and Aharona

Contents

Preface

THE PAPERS in this volume were originally delivered as lectures in the Benjamin Cohen Memorial Lecture Series of the Center for Judaic Studies of the University of Denver in 1978. The lecture series, as well as the publication of this volume, was made possible through the generosity of Dr. Shep Cohen, in memory of his father. The Center for Judaic Studies, the University of Denver, and the Denver Jewish community are deeply grateful to Dr. Cohen for his continued and generous support of Jewish educational and cultural programs, for sharing the vision that the Center for Judaic Studies must combine academic scholarship with community involvement, and for helping to ensure the realization of that vision.

The editors also wish to thank the authors for giving so generously of their time in preparing the original lectures, for their willing and friendly cooperation in revising the papers when necessary, and for their dedication to the concept of a unified volume presenting a study of six of the most serious internal conflicts in Jewish history.

Raphael Jospe

Tevet 5740/January 1980

Introduction

WEBSTER'S DICTIONARY defines "schism" as "division, separation, discord, disharmony, or formal division or separation . . . from a church or religious body, a condition of disagreement in opinion, (or) a division of a group into two discordant groups."[1] In one form or another, and at one time or another, these definitions all applied to the dynamics of Jewish life.

The existence of "splinter groups" is as old as the Jewish nation itself. Division and divisiveness can, in a way, be traced back to the controversy between the "herdmen of Abram's cattle and the herdmen of Lot's cattle,"[2] which resulted in Abram's suggestion, "Separate thyself, I pray thee, from me; if thou wilt take the left hand, then I will go to the right; or if thou take the right hand, then I will go to the left."[3] Throughout the ages, divisiveness has been a characteristic of the people of Israel, with part of the Jewish corpus on the "left" and the other on the "right" of the argument as to what constituted "authenticity" in Judaism.

The Torah describes the Jews' continual murmuring against the leadership of Moses and Aaron. But the greatest rebellion, led by Korah and his company,[4] may well have represented a differing and rival conception of legitimate political leadership of the nation, although, according to tradition, it was a religious dispute, for Korah and those with him were demonstrating against Moses for the inconsistencies and irrationality of "his" Torah.[5] As an organized ideological revolt, this may have been the first "schism" in Jewish history.

So was it through the ages. Separate and distinct from forms of personal or individualistic nonconformity, dissidence, and even heresy, groups always arose, calling for new allegiances, divergent approaches to Judaism, and new sets of discipline, which claimed exclusive Jewish authenticity and traditional authority, while branding the other groups as "defectors," "separatists," "protestants," "sectarians," or "heretics." The divisions in biblical Israel may have set the stage for the Jewish sectarianism marked by "groundless hatred" (*sin'at ḥinam*) between Jews that traditionally has been regarded as contributing to, or even causing, the destruction of the Second Temple and the dissolution of the Jewish State.[6]

It was more of a hope than a reality when the Talmud pronounced:

> The Holy One, blessed be He, said to Israel: You have made me one entity [*ḥativah aḥat*] in the world, and I have made you one entity in the world. You have made me one entity in the world, as it is said: "Hear, O Israel, the Lord our God, the Lord is one." And I shall make you one entity in the world, as it is said: "And who is like Thy people Israel, a nation one in the earth."[7]

It appears almost as if the Jewish people flew in the face of the biblical injunction, *lo titgodedu*, "ye shall not cut yourselves,"[8] as interpreted by the Sages, "ye shall not divide yourselves into many groupings."[9] Indeed, prior to the destruction of the Second Temple, so divided was the Jewish community that there were no less than twenty-four groups of Jewish sectarians.[10] Even at the height of medieval corporativism, Jewish life was far from monolithic, and in modern times, without the embracing benefit of a formal "organic" community structure, the divisions have become institutionalized as rival movements, organizations, and denominations.

This volume, *Great Schisms in Jewish History*, attempts to describe only those divisions in Jewish life of such magnitude that they could be considered convulsive. From it, many fascinating insights flow which enhance our perceptions of Jewish history and Jewish life. Schisms, it will be seen, are of a diverse nature. The Jewish community could be "fractured" in several ways:

1. *Geographically*, the Diaspora almost reduced the Jewish people to a scattering of tribes. The Judaism of Christian Europe

and the Judaism of the world of Islam, for example, often developed differently, not only halakhically and liturgically, but also in terms of the Jews' education and values. For example, the Jews of Christian Europe were often unexposed to the secular learning, philosophy, and science of their brothers in the Arab world, and the medieval controversy over philosophy often represents the European Jewish reaction—sometimes violent—to pursuits long accepted as legitimate by Jews living under Islamic rule.

2. *Sociologically,* the clashing strata within Jewish society—in Second Commonwealth times, the urban Jew and the rural Jew, the priestly aristocracy and the middle-class scholars; and in America, two millenia later, the Eastern European Jewish immigrants and the earlier Jewish immigrants from Central Europe—ruptured the harmony of Jewish communal life.

3. *Politically,* "zealots" for political causes and their opponents were often responsible for serious eruptions in Jewish life, as in conflicts arising out of Israel's need to establish an alliance with Egypt or Babylonia in biblical times, the question of the wisdom of rebelling against Rome in the first century, leftist commitment to the class struggle versus Zionism and other nationalist ideologies, support for civil rights and the struggles of other groups, or insistence on "what's good for the Jews."

4. *Ideologically,* is "faith" supreme above "reason"; should the Jewish community be "isolationist" in order to survive, or can it successfully synthesize or syncretize alien cultural elements without compromising its spiritual integrity? Should the Jews embrace or resist secular modernity, in the form of enlightenment and emancipation?

5. *Spiritually,* the binding authority of the oral law, and which oral laws; the validity of "tradition," and which traditions; the principles of continuity and change in ritual practice and worship; the need to preserve traditional interpretive authority versus democratic or individualistic interpretation—all these are questions which continually agitated the Jewish community.

It is interesting to note that in almost every case, the internal schism in Jewish life was precipitated or enlarged by external factors or circumstances. The intrusion of the Canaanite culture on the Israelite community living in the Holy Land, for example, was but the precursor of subsequent cultural incursions— Hellenistic, Christian, Islamic, and secularist—which were responsible for varied and divergent organized responses to those challenges to Jewish survival. Similarly, Jewish exile and homelessness, the massacres, pogroms, and persecutions to which Jews were invariably subjected, and the political context in which Jews lived, all played a significant role in shaping the assorted attitudes and positions, the propensities and philosophies which divided Jews from Jews. In this sense, a companion volume to this work is the Center for Judaic Studies' *Great Confrontations in Jewish History*,[11] which describes the nature of these sometimes cataclysmic encounters.

Judaism has persevered despite the allure of pagan cultures, the hostility of worlds set against it, and, most importantly, its worst enemy, internal divisiveness. On occasion, schisms perpetuated themselves, as in the case of the Pharisee-Sadducee, Rabbanite-Karaite, and Orthodox-Reform controversies as to the binding character of the Oral Law, with a similar scenario, but new players on the stage of Jewish history. In some instances, disputes became virulent, venomous, and even violent, involving book burnings, bodily harm, and excommunications, and thus caused irreparable damage to the fabric of Jewish life. In some cases, the schism affected the Jewish masses, in others only the Jewish elite.

The history of ideological schisms in Judaism is a reminder of the promise of Israel's eternity, the genius of Jewish leadership, and the resiliency of a community committed to its Covenant. Also recorded are the wholesome and beneficial by-products of schism—the facility of the Jews to repel an opponent with one hand, and to embrace him, willingly or unwillingly, with the other, by opening themselves up to his influence, for these are ideological conflicts which temporarily divided the Jews but permanently enriched Judaism.

It will certainly be more difficult, after reading this study, to answer the question "Who is a Jew?", but it will be possible to discover the strengths which enabled various definitions of Judaism to become "normative" at one time or another.

We may also discern what constitutes a schism within the Jewish fold and what factors determine when total severance from Judaism takes place. As Salo Baron observes in connection with Christianity: "In its first stage, the new movement was hardly more than a sectarian current within Judaism, no more apart, for instance, than the Essenes. The second stage began with a definite schism and ended in a new religion, which received in its third stage its definition organization."[12] When, indeed, does a Jew drift so far from his spiritual moorings that he is considered not a schismatic, but a "deserter"?

We are indebted to those scholars whose investigations of this intriguing subject, included in this book, have shed light on a heretofore insufficiently explored area of Jewish life and history.

Stanley M. Wagner

NOTES

1. *Webster's Third New International Dictionary* (1969), s.v. "schism."
2. Genesis 13:8.
3. Genesis 13:9.
4. Numbers 16.
5. Louis Ginzberg, *Legends of the Jews* (Philadelphia, 1946), Vol. III, pp. 286–298. See also notes, ibid., Vol. VI, pp. 100–102. Compare J.T. *Sanhedrin* 27d–28a.
6. *Yoma* 9b.
7. *Berakhot* 6a.
8. Deuteronomy 14:1.
9. *Yebamot* 14a.
10. J.T. *Sanhedrin* 29c.
11. *Great Confrontations in Jewish History*, edited by Stanley M. Wagner and Allen D. Breck (University of Denver, 1977).
12. Salo W. Baron, *A Social and Religious History of the Jews* (Philadelphia 1958), Vol. II, p. 63.

Jewish Sectarianism in Second Temple Times

LAWRENCE H. SCHIFFMAN

New York University

I. Historical Background

IN THE FALL of 540 B.C.E., Cyrus (II) the Great, already king of Persia and Media, vanquished Babylonia's army and soon controlled the entire area of Mesopotamia. He immediately adopted a policy which was to be characteristic of his reign; he encouraged the repatriation of exiles and the rebuilding of shrines, all in a benevolence which seemed to sit well both with his temperament and with the need to govern a large and far-flung empire. In 538 B.C.E. Cyrus decreed that the Temple of the Jews in Jerusalem be rebuilt and that all the exiles who wished might return to Judea.[1] It was this decree that inaugurated the period of the Second Temple or Second Commonwealth.

But the period of the Second Temple cannot be understood without reference to the seven hundred years before.[2] In about 1250 B.C.E., the Hebrews had escaped from servitude in Egypt to begin a long trek through the desert. This was the formative period of their national and religious character. A common ancestry, history, and the belief that God had revealed His will to them at Sinai all contributed to the molding of the Israelite nation. While the period of the conquest and the Judges was one of relative political and religious instability, the Israelites emerged from it ready to become a great empire and to receive the message of the prophets.

The great kingdom of the united monarchy under David and Solomon unfortunately gave way to regionalism, and the result was the split of the kingdom. This led in turn to the political, economic, and military weakening of the country and eventually

1

to the conquests of Israel by Assyria in 722 and of Judah by Babylonia in 586. Each conquest resulted in the exile of substantial groups of people to Mesopotamia. Even worse, the combined depredations of both enemies brought about the destruction of the economy, so that life in the Land of Israel was, to say the least, very difficult. It was now that Cyrus came on the scene.

The rise of Cyrus and the fall of Babylon in 538 B.C.E. were viewed by the Jews as God's work.[3] Immediately after his conquest of Babylonia, Cyrus issued the aforementioned edict allowing the return of the Jews to Judea and the rebuilding of the Temple of Jerusalem. While then, as today, settling in Israel was an option exercised by a small and devoted minority, the entire Jewish Diaspora gave financial and moral support to the newly reestablished community.[4]

With the rise of Cyrus we enter the Persian period. A new kind of bureaucracy was now ruling.[5] While at times the Judeans had trouble with the ruling powers, Jews were able to rise in the civil service and even constituted military units employed by the Persian Empire at the frontiers.[6] The Persian period was formative for the Second Jewish Commonwealth in that Jerusalem was rebuilt and its sacrificial cult reconstituted. A final important development was the granting of temporal (not merely religious) authority to the high priesthood. Little is known of the period between the rebuilding of Jerusalem under Ezra and Nehemiah and the coming of Alexander the Great,[7] which was to begin a new period in the history of the Near East.

The Hellenistic period begins officially with Alexander's arrival in the Near East in 334 B.C.E.[8] It is common to think of Hellenization as the sudden importation of Greek culture into the Near East. Nothing could be further from the truth. First, commercial contacts and their attendant cultural effects had already been developing for several centuries. Second, Alexander and his armies did not represent native Greek ways. Alexander was a Macedonian. As his armies moved through the East, native soldiers (with their cultural baggage) were added to his units. In his wake a new Hellenistic culture was created which was, in fact, an amalgam of Alexander's Macedonian Greek culture with the ways and beliefs of the Near Eastern peoples.[9]

After Alexander's death his empire was divided by his generals.[10] Henceforth, until the coming of the Romans in 63 B.C.E., the Land of Israel was to be ruled by the Ptolemaic (Egyptian) and Seleucid (Syrian) kings in alternating succession. It was during this period that Judaism suffered strife and war to determine its ultimate relation to Hellenism. A small minority had sought to gain control of the nation and to impose extreme Hellenism on the people. This would have meant the abandonment of the Torah as the national constitution and the norm of Jewish life. In its stead would have been the Hellenic cosmopolitan ideal and the Greek city-state, the *polis*. When intermittent civil war over this issue began, Antiochus Ephiphanes, the Seleucid ruler, reacted by supporting the Hellenists. His tactic was to outlaw Jewish practice and then mandate extreme Hellenization. It was against this policy that the Maccabees rose in revolt (167–164 B.C.E.). Their struggle has become for Jews a reminder of their ability to overcome persecutions, no matter how dire.[11]

It is not uncommon for the victor to become the vanquished. When ancient Rome conquered Greece, native Roman culture soon gave way to that of Hellas. When Alexander conquered Iran, he soon became a Persian monarch, wearing Persian clothes and keeping a Persian harem. So went the Hasmoneans, the later descendants of the Maccabees. Ultimately, the descendants of those who had risen so defiantly against extreme Hellenization became so Hellenized as to alienate their subjects.[12]

It was a relief to the Jews, then, when Pompey took control of Judea for Rome in 63 B.C.E. Two Hasmonean pretenders had both appealed to Pompey for help in ascending the throne, and he saw an easy opportunity to take control.[13] Roman rule took several different forms. For most of the time, the Empire was represented in Judea by procurators. Many of these were opportunists who had little concern for their responsibilities. Others, however, were genuinely sincere in trying to rule wisely and fairly. At other times, the country was ruled by the Herodians, a puppet dynasty of "Jewish" kings controlled by Rome, and totally acculturated to Roman ways. Constant strife characterized this period as Rome showed little ability to understand or respect the religious sensitivities of the Jews.[14]

Further, by this time the Hasmonean period had been idealized in the minds of the people, and a staunch desire to attain political freedom from foreign domination had become widespread. By 66 C.E. the Jews had begun their revolt against Rome, which was to end by 74 C.E. in total destruction and defeat. The Temple of Jerusalem was destroyed in 70. With this revolt, the Second Commonwealth comes to an end.[15] The Rabbis of the Talmud claimed that the revolt failed because of dissension among Jewish groups,[16] probably a result of the sectarianism of the Second Commonwealth to which we now turn.

II. Problem and Sources

Our study of the sectarianism of the Second Jewish Commonwealth will seek to fulfill two primary purposes. First, it will describe the main sects and their relationships to one another. Second, it will investigate the underlying cause of the deep divisions which we will see in the period under discussion. Others have seen the causes of the rift in the political, social, or religious circumstances of the Hellenistic period.[17] We will argue, however, that almost every sectarian trend was already present in biblical times, and that Hellenism, while certainly a factor in encouraging sectarianism, was not its overriding cause. Hellenism simply heightened conflicts which had begun centuries before. In demonstrating this thesis, we will avoid the usual cataloguing of sects, choosing instead to concentrate on basic issues among the sects and how each group reacted to them.

A word is in order about sources. Two major characteristics may be mentioned for the sources we have regarding the sects and their biblical background. First, we are very often reading the works of opponents, whose writings may be colored by their negative view of what they describe or by the polemical purpose for which the material was written. Second—and this applies both to the biblical and post-biblical data—the literature often shows evidence of a complex literary history which involves editing and revising and which is usually far removed chronologically from the subject matter. At many points, therefore, we will have to pause to assess the reliability of the sources and traditions which form the basis for our inquiry so as to be able properly to evaluate the degree of certainty we may rightfully ascribe to our conclusions.

Let us now survey the sources we will use in our inquiry. First, there is the Bible itself. It is from the Bible that we will seek to identify the conflicts which lie at the root of the sectarianism of the Second Commonwealth. After all, the thesis of this study is that the central issues of Second Temple times were already factors in the biblical period.

Here we must take several factors into consideration. First, the biblical materials have gone through a long process of editing and transmission, which means that we cannot be certain that the reports are accurate.[18] More important, though, this process has clearly been influenced by the ideological stance of those who handed down the material.[19] Specifically, the Bible was edited by Judeans who espoused pure monotheism and loyalty only to the God of Israel. As we shall see below, others disagreed. Further, these editors were convinced that Jerusalem and its Temple were the only place in which sacrifice might take place.

The earliest postbiblical Hebrew sources at our disposal are the Dead Sea Scrolls. These texts were found in the caves of Qumran, at the shore of the Dead Sea.[20] They clearly describe the religious life and theology of some group within the Judaism of the Second Commonwealth. Various considerations have led to the conclusion that the texts date from the second century B.C.E. through the first century C.E.[21] Besides the texts of a clearly sectarian nature, there are also biblical manuscripts as well as copies of some books of the Apocrypha and pseudepigrapha to which we shall presently turn.[22]

Scholars are divided regarding the identity of the sect which authored these texts and inhabited the caves and buildings of Qumran.[23] The majority opinion sees these texts as the literature of the Essenes.[24] Since this view remains unproven, this study will simply refer to the authors of these texts as the Dead Sea Sect.

"Apocrypha" and "pseudepigrapha" are loose designations

covering a wide literature composed by Jews during the Greco-Roman period in Palestine and in the Diaspora.[25] By far the majority of these books were written during the same period as the Dead Sea Scrolls.[26] These works were composed in Hebrew, Aramaic, and Greek. Because later Judaism for the most part rejected these works,[27] they survive only in Greek or in Christian translations from late antiquity or the Middle Ages.[28] The ideology of much of this literature represents Hellenistic Judaism.

Since we are dealing with translations and not original compositions, we are presented with numerous textual and linguistic problems. We cannot determine with precision the dates of composition or the identity of the author(s) of these books. These works are of great value, however, in that they shed light on the general religious and intellectual climate in the Jewish communities of the Greco-Roman period.

An extremely important source regarding Hellenistic Judaism in the Diaspora is Philo Judaeus (ca. 20 B.C.E.–50 C.E.). Philo lived in Alexandria, the center of Hellenistic culture. While he himself espoused a Judaism which synthesized the law and theology of the Torah with the philosophy of the Greeks, he described other Jews who had abandoned the ancestral law and lore under the influence of Greek ways.[29]

The New Testament is also of value to our study. Although even the earliest material in the Gospels was not edited until somewhat later, Jesus lived in the last years of the Second Temple period. Much of what the New Testament says about the history of this period can be corroborated by other sources. However, we must exercise great caution, particularly in regard to the description of the Pharisees. The New Testament writers clearly polemicize against the Pharisees and attempt to present them in an unfavorable light.[30] The same may be said of the New Testament descriptions of the priests and the Temple officials.

Then there is Josephus Flavius (ca. 38–after 100 C.E.), the famous Jewish historian.[31] His works are indispensable to the study of this period, yet he is not unimpeachably reliable. First, while he himself claims to have been a priest of aristocratic lineage and to have studied with the Sadducees (as well as the Pharisees, the Essenes, and a desert hermit named Banus), he states that he was a Pharisee. Hence, he can be expected to have prejudices against the Sadducees. Second, he described the Jewish sects of the Second Commonwealth in such a way as to make them resemble Greek schools of philosophy in an attempt to present the Jewish traditions in a good light to his non-Jewish readers. Third, he seems to have had first-hand familiarity with the major sects in his own day, and it would seem that he considered this experience sufficient to project back data into the early Hasmonean period. Finally, he was writing after the abortive Jewish revolt against Rome, during which he switched to the Roman side. Thereafter, the alignment of sects in Judaism was changed radically, as we shall see later on.

The last major literary source is Rabbinic literature—Mishnah, Talmud, and Midrash. Here we encounter three problems. First, the Rabbis regarded themselves as the spiritual heirs of the Pharisees. Hence, the Sadducees were the opponents. Second, as a result of censorship of Jewish texts by Christians in the Middle Ages, the word *ṣeduqi* ("Sadducean") was often introduced into the text of the Mishnah and Talmud to replace words for "Christians" or "heretics." Therefore, many of the alleged references to the Sadducees in Rabbinic texts have no bearing on them.[32] Third, the earliest strata of talmudic literature are, in their present form, like Josephus, far removed from the early years of the Hasmonean period and can at best be considered reliable for the last years of the Second Temple period.

Recent years have seen increasing evidence of our period emerging from archaelogical research.[33] While Palestinian archaeology began as an attempt to uncover the realia of biblical times, it has increasingly concentrated on the Second Temple period. Archaeology has revealed the material culture of the times and has greatly illuminated the extent of Hellenization in Palestine as well as the general religious climate, specifically the amount of foreign worship. Because the artifacts were buried and are found *in situ*, the information which they yield is not subject to as much suspicion as is the literary evidence. Questions do arise, however, about the dating of what has been uncovered and its evaluation.

In view of the nature of our sources and their composition after the events they describe, it is important to remember that what follows is, of necessity, a reconstruction of the sectarian controversies based on the available data. It would be nearly impossible to study this period by using only information which can be proven without question. It is hoped that the careful weighing of the material has allowed us to come close to an understanding of this difficult and formative period in the history of Judaism, despite the many historical problems and uncertainties which remain.

III. ONE GOD OR MANY

What then are the basic issues in the biblical period, and how do they manifest themselves later on? A major conflict concerned the very nature of Israelite religion. Was the God of Israel to be worshipped alongside "other gods," or was He to be venerated exclusively?[34] Along with this issue went the question of the centralization of worship. In an attempt to root out syncretistic worship and to control the priesthood, the Deuteronomic tradition, as followed by Hezekiah and Josiah, stood for limitation of sacrificial worship to the Jerusalem Temple. Further, only Zadokite priests (descendants of one of Solomon's high priests, Zadok) were to offer the sacrifices.[35] Needless to say, those believing that the God of Israel was to be one among many saw no reason to centralize worship or to limit membership in the legitimate priesthood.

Behind these political and religious questions lay a larger cultural question which was to concern the Jews in the Second Commonwealth. It may seem strange to those of us who are familiar with Rabbinic Judaism, but in the biblical and Hellenistic periods a fundamental question was whether Israelite religion should be a total way of life which left no room for outside elements, or whether it was to be only a part of the life of the individual and the nation. Whether it was the paganism of the Canaanites or the Hellenism of the later period, the question was the same.

It ought to be made clear that despite some of the rhetoric to the contrary, the question was not a black-and-white one. The issue was never whether or not to reject outside influence. The question was rather whether to assimilate some elements not considered harmful or to allow the wholesale entry of foreign elements into the way of life of the Jews. Those seeking exclusive worship of God in both the biblical and Hellenistic periods felt that adoption of foreign elements without restriction was nothing more than apostasy and the abandonment of Judaism. Others, against whom our sources so often polemicize, disagreed.

IV. THE SAMARITANS

This complex of issues was to manifest itself early in the Second Temple period. As the returning Jews began to rebuild the Temple, the Samaritans offered to help and were rejected.

When we come to discuss the Samaritans, we are immediately plagued by the problem of sources. While the Bible describes the origins of Samaritanism,[36] we must remember that the Scriptures were handed down by Jewish groups which were fundamentally anti-Samaritan. It is therefore probable that there is some bias in these materials. Second, all the Samaritans' own traditions appear in writings which are of very late date and many of which have been clearly influenced by Islamic sources. Finally, the material in Rabbinic literature and in Josephus is also subject to the claim of bias.[37]

From these various sources, we can reconstruct the following account. The Samaritans were a mixed people made up of strains of Northern Israelites who had not been exiled in 722 and the various foreign nations that the Assyrians had brought into the area in an attempt to ensure that national aspirations could not again come to the fore. This mixed group, the Samaritans, had adopted a syncretistic form of Judaism. They seem to have maintained the old Northern traditions and to have combined them with those of the nations settled among them. More important, however, was the genealogical problem.

In First Temple times it was possible for foreigners to join the

Jewish people in an informal way by moving physically and socially into the land and adhering to its religion and laws. During the exile, Judaism had been transformed from a nationality which depended on connection to the land and culture to a religion which depended upon descent. For how else could Judaism ensure its continuity when deprived of its homeland? The returning Jews from Babylonia could not accept the questionable genealogy of the Samaritans. On the other hand, there was not yet a system for religious conversion as developed later on in the Second Temple period. Hence, there was no choice but to reject the Samaritans, even had they agreed to abandon their syncretistic practices.[38]

This issue had political overtones as well. The Samaritans attempted, although with limited success, to influence the Persian authorities to stop the building of the Temple and to limit the powers of the priestly and temporal government of the Jews.[39] This split between the Samaritans and the Jews was final, the Samaritans remaining a separate community to this day.

The Samaritan problem was, no doubt, complicated by another long-smoldering issue. There can be no question that as far back as the earliest days of the monarchy, there was division between North and South. It was this division that eventually led, after Solomon's death, to the split of the kingdom.

There were several aspects to this problem. First, after David's death, the South accepted the idea that the monarchy was hereditary. The North, on the other hand, did not. Apparently, this difference characterized the two kingdoms, for the South maintained the Davidic dynasty while the North repeatedly changed dynasties.[40]

A second aspect was religious. We cannot doubt that there was Northern opposition to the centralization of the cult at Jerusalem. This opposition must have surfaced already in the time of Solomon, even when worship at the *bamot* ("high places") was still considered legitimate. The North rejected the constant efforts to centralize worship at the Jerusalem Temple and to restrict the priesthood to the Aaronides. Accordingly, after the split of the kingdom, the North set up sanctuaries at Bethel and Dan.[41] The opposition of Southern, Judean circles to these sanctuaries and the bull-images which were erected in them is clearly stated in the books of Kings.[42] We will explain below how the same Northern opposition to centralization of the cult was bolstered by a Northern calendar reform.

From the linguistic point of view, we know that the Northern and Southern Israelites spoke somewhat different dialects, as these differences are in evidence in the Bible.[43] The Hebrew Scriptures, however, were generally edited to conform to the dialect of Judah in the last years of the First Temple. Later on, in the Second Temple period, the Northerners would shift more quickly to Aramaic, while Hebrew would hold on for much longer in the southern regions.[44]

Thus, the issue of the Samaritans in the Second Temple period may be viewed, to some extent, as a continuation of the North-South schism of the First Temple. Like their Northern predecessors, the Samaritans insisted on the right to sacrifice outside of Jerusalem. Evidence seems to point to their adoption of Aramaic at an earlier stage than their Judean counterparts. Under Persian rule, the Judeans had rejected the Samaritans due to their syncretistic worship and the presence among them of non-Israelite elements. Clearly, the Judeans had chosen to follow in the footsteps of those who believed that only the God of Israel was to be worshipped, and that this worship was to be done only according to the ancient traditions of Israel. The same question was to arise again in the Hellenistic period.

The issue of Hellenism, then, can be seen as a larger issue of openness to foreign cultures and influences, a conflict which was foremost in biblical times and which continued into the Second Temple period. As the constellation of world politics and culture changed, Judaism first found itself in confrontation with the Canaanite culture and then with the phenomenon of Hellenism.

V. Major Sects of the Greco-Roman Age

Generally speaking, there were five groups in the Jewish population of Palestine during the Hellenistic period. (It must be remembered that many Jews in the Diaspora were very thoroughly

Hellenized.[45]) There was a small group who clearly believed that Jews ought to enter into the mainstream of Hellenistic culture. They believed that Greek educational and cultural forms ought to be imposed on the biblical heritage so that Jews might enter into the *cosmos* as Hellenistic citizens. Judaism would then become one of the Hellenistic cults, and the God of Israel just one of the many manifestations of Zeus, the major god of the Greek pantheon.[46] After all, throughout the rest of the Hellenistic world, the local deities were identified with the gods of the Hellenic pantheon. It was against this extreme Hellenization that the Maccabees revolted, as we have said. With time, those holding these views, whether in the Land of Israel or in the Diaspora, probably assimilated so totally into the Greek way of life that they and their descendants were lost to the Jewish people.

A second group of somewhat Hellenized Jews is that of the Greek-speaking Jews. Their primary loyalties were to the Jewish tradition, but their culture was very much influenced by the atmosphere in which they lived. Alexandria, Egypt, was certainly a center for this kind of Hellenization,[47] typified by Septuagint (Greek translation of the Bible)[48] and the writings of Philo Judaeus (ca. 20 B.C.E. 50 C.E.), who attempted to synthesize the revelation of the Torah with Platonic thought.[49] This moderately Hellenistic Judaism also found a place in Judea, as represented, for example, by Josephus and the Greek-speaking Jews.[50] Many of the Greek books of the Apocrypha and pseudepigrapha are products of this approach. Among this group were, no doubt, many aristocrats and members of the Sadducean priesthood.

In speaking of the Sadducees, the problem of sources is especially acute for the reasons mentioned above. Nonetheless, considerable data can be gleaned about the Sadducees, and in the main, it seems to be reliable. Josephus explicitly mentions the Sadducees (along with the Pharisees and the Essenes) as existing as early as the time of Jonathan Maccabee (ca. 150 B.C.E.).[51]

The most repeated characteristic of the Sadducees is their aristocratic aspect. Most of them were apparently priests or those who had intermarried with the high priestly families.[52] The Sadducees derived their name from that of Zadok, the high priest of the

Jerusalem Temple in the time of Solomon.[53] It was this family of high priests who served at the head of the priesthood throughout First and Second Temple times, the only interruptions being when foreign worship was brought into the Temple and when the Hasmoneans took control.[54] Further, according to Josephus, the Sadducees rejected the "traditions of the fathers" observed as law by the Pharisees.[55] These traditions seem to have been a forerunner of the later Oral Law.[56] For the reasons described above, it is difficult to evaluate the many legal differences between the Sadduccees and the Pharisees mentioned in the tannaitic sources.[57] The Sadducees also differed to some extent in theological matters with the Pharisees, a subject to which we shall return.

Closely allied with the Sadducees were the Boethusians. This group seems to have adopted similar views to those of the Sadducees. Scholars ascribe the origin of the Boethusians to Simeon ben Boethus, appointed high priest by Herod in 24 B.C.E. so that he would have sufficient status to marry Herod's daughter Mariamne (II). There certainly were some differences between the Sadduccees and the Boethusians, but it is probable that the Boethusians were a subgroup of the Sadduccees.[58]

It is clear that many of these Saducean and Boethusian priests and their families were considerably Hellenized. They, therefore, represent the focal point of a group which accepted many aspects of Hellenistic culture while remaining loyal to the Jewish tradition.

A third group may be said to have rejected almost all aspects of Hellenistic culture. This is not to say that they had not picked up Greek vocabulary in their Hebrew and Aramaic speech or that the intellectual traditions of the *oikuméne* (the Hellenistic world) had not affected them at all. Rather, this group seems to have remained primarily Near Eastern in culture. We refer here to the Pharisees. The name of this sect is derived from the Hebrew *perushim*, "separate." This designation most probably refers to their separation from levitically impure food and from the tables of the 'am ha-'areṣ, the common people, who were not scrupulous regarding the laws of Levitical purity or tithes.[59]

For the Pharisees as well we face the problem of sources. Little can be said with certainty about the Pharisees in the pre–70 C.E. period.[60] Three major characteristics seem to emerge from the sources before us. First, they represented primarily the middle and lower classes.[61] Second, and perhaps as a consequence of their social status, they were not really Hellenized. To be sure, certain Greek words or intellectual approaches may have been part of their lives. However, they viewed as authoritative only what they regarded as the ancient traditions of Israel.[62] Third, they accepted the "traditions of the fathers." The laws of purity, tithing, and Sabbath were of primary interest to the Pharisees.[63]

The Pharisees first appear by name in the time of Jonathan Maccabee (ca. 150 B.C.E.).[64] Many scholars have attempted to identify the Pharisees with the Hasidim who appear as allies of Judah in the Maccabean revolt.[65] This theory, however, cannot be substantiated. Further, our knowledge of the Hasidim in this early period is very limited. It is most probable that they were not really a sect or party, but rather a loose association of pietists such as are denoted by this term in talmudic literature.[66]

Rabbinic sources trace the history of the Pharisees back to the Men of the Great Assembly, who are said to have provided the religious leadership for Israel in the Persian and early Hellenistic periods.[67] Some modern scholars have associated the Soferim ("scribes") with the Men of the Great Assembly. The Soferim would then be forerunners of the Pharisaic movement. Unfortunately, historical evidence does not allow any definite conclusions here.[68] All that can be said is that the Pharisees cannot have emerged suddenly, full-blown in the Hasmonean period. Their theology and organization must have been in formation somewhat earlier. How much earlier and in what form, we cannot say.

A fourth group seems to have eschewed Hellenism much more thoroughly than the Pharisees. While Pharisaic Judaism seems to have been Hellenized to at least a minor degree, the Dead Sea sect used no Greek words in its writings and, despite some views to the contrary,[69] was in no way Hellenized. This sect was apparently founded at about the time of the Maccabean uprising.[70] From the role of Zadokite priests in the legal teachings of the sect,[71] one would assume that such priests made up the nucleus of the sect. Two possible explanations can, therefore, be offered for its founding. It may have been founded by Zadokite (perhaps Sadducean) priests who left the Temple and Jerusalem in protest and disgust over what the Hellenizing priests were doing in the sanctuary. Alternately, it may have been founded by righteous Zadokite priests who were expelled from Temple service when the Maccabees arrogated to their family the right to officiate as high priests. At any rate, this group went off to the desert, where they lived at the shore of the Dead Sea in Qumran and some surrounding settlements.[72] They left us a series of scrolls, dating from about 150 B.C.E. to 70 C.E., which clearly outline the life and doctrines of this sect to which we will return so many times below.[73]

Among the most important characteristics of the Dead Sea or Qumran sect is its rejection of the validity of extra-biblical traditions for the derivation of law. This group derived its law solely from biblical exegesis, an activity which occupied a major part of the daily life of the sect.[74] In this respect, they shared the Sadducean daily view. On the other hand, they seem to have reached conclusions very much like those to which the Pharisees adhered as part of their "traditions of the fathers," later part of the Rabbinic Oral Law.[75]

It should be noted here that the Dead Sea sect wrote down legislation. Later talmudic sources forbade the writing of Oral Law and ascribed such a proscription to Second Temple times.[76] There is no way of knowing whether the Pharisees would have written down their extra-biblical "traditions of the fathers."[77] We can say with certainty that no clearly identifiable Pharisaic legal manuscript from the Second Temple period has come down to us, but neither has any Sadducean manuscript.[78]

Many scholars have identified the sect of the Dead Sea Scrolls with the Essenes described in Philo and Josephus.[79] Indeed, this suggestion has the merit of solving the problem of why Josephus does not mention such a major sect as that of the Qumranites. The Essenes, however, cannot be identified with the Qumran sect except by correcting Josephus in light of the Dead Sea Scrolls. Such a process is somewhat circular, so that the most we may say is that the sect of Qumran *might* be the Essenes. Josephus mentions Essenes as existing as early as 150 B.C.E.,[80] but we must remember again how much later he was writing. No information as to the founding of this group is given, and no convincing etymology of the name has been proposed.[81] Further, Josephus might have generalized numerous smaller groups under the heading Essenes.[82] It is a pity, as well, that there is no mention of the Essenes in talmudic literature—at least not by name. The most prominent characteristic of the Essenes seems to have been the community of property; some practiced celibacy.[83]

With regard to the Hellenistic continuum, we have a problem concerning the Essenes. If they are to be identified with the Dead Sea sect, then Hellenistic influence would seem out of the question. If, however, they are a separate group, and Josephus' description is accurate, Hellenistic influence might account for many of their divergences from the Pharisaic approach.[84] Further, Philo describes the sect of the Therapeutae,[85] located at Lake Mareotis in Egypt, clearly an area of strongly Hellenized Judaism, and this sect has many affinities with the Essenes.

We have omitted discussion of a number of minor sects mentioned in Rabbinic literature. Information on these is too scant and it is often not possible to tell if we are dealing with an organized group or not.[86]

All the groups we have discussed probably altogether accounted for less than ten percent of the Jewish population of Palestine in the Second Commonwealth. Who were the rest? Most people belonged to a class called by the Bible and the later Rabbis the *'am ha-'areṣ*, "the people of the land."[87] This group was primarily rural and of the lower economic class. Their faith was probably a simplified version of the teachings of the Bible, and their observance was similar to that of the Pharisees except that tithing and purity laws were widely disregarded. Nevertheless, we can safely assume widespread Sabbath observance and abstinence from forbidden foods.[88] Regarding prayer and the status of the synagogue at this time, evidence is scant, and no definitive conclusions can be reached.[89]

The *'am ha-'areṣ* was probably affected by Hellenism only in regard to what we may call surface culture, i.e. some vocabulary terms of a technical nature, and material culture, as shown by the widespread finds of Greek pottery and wares in Palestine of this period.[90] We know that after the Great Revolt of 66–73 the bulk of this group followed the Pharisees into the Rabbinic movement.[91] It may perhaps be said that this was only the end of a long process. This group, regarding Hellenism and the Hellenists as interlopers into their ancient way of life and culture, had greatest sympathy for the Pharisees in our period. Indeed, such an impression is certainly given by Josephus,[92] but it may be the result of post–70 c.e. developments or of his own prejudices.

VI. Centralization of the Cult

We have already seen that the issue of centralization of the sacrificial cult, i.e. the prohibition of all sacrificial worship except in the Jerusalem Temple, was linked to that of the exclusive veneration of the God of Israel. In order to ensure the proper worship of the Israelite God, the author of Deuteronomy, followed by Hezekiah and Josiah, prohibited worship elsewhere.[93] Further, Josiah had reduced the priests from outlying areas, whose worship was often syncretistic, to a secondary status at Jerusalem.[94] Ezekiel, in his vision of the restored Second Temple, for the same reason, expected only Zadokite priests to minister, with others relegated to a secondary status.[95] This seems to have become the practice in Second Temple times.[96]

Various exceptions to the centralization of sacrificial worship can be observed in the Second Temple period. Before investigating them we must note how insignificant these exceptions are. By and large, from the Josianic reformation on, Jews did not attempt to sacrifice except in Jerusalem. Hence, the Babylonian exiles made no attempt to sacrifice in Babylonia. Of the exceptions we will mention, only the Samaritans are actually to be considered a sect. Nevertheless, the other examples provide the background for understanding the Samaritan position on this issue.

Three exceptions should be mentioned. In the Persian period, a Jewish garrison was established at Yeb or Elephantine, now

Aswan, on the Nile. This garrison had a somewhat syncretistic cult including not only the God of Israel but some local gods as well. Their temple in Egypt included sacrifices offered to the God of Israel, who was the head of their pantheon.[97] This is probably a late survival of the syncretistic worship of the *bamot* ("high places") of First Temple times.

A second Egyptian cultic place to the God of Israel is the so-called Temple of Onias at Leontopolis. Founded in the mid-second century B.C.E., this temple was probably established as the result of internecine strife among candidates for the high priesthood in Jerusalem. At any rate, its priests were Zadokite, and it was built on the model of the Jerusalem Temple. There is no reason to doubt its exclusive worship of the God of Israel, especially if the talmudic traditions are to be accepted.[98]

A third example is the Samaritan temple on Mount Gerizim. According to a report of Josephus,[99] the veracity of which has been questioned by many scholars,[100] this temple was also founded as the result of strife within the priesthood. Manasses, a brother of the high priest Jaddua, married Nikaso, daughter of Sanballat, governor of Samaria. Because of his marriage, Manasses was expelled from Jerusalem. His father-in-law built him a temple on Mount Gerizim (modern-day Nablus on the West Bank) with the permission of Alexander the Great. It seems, at the very least, that this date can be accepted for the building of the Samaritan temple. Additional confirmation comes from the recently discovered papyri from Wadi el-Daliyeh.[101]

The exact details given by Josephus regarding the cause of the founding of this temple may be fictional. However, it certainly took place after the success of the Judeans in building the Jerusalem Temple. After all, the attempt of the Samaritans to join in the building of the Jerusalem sanctuary had been rebuffed by the Judean authorities. This rejection must have resulted in the founding of an independent temple.

It is impossible to reconstruct the cult of the Samaritan temple since the texts we have are of so much later provenance. It seems, though, that only the God of Israel would have been worshipped there, and that the sacrificial system would have been very much in accord with the biblical cultic codes as found in the Samaritan version of the Pentateuch.[102]

VII. The Biblical Canon

An important area of divergence among the Jews of the Second Commonwealth concerns the biblical canon and text. By canon we mean those books which are considered authoritative and holy.[103]

The Pharisees probably accepted as sanctified and authoritative the Torah, Prophets, and a corpus of writings.[104] Only in Mishnaic times, however, was the final decision made on certain of the writings.[105] The Sadducees were said by the Church Fathers to have accepted only the Pentateuch,[106] yet there is no evidence for this claim.[107] While we cannot be sure, it seems that the Sadducees would have shared at least the canon of the Pharisees.[108] It is also possible that they accepted even more books as authoritative. The canon of the Hellenistic Jews of Alexandria, as evidenced by the Greek Bible (and followed in the Catholic tradition), includes the books classified as Apocrypha.[109] These additional books were written during the Hellenistic and Roman periods, some in Hebrew and most in Greek. Some of the apocryphal books are representative of the point of view of the Hellenistic Jews of Alexandria. It is therefore possible that the Hellenized Sadducees may have also been attracted to these books and included them in their canon. Some of the apocryphal books, on the other hand, were written in the last days of the Second Temple, and there seems little chance that the Sadducees would have considered these works canonical.

The Samaritans regarded as canonical only the Pentateuch.[110] Some scholars have argued that this limited canon shows that the Samaritans broke away from normative Judaism before the Prophets had been canonized. This claim, however, has been seriously challenged.[111]

At Qumran every biblical book has been found except Esther. There are also various apocryphal or pseudepigraphical books.[112]

The problem is that we cannot be sure whether the Dead Sea sect had a concept of canon. Perhaps at Qumran the canon was open, with new books being added at times.[113]

Regarding the biblical text, it has been established that three basic text types existed side by side during our period.[114] Evidence for this comes primarily from the Dead Sea Scrolls, but also from the ancient translations of the Bible. The three recensions were as follows: (1) The Alexandrian recension is that which served as the basis for the Septuagint, the Greek translation of the Bible. This text was used by Hellenized Jews, including many of the Sadducees. It was later a factor in facilitating the spread of Christianity. (2) The Palestinian text can also be described as proto-Samaritan. This version was similar to the Samaritan Pentateuch as we know it except that it did not contain the tendentious variants which supported the Samaritan doctrines regarding the sanctuary at Mount Gerizim.[115] Finally there is (3) the Babylonian recension, which was used by the Pharisaic forerunners of the talmudic Rabbis. This last version served as the basis for what was later called the Masoretic Text, the Hebrew biblical text in use until this day.

Among the Qumran scrolls were found biblical manuscripts in both the square Hebrew script as well as in the paleo-Hebrew script. From later sources we know that the Samaritans wrote their biblical texts in paleo-Hebrew script.[116]

VIII. THE CALENDAR

Still another aspect of the divergence among sects at this time is the calendar. In the history of religions, calendar reform or variation has often played a part in religious schisms. To mention some familiar cases, there is the Christian shift of emphasis from Saturday to Sunday, the elimination of the intercalation of the month in the Moslem calendar, and the variations between the Eastern and Western Churches in Christianity. Such a variation or change is found in the Bible, and it will not surprise us to see a calendar dispute play a part in the Second Commonwealth as well.

Jeroboam, ruler of the Northern Kingdom of Israel (928–907

B.C.E.), had already attempted to use a calendric change as part of his efforts to separate the people of the Northern Kingdom from their Judean coreligionists. To this end, he postponed the celebration of Sukkot from the seventh to the eighth month.[117] Even if this adjustment may have been more in accord with the agricultural realities of the North, with its somewhat colder climate than the South,[118] the fact remains that his purpose was to complete the shift of allegiance from the sanctuary at Jerusalem to those of Beth El and Dan to shore up his political structure.

Calendar controversy was also prominent in Second Temple times. The major issue now revolved about whether to use a series of twelve lunar months periodically adjusted by intercalation of a thirteenth to constitute a year (lunar-solar) or to use a fixed calendar of thirty-day and thirty-one-day months, twelve of which would constitute the solar year (solar). While Jewish tradition assumes that the former was the ancient Israelite calendar, and that the latter was an innovation, rightly opposed, some scholars have held the less likely view that it was the lunar month which was the innovation. In any case, the calendar of the Pharisees must have been the lunar-solar, while the Dead Sea sect and the pseudepigraphic books of Jubilees and Enoch followed solar calendars. (We cannot be sure about the Sadducees.)[119] It is possible that this 364-day solar calendar had as its purpose ensuring that the festivals would not fall on the Sabbath as this entailed numerous problems regarding Temple and home observance.

A related calendar dispute pertained to the date of the festival of Shavuot.[120] The Bible commanded that forty-nine days be counted from the "day after the Sabbath" (Lev. 23:15). The Pharisees, according to later sources, took "Sabbath" here, based on context, to mean the first day of Passover (a day of rest, or "Sabbath"); hence, the fiftieth day after Passover was the date of Shavuot. The other groups took this passage as referring to the Saturday after either the first or last day of Passover.[121] That these variant calendars were actually put into practice by the different groups is shown by the Habbakuk Commentary from Qumran, which tells of how the Jerusalem high priest attacked the sect on a day which they regarded as the Day of Atonement.[122]

IX. URBANIZATION

The character of the various groups was also influenced by the degree of urbanization each group accepted. When the nomadic tribes of Israel invaded the land of Canaan, they were confronted with large urban centers. Most Israelites accepted at least limited urbanization as conducive to their way of life.[123]

One group already took strong exception in First Temple times. The Rechabites were a group tracing themselves back to the early monarchical period. They did not drink wine, cultivate vineyards, or even own fields or houses. They remained pastoral tent-dwellers until the invasion of Nebuchadnezzar, when they were forced to take refuge in Jerusalem. The Rechabites must have lived much in the style of Bedouin. In other words, this group either maintained or imitated the pre-conquest way of life of ancient Israel. There is evidence that at least the progenitor or spiritual ancestor of this group took action against the worship of Baal in the early days of the divided monarchy.[124]

Descendants of the Rechabites certainly survived into the Second Commonwealth period.[125] In Second Temple times, not everyone was content with the increasing urbanization and the changes it introduced into the agricultural way of life. Much later the Talmud was to remark that the signs of urbanization were robbery, sexual immorality, and deceitful oaths.[126] The rural environment was regarded as fostering scholarship and the piety which went with it. This attitude must have been widespread in the Hellenistic and Roman period, as the mores of these foreign societies, with their disdain for sobriety and moderation, became increasingly familiar to the Jews of Palestine.[127] Unfortunately, the Sadducean priests, with time, seem to have surrendered themselves totally to the lure of the city and its attractions.[128] The Pharisees, despite the widespread support they had among city-dwellers, must have stood fast against much of this.[129] It was the Dead Sea sect that made clear its opposition in its writings, attacking the Jerusalem establishment for fornication, materialism, and impurity.[130] This opposition was no doubt manifested in the way of life of the group which set up its headquarters at Qumran.[131] To be sure, the sect allowed the use of wine,[132] although we may assume that it shared the biblical view that wine had to be taken in moderation.[133] Nonetheless, the sect had physically relocated in an environment which made contact with the evils of urbanism impossible.

Particularly important is the Dead Sea sect's view of property.[134] While not rejecting the concept of private property so important to the society envisaged by the Hebrew Bible,[135] the sect required that the use of all property belonging to members be common. In other words, the use of all property was shared while ownership remained in the hands of the individual. Certainly, an approach such as this would eliminate the need to accumulate large amounts of personal wealth, often at the expense of those less advantaged. Most important, it constituted a sharp denial of the materialistic attitude so prevalent in the increasingly Hellenized cities.

It is of interest as well that while certain communal buildings were built by the Dead Sea sect at Qumran, no individual houses were found. Scholars have been forced to speculate on where the Qumranites lived. Two views have emerged: Some have seen the caves in which the scrolls and other material remains were found as the dwelling places, while others have assumed that individual tents would have been pitched around the main buildings.

We have noted that it cannot be determined with certainty whether the Essenes and the sect of the Dead Sea Scrolls were one and the same. The Essenes, as described by Philo and Josephus, went even further than the Dead Sea texts. The Essenes denied private ownership and held all property in common.[136] Indeed, such an approach would later be seen in the emerging Church.[137] The Essenes clearly denied the urban materialism, and many are described as having shunned towns because of the immorality of their inhabitants.[138] We know from Josephus and the New Testament that in the period under discussion, there were also hermit-like holy men who had left society and separated themselves from its evils,[139] but we must emphasize that this phenomenon is very different from that of organized groups.

We have pictured the Dead Sea sect as to a great extent anti-urban in its outlook. Even so, despite its sectarian organization and particular economic system, the settlement at Qumran and its offshoot at Ein Fashka[140] in many ways may be regarded as a mini-city, or what might be called in Israel today a development town.

X. God, Man, and History

Another area in which the various sects disagreed was that of theology and the future of man. The Bible speaks of a Hades-like existence in Sheol after death. This kind of afterlife concept makes no distinction between body and soul, as the location of Sheol is below ground, and that is where Jews have always interred their dead.[141] Indeed, the Bible regards the individual as a unitary being, making no distinction between man's physical and spiritual aspects.

When the Jews found themselves in the Hellenistic environment, the Greek concepts of body and soul began to have an influence on Judaism.[142] If we can believe Josephus, the Sadducees, the most Hellenized group of Jews, rejected this concept,[143] and, hence, retained the biblical concept of afterlife. While it is indeed hard to believe that the Hellenized Sadducees would have rejected this Hellenistic concept, it is possible. After all, the Sadducees were a very conservative group in religious matters. The Pharisees, gradually accepting the Greek division of body and soul, modified their concept of life after death. They came to believe that the body ceased to function at death, while the intangible soul continued in existence. During this afterlife, people would be rewarded or punished. Eventually, the righteous would be resurrected to eternal life in the end of days.[144] The views of the Essenes of Josephus are almost the same as those of the Pharisees.[145] The Dead Sea sect had no problem with afterlife as they believed that they were living on the verge of the future age. They would still be alive for the dawn of the Messianic era.[146] Nonetheless, they seem to have viewed the person of man in the old biblical sense, making no distinction between body and soul.[147]

Interesting in this connection is the question of fate and the free will of man. The Sadducees are said by Josephus to have believed in absolute freedom of the individual, with providence playing no part in the affairs of men. The Essenes, according to him, believe that all is "in the hands of heaven." The Pharisees are pictured as occupying a middle ground, believing that man's free will interacts with the force of divine providence.[148] Some scholars have questioned this schematization, believing it to be influenced by Josephus' knowledge of Greek philosophy.[149] Nonetheless, it is important to observe that the Dead Sea Scrolls deny man free will, and accept predestination. These texts go so far as to blame men for their transgressions, and yet to assert that it is predetermined whether one is to be in the camp of the "sons of light" or that of the "sons of darkness."[150] Apparently, along with the sect's constant calls for repentance goes the idea that only those whom providence has so designated are capable of repentance.

In light of later developments, Messianism is of central concern. The extent to which Messianic belief is enshrined in the Hebrew Scriptures is the subject of great controversy. On the one hand, already by the time of Isaiah, there is the concept that there will eventually arise a future Davidic king who will have excellent qualities and whose reign will usher in a period of great tranquility and peace. Further, the prophets foretell a great day of the Lord on which all the evildoers will receive their due. This day of the Lord will be accompanied by earth-shattering, cataclysmic events. The followers of the way of God will reign supreme at its conclusion. Finally, by the Second Temple period, as shown by the Book of Daniel, there was an apocalyptic notion that the deliverance of Israel would come only after a succession of divinely appointed kingdoms had reigned. After this, the Messianic era would dawn.[151]

These ideas represent a complex of notions, and we must assume that in the First Temple period there were various differing views and conflicts regarding them. There is no way, however, to pinpoint the various views or the parties that held them.

By the Second Commonwealth, fortunately, we can be more specific. First, we have various sectarian apocalyptic works such as are found in the Apocrypha and pseudepigrapha.[152] It would seem that to many of these writers what was important was the idea of the coming of the Messianic age and not necessarily the personal Messiah. The apocalyptic groups emphasized the war and the punishment of evildoers that would inaugurate the coming end of days, while the Pharisees, we may presume, emphasized the utopian kingdom to be established by the Davidic Messiah.

Another position was taken by the Dead Sea sect and some pseudepigraphical texts. They believed that the coming age would indeed begin with a great war and punishment, yet they saw the leadership of the people in the hands of two Messianic figures. A priestly Messiah would take precedence and reestablish the Jerusalem sacrificial cult. Along with him, a Davidic Messiah would rule over the reestablished temporal kingdom.[153] The precedence given to the priestly, or Aaronide, Messiah was, no doubt, the result of the priestly origins and dominance of the Dead Sea group which we have already discussed.

Many scholars have taken the view that the Sadducees did not believe at all in Messianism.[154] Their conclusion is based on the Sadducean denial of fate, divine providence, immortality of the soul, and resurrection. On the other hand, the Sadducees may have adhered more closely to First Temple sources and expected a more natural turn of events which would lead to the restoration of ancient Jewish glory.

Of course, the issue of Messianism really comes to the fore in the rise of Christianity. Early Christianity seems to have combined the apocalyptic view of the sects with a heavy emphasis on the Davidic Messiah, apparently the hallmark of the Pharisaic approach. From this combination emerged a concept that the Messianic era was in fact at hand as Jesus was identified as the Davidic Messiah. When his mission failed to bring about the expected results foretold in the Hebrew prophets, nascent Christianity revised those prophecies through the medium of exegesis and so was able to preserve the concept of the Messiahship of Jesus despite the disappointment. Christianity went even further and saw the Messiah as a divine or semi-divine being.[155] Soon Christianity abrogated Jewish law and so took the steps which would separate it decidedly from Judaism. When this breach became fully apparent, the Christians realized the deep gulf separating them from Judaism and began to shift their mission toward the gentiles. The Christian view that Jewish law had been abrogated served to make gentile Christianity a realistic possibility.

XI. INTERRELATION OF THE SECTS

Palestine was a small country in which the bulk of the populace lived a simple rural life. Nevertheless, Judaism is a communally practiced religion, necessitating cooperation and consensus in the manner of discharging religious duties. For this reason alone, sectarian divisions might become sources of tension and aggravation within a community. Add to this a central sacrificial sanctuary, for control of which various groups might vie, and here are the necessary ingredients for the extension of sectarianism from the philosophical and intellectual realm into real conflict.

On the other hand, the common national heritage and a common foreign enemy often galvanized the people into overcoming and rising above their internal divisions. Further, most of the people belonged to the class called by the Talmud the 'am ha-'areṣ, the common people. This class must have been for the most part unaware of such matters.

Relations between the sects in the Greco-Roman period ranged from cordial disagreement to armed conflict. Let us survey a few examples.

The Maccabean revolt can certainly be seen as beginning with a civil war between pro- and anti-Hellenistic factions within Judea.[156] This civil war eventually resulted in the arrogation of high priestly and royal powers by the Maccabees and their Hasmonean descendants. It was probably as a reaction to this usurpation that righteous Zadokite priests went to the desert to live at Qumran. There one of the Jerusalem priests, by now Sadducean in outlook, attacked the sect's leader on the day which was Yom Kippur according to the sectarian calendar.[157]

The Pharisees eventually raised their objection to the Hasmonean usurpation of the priesthood and kingship, and this resulted in the slaughter of many Pharisees by the Hasmonean king.[158] At the same time, the Hasmonean rulers fought the Samaritans and destroyed the Samaritan temple on Mount Gerizim.[159]

Many differences existed between the Pharisees and Sadducees in regard to Temple service. We know of later scuffles and even riots in the Temple regarding these practices.[160] There is no reason to suspect that such conflicts did not also erupt in earlier times.

On the other hand, the Mishnah portrays cordial dialogues between Pharisees and Sadducees regarding questions of Jewish law.[161] There is again no reason to doubt that such discussions took place, especially in times when tensions were eased for one reason or another. Talmudic reports, however, paint the Boethusians as sabotaging the Rabbinic proclamation of the new moon in an attempt to confuse the Pharisaic calendar, which the Boethusians regarded as illegitimate.[162] We must remember, however, that the Rabbinic dislike for the priestly house of Boethus[163] may have colored their opinions of the Boethusians.

Relations between Jews and the early Christians seem to have been friendly at first. Many peaceful dialogues relating to religious matters are recorded in the New Testament. As the divergences of Christianity from Judaism became increasingly clear, Jews and Christians began to turn against each other. This is already evident in the priestly opposition to Jesus. By the year 70 c.e. the Christian community of Jerusalem would see their national destiny as separate from that of the Jews.[164] It may be that Messianic overtones to the revolt against Rome (of which we shall speak below) made it impossible for the Christians to participate fully in the revolt.

What was the impact of these conflicts on daily life? First, we know that some of the groups, namely the Pharisees and the Dead Sea sect, had special purity laws which required that they eat only food prepared according to regulation.[165] Sadducees would have observed similar laws in regard to the eating of Temple offerings. These groups would have abstained from the food of the 'am ha-'areṣ, who were not careful in regard to purity or tithes. The social consequences of these differences are readily apparent. What needs to be stressed is that, with the exception of the priesthood, one could join another group simply by adopting the rules of the sect. These were not closed groups.[166]

Regarding marriage, we have already seen that beginning in the early years of the Second Commonwealth, the genealogical conception of the Jewish people did not allow their marriage with non-Jews. Hence, marriage with the Samaritans was prohibited, and it remains even so today.

In the case of Christianity, the matter is more complex. Jews and Jewish Christians would probably have married one another in the early years of Christianity. Once Gentile Christianity became the norm, the Jews defined Christians as non-Jews and prohibited marriage with them. Beyond this, we know of no other prohibitions on marriage between the sects. On the other hand, the tendency of people to marry within their own socio-economic group must have operated then as it does today. Indeed, aristocratic and Sadducean priestly families tended to intermarry throughout our period.[167]

Some Jews, those holding the views of extreme Hellenizers desiring complete assimilation into the mainstream of the Greco-Roman world, would have ignored the prohibitions on intermarriage. A small number of individuals would have also found themselves intermarrying for purely personal reasons.

There was, as we mentioned, some disagreement about the dates of holidays. We cannot be sure which dates were followed, except that the Sadducees must have controlled Temple worship. Rabbinic sources and Josephus, however, portray the Pharisees as in control, at least from the time of Salome Alexandra (79 B.C.E.). This account may be idealized, as it is hard to see the Sadducees accepting Pharisaic domination of the Temple.[168] It is not impossible, though, that the immense popularity of the Pharisees gave them considerable leverage over the less popular Sadducean officials of the Temple.

In spite of these accounts of struggles, we must not lose perspective on the extent of these conflicts. Our sources tend to highlight conflicts and disagreements. The fact is that there were affinities among all the groups since they shared many religious principles and practices and a common nationality.

Here we come to a central question. Why do we regard the Samaritans and Christians as having left the Jewish fold while regarding the others as sects within Judaism? There is no general rule. Rather, the answer must be investigated for each specific case.

Regarding the Samaritans it was a combination of their questionable lineage and their religious syncretism which led to their initial rejection by the Judeans. Once they established their own sacrificial sanctuary and adopted a radically limited canon, there was no longer any question of their being considered Jewish. Eventually, political and social developments in the Land of Israel strengthened this division, and it remains permanent to this day.

Regarding Christianity, it was initially the belief in the doctrine of Jesus as the Messiah which divided the Jewish-Christian from the Jew. Given time alone, this disagreement would probably have resulted in a complete and permanent schism. Nonetheless, the relationship between the Jews and early Christians did not result in unreconcilable differences until Christianity increasingly turned toward the gentiles. To this end, the Christians abrogated Mosaic law, the cornerstone of Judaism. They, therefore, would be regarded henceforth as non-Jews.

XII. Foreign Rule and Revolt

In the last years of the Second Commonwealth, as Roman rule became more and more intolerable, different revolutionary groups began to spring up. Foreign domination was nothing new for the Jews. In First Temple times there never ceased to be disagreements about how to relate to the dominant empires. Often, it was assumed that a revolt against the Mesopotamian power would be supported by Egypt, or vice versa. More often than not, these were but vain hopes. Such an assumption led in part to Zedekiah's rebellion against Babylonia, which resulted in the destruction of the nation and its Temple in 586 b.c.e.[169] Indeed, there can be discerned at this time pro-Egyptian and pro-Babylonian parties. The former counseled rebellion as their ally, Egypt, was expected to lend support. The latter, including the prophet Jeremiah, advised the king to pay tribute to Babylonia. After all, they reasoned, foreign or military domination was but a small price to pay for internal self-government and the freedom to pursue their ancient way of life.

In the Maccabean uprising, the lines had been drawn more clearly. The rebellion had begun in a civil war regarding the extent to which Judea was to be Hellenized. At the outset there were the Hellenizers and their opponents. Once Antiochus stepped in and outlawed certain basic Jewish practices and defiled the Temple, the masses of Jews rallied behind the Maccabean family, leaving only the extreme Hellenizers and the armies of Seleucid Syria on the other side. Thus, the revolt became primarily that of the Jewish people against their Greco-Syrian overlords.[170]

With Rome the situation was much more complex. Josephus speaks of the so-called Fourth Philosophy (alongside Pharisees, Sadducees, and Essenes).[171] This group seems to have been identical with the Sicarii ("dagger-carriers"), who played so important a role in the revolt against Rome. These were primarily Galileans who, under Judah the Gaulanite, began to attack the Romans in 4 B.C.E. This faction must have continued its operations and stayed under the leadership of the same family through the Great Revolt of 66–74 C.E. They held that Israel had no master but God Himself and steadfastly refused to accept foreign domination. Josephus states that these men agreed in other respects with the Pharisaic approach. It should be remembered that the revolt against Rome was brewing from the very start of the century, and guerilla groups such as the Sicarii were active throughout this period. The Fourth Philosophy, then, seems to be a Pharisaic-like group especially dedicated to the revolt against Roman domination.[172]

Another group involved in the rebellion was the Zealots. Some have tried to see the Zealots as identical with the Sicarii, but this view is unacceptable. Further, it cannot be argued that the description Josephus gives us of the Fourth Philosophy is a composite portrait of several revolutionary groups (as was argued above regarding the Essenes). After all, Josephus was himself a participant in the revolt and gives us elsewhere very detailed accounts of the revolutionary groups and specifically differentiates them from one another.

The Zealots were a group that crystalized quite late in the revolt. Its main leadership came from lower-level priests of the Jerusalem Temple. Indeed, it was they who suspended the twice-daily sacrifice for the welfare of the Roman emperor—an act tantamount to a declaration of war (66 C.E.). Like the Sicarii their methods were those of terrorists. For both groups terrorism, including assassination of moderate Jews whom they regarded as Roman sympathizers, ultimately may have caused the populace, at least in Jerusalem, to turn against them.[173]

Simeon bar Giora and John of Giscala (Gush Ḥalav in Galilee) stand out as individuals who led factions in the revolt. Both of these men seem to have been charismatic leaders who headed private armies. Simeon was closest in approach to the Sicarii and John to the Zealots, although these leaders cannot be identified with these two groups. Simeon seems to have embodied Messianic dreams to some of his followers, like the later Simeon bar Kosiba (bar Kokhba), who led the revolt against Rome in 132–135 C.E. John, on the other hand, seems to be have been more moderate and was friendly with Simeon ben Gamliel, the leading Pharisee.[174]

The Essenes are mentioned by Josephus only once in regard to the revolt. A certain John the Essene appears as a revolutionary commander.[175] While there is no other direct evidence of Essene participation in the war, the reports that the Romans tortured the Essenes would seem to indicate that the Essenes had thrown in their lot with the rebellion.[176] To be sure, Philo had pictured the Essenes as pacifists,[177] but we must assume that they saw this war as the eschatological battle and, therefore, that they had no qualms about participating in it.[178]

We have discussed above the issue of whether the Essenes are to be identified as the sect of the Dead Sea Scrolls. Here we should say that various theories regarding participation by the Qumran sect in the revolt have been proposed. The *War Scroll* has been seen as a description in eschatological terms of the already-brewing revolt. The *Copper Scroll* has been viewed as indicating where the Temple treasures were hidden at the outbreak of war.[179] These are but speculations. We do know that Qumran was destroyed in the aftermath of the revolt and that some of the sectarians probably fled to Masada, where they perished in the final conflagration.[180]

Who opposed the revolt?[181] The aristocratic leaders, most probably high-level Sadducean priests and their supporters, as well as the extremely Hellenized Jews supported Roman rule, from which, no doubt, they gained commercial and financial advantage. In addition, the moderate Pharisees believed, as did Jeremiah so many years before, that it was better to submit to the military domination of Rome than to risk subjecting religious freedom and the Temple to the wrath of the Empire. Rabbi Johanan ben Zakkai, who established an academy at Yavneh in the last hours of the revolt, certainly took this view.[182] It was as a consequence of the Pharisaic tolerance of Roman rule that the descendants of Rabban Gamliel were entrusted by the Romans with the internal self-government of the Jewish people, usually termed the Patriarchate.[183]

What emerges from this picture is an alignment which cut across sectarian lines. It seems that the Sicarii represented those followers of the Pharisaic order who actively supported the revolt. This was despite the much more moderate, almost pacifist view of some members of the Pharisaic leadership. Whereas the upper-level Sadduceans would have preferred peaceful coexistence with Rome, it was lower-level priests, also of the Sadducean order, who formed the Zealots and effected the formal declaration of revolt. Whereas the sectarian group at Qumran seems to have sat out the war, although ultimately engulfed and destroyed by it, some Essene sectarians were actively involved. While some Judeans saw the revolt as the culmination of the apocalyptic movements of Second Temple times,[184] this was certainly not the view of most rebels or their supporters among the population. Finally, both rebels and moderates had urban and rural, rich and poor constituents. With all we have said, though, it is doubtful whether the revolt could ever have gotten as far as it did if not for the support of the majority of the Jewish population of Judea.

XIII. Conclusion

From this cursory survey, in which we have covered only a small number of issues, it is already clear that Palestinian Judaism in the Hellenistic period was variegated and certainly not monolithic. This situation continued until the destruction of the Temple in 70 C.E. The Talmud gives its reason for the destruction as the Jews' lack of ability to function as a unified people.[185] In fact, Rabbinic tradition looked askance at the entire phenomenon of sectarianism. Its view was that Pharisaism, the intellectual and religious approach the Rabbis had inherited, was in direct continuity with the Mosaic oral tradition.[186] From the vantage point of Rabbinic Judaism, everyone else was a schismatic. Had Israel only adhered to the tradition of the Pharisees, there would have been no Hellenization, no revolt, and no destruction. Just as the Deuteronomic editor of Kings saw the misfortunes of the Israelites in biblical times as stemming from deviation from the teachings of the Lord, so it was this deviation, in the form of the rejection of the true tradition, that led, in the talmudic view, to the destruction in 70 C.E.

We must inquire here as to whether this evaluation is valid. We have seen that the issues raised by the sectarian movements in the Second Temple period were not, in almost every case, new questions. Rather, they constitute a series of unresolved problems remaining from First Temple times. What was new was the venue. It was no longer the Israel surrounded by Semitic paganism that would argue these issues. It was now a nation of Jews first in the Persian, and then in the Hellenistic or Greco-Roman world. This new environment, culturally and historically, gave new impetus to some conflicts and modified others. By and large, though, it did not bring about the schisms; they were already present in biblical times.

So the sectarianism of the Second Temple period is really a

continuation of earlier divisions. If so, can we speak of a normative tradition at any time in pre-Rabbinic times? I think not.
Despite the Rabbinic ideal, it seems that the Jewish people always
had room for differences and for movements within it. These
could be religious, political, or socio-economic.

Were these divisions beneficial or harmful to Jewish life? There
is no question that from a political or military point of view they
were a disadvantage. Had the Jewish people been unified, there
would have been a better chance of holding out longer against
Rome, although there can be no question that enough Roman men
and materiel would have eventually been victorious.

But Judaism was not meant to be simply a military or political
entity. It was and is a way of relating to God and man, of
bringing meaning and purpose to human existence, and of explaining the world around us. The emergence of the Jewish people
into the Hellenistic period was in many ways analogous to its
emergence into modern times. The world in which the Jews lived
was suddenly changed. This new world intensified the old
conflicts. At the same time, the Hellenistic environment created a
greater need to answer the pressing questions Judaism raised. As
such, this was a period in which Judaism was not sure in which
direction to go. What Judaism and the Jewish people needed was
to experiment by playing out the results of the old conflicts to see
how the various approaches would work in this new era. Thus,
the sects were a proving ground from which emerged an answer to
which way Judaism would move in the post–70 C.E. period.

It was the destruction in 70 C.E. which served as the time of
decision. It must be remembered that the destruction of the Temple was not just a religious tragedy. By the time Jerusalem and the
Temple fell, the entire country had been devastated by years of
war and pillage. The entire socio-economic, political, and religious
order had been overturned. Finally, the conflicts that had seethed
above and below ground in Second Temple times needed to be
resolved. It was here that history played its usual role. It decided.

Apocalypticism and the approach of such groups as the Essenes
and the sect of the Dead Sea Scrolls had already served as the
background for emerging Christianity. After all, it was these

groups that had seen the end of days about to dawn. Their energies and many of their ideals, from an historical point of view, found their way into the nascent Christian Church, and these approaches were no longer to be considered Jewish. The mainstream of Jewish life would confront this approach again only in the guise of false-Messiah movements, most notably that of Shabbatai Zevi, or in the form of Christian conversionist preaching.

The Sadducean movement was so tied up with the priestly aristocracy and Temple worship that when the Temple was destroyed and the social order decimated, the priestly, Sadducean approach simply could not endure. Perhaps its emphasis on the primacy of the Temple made its views untenable in the new situation. Perhaps it was the religious victory of the Pharisees and the attendant recognition of their political powers (which we shall mention below) which further weakened the Sadducees. There are some references to Sadducees in post-70 times in talmudic literature, but, as we have said, these are often the result of Christian censors in the Middle Ages who changed words meaning "Christian" or "heretic" to "Sadducee."

We must also consider a theory suggested in the nineteenth century. It is possible that Sadducean sectarians or beliefs went underground and survived to emerge later in the literalist sect of the Karaites.[187] In view of the many similarities which scholars have noted between the Dead Sea sect and the Karaites,[188] it is more likely that if there were any survival of Second Temple sectarianism in the early development of Karaism, it was that of the Dead Sea sect. The confluence of several of these disenfranchised traditions is also possible.

What of the Pharisees? It seems that a combination of their religious and political views made them uniquely able to serve as the continuers of the Jewish tradition. On the political front, they had always counseled cooperation with the existing authorities, and it was through them after the catastrophe of 70 that the Romans set up a system of local Jewish self-government known as the Patriarchate.

On the religious front, of all the sects of the Second Commonwealth, the Pharisees seemed best able to command the allegiance of the common people, the *ʿam ha-ʾareṣ*. Most important, the Pharisaic approach to *halakhah*, Jewish law, was flexible. By allowing it to change with the times, at least in terms of practical applications, they made it a livable system, denying the later Pauline view that Jewish law was an insuperable burden. Thus, Judaism never faced the problems it might have, had a literalist approach to Jewish law become the norm. In regard to theological questions, the Pharisaic beliefs had long accorded with those of most Jews, for in times of trouble, the Jewish people longed to believe in such ideas as afterlife and the Messianic era. If life in this world was not what it should be, they would be rewarded in the next for their observance in this world.

And so it was that after the destruction, the Pharisaic approach, as interpreted by the Rabbis of the Mishnah and Talmud, furnished the groundwork for what we have come to call Rabbinic or normative Judaism. This Pharisaic heritage in the Middle Ages, when Judaism faced the challenges of the Islamic and Christian worlds, was again able to prevail and to flourish by the process of organic, subtle, and imperceptible self-modification and adaptation. Rabbinic Judaism has again had to face alien values in the modern world. It still remains to be seen how the heritage of the Pharisees will continue, but there can be no question that it will.

NOTES

1. J. Bright, *A History of Israel* (Philadelphia: Westminister Press, 1972), 360–363: M. Noth, *The History of Israel* (New York and Evanston: Harper & Row, 1960), 300–308. For the text of the decree see Ezra 1:1–6, 2 Chron. 36:22 f., and cf. Cyrus' inscription in *ANET*, 315 f. which confirms the plausibility of the biblical material.

2. For thorough accounts of biblical history see Bright, *History of Israel*, and W. F. Albright, *From the Stone Age to Christianity* (Garden City, N.Y.: Doubleday Anchor Books, 1957).

3. See Isa. 45:1–13, U. Rappaport, "Cyrus," *EJ* 5, 1184–86.

4. Bright, 363, 377 f.

5. See C. Huart, *Ancient Persia and Iranian Civilization* (London: Routledge & Kegan Paul, 1927), 73–79.

6. This was the case of Elephantine, on which see below, p. 11, and the thorough study by B. Porten, *Archives from Elephantine: The Life of an Ancient*

Jewish Military Colony (Berkeley and Los Angeles: University of California Press, 1968).

7. Rabbinic tradition saw the period of the Second Temple under Persian rule as lasting only thirty-four years, thus losing almost a century in its chronology. See J. Z. Lauterbach, "Midrash and Mishnah," *Rabbinic Essays* (Cincinnati: Hebrew Union College Press, 1951), 253 f.

8. V. Tcherikover, *Hellenistic Civilization and the Jews* (Philadelphia: Jewish Publication Society, 1966), 1–7.

9. See H. Jonas, *The Gnostic Religion* (Boston: Beacon Press, 1963), pp. 3–27, Albright, *Stone Age*, 334–344.

10. Tcherikover, 7–10.

11. Ibid., 152–234.

12. One of the major objections to the Hasmoneans was their assumption of the high priesthood and kingship at the same time. See the talmudic story in B. Qiddushin 66a.

13. E. Schürer, *The History of the Jewish People in the Age of Jesus Christ*, ed. G. Vermes and F. Millar (Edinburgh: T. & T. Clark, 1973), 233–242.

14. Ibid., 267–470.

15. Ibid., 484–513. On the date of 74 C.E. for the fall of Masada, see p. 512 and n. 139.

16. See B. Giṭṭin 56a.

17. See, for example, L. Finkelstein, *The Pharisees* (Philadelphia: Jewish Publication Society, 1966), 2 vols., and M. Hengel, *Judaism and Hellenism* (Philadelphia: Fortress Press, 1974), 2 vols.

18. Cf. J. Maxwell Miller, *The Old Testament and the Historian* (Philadelphia: Fortress Press, 1976), 1–39 on the literary evidence of Scripture.

19. M. Smith, *Politics and Parties that Shaped the Old Testament* (New York: Columbia University Press, 1971), 1–14.

20. The best account of their discovery is in Y. Yadin, *The Message of the Scrolls* (New York: Simon & Schuster, 1957), 15–30.

21. R. de Vaux, *Archaeology and the Dead Sea Scrolls* (London: Oxford University Press, 1973), 97–99.

22. For surveys of the material from Qumran, see F. M. Cross, *The Ancient Library of Qumran* (Garden City, N.Y.: Doubleday, 1961), 30–47, and J. T. Milik, *Ten Years of Discovery in the Wilderness of Judaea* (London: SCM Press, 1959).

23. De Vaux, 126–128.

24. Cross, 51–106, de Vaux, 128–138, Yadin, 160–189.

25. For definitions, see J. M. Grintz, "Apocrypha and Pseudepigrapha." *EJ* 3, 181 f. These works are, for the most part, collected in R. H. Charles, *The Apocrypha and Pseudepigrapha of the Old Testament*, 2 vols. (Oxford: Clarendon Press, 1913).

26. On the dating of the individual books, see the introductions in Charles and the many individual articles in the *Encyclopaedia Judaica*, which, in most cases, provide an up-to-date consensus. For apocryphal and pseudepigraphal material found at Qumran, see the sources in n. 22. For a thorough but sometimes outdated study of this literature, see E. Schürer, *A History of the Jewish People in the Time of Jesus Christ* (New York: Scribners, 1891), vol. III.

27. For various views on why Judaism rejected these texts, see the essays of

G. F. Moore, L. Ginzberg, S. Zeitlin, J. Bloch, and M. Haran in S. Leiman, ed., *The Canon and Masorah of the Hebrew Bible* (New York: KTAV, 1974), 115–253.

28. For later Jewish relationship to the Apocrypha and pseudepigrapha, see Y. Dan, "Apocrypha and Pseudepigrapha, In Medieval Hebrew Literature," *EJ* 3, 186 f.

29. Schürer (1891) III, 321–381; H. A. Wolfson, *Philo* (Cambridge, Mass.: Harvard University Press, 1968) I, 1–86.

30. J. Neusner, *From Politics to Piety* (Englewood Cliffs, N.J.: Prentice-Hall, 1973), 67–80.

31. See A. Schalit, "Josephus Flavius," *EJ* 10, 251–263, bibliography, 265; Schürer I (1973), 43–63.

32. K. Kohler, "Sadducees," *JE* 10, 633.

33. Most notable is E. R. Goodenough, *Jewish Symbols in the Greco-Roman Period*, 13 vols. (New York: Pantheon Books, 1953–68).

34. This is the theme of Smith, 15–56.

35. Bright, 280–282, 318–323.

36. 2 Kings 17.

37. For a thorough examination of these sources, see R. J. Coggins, *Samaritans and Jews* (Atlanta: John Knox Press, 1975). Our conclusions, however, are not the same as his.

38. Y. Kaufmann, *Toledot Ha-'Emunah Ha-Yisra'elit* (Jerusalem: Mossad Bialik, Tel Aviv: Dvir, 1966/67) IV, 296–301.

39. Bright, 382–384.

40. Bright, 191–193, 226 f.

41. Bright, 233 f., cf. Smith, 22 f.

42. 1 Kings 13:1–10, 33 f.

43. Northernisms are the pl. -*in* (for examples see Gesinius § 87e), and fem. singular pronominal suffix, -*ekhi* (for examples see Gesenius § 91e). It is true that most of these examples occur in late biblical books (C. Gordon, *Ugaritic Textbook* [Rome: Pontifical Biblical Institute, 1965], 99, n. 1, and "North-Israelite Influence on Post-exilic Hebrew," *Eretz Israel* 3 [1954], 85–88), but early examples can be cited.

44. C. Rabin, "Hebrew and Aramaic in the First Century," *The Jewish People in the First Century*, ed. S. Safrai and M. Stern, II (Philadelphia: Fortress Press, 1976), 1033–1037. Cf. also J. Greenfield, "The Languages of Palestine, 200 B.C.E.–200 C.E.," *Jewish Languages: Theme and Variations*, ed. H. Paper (Cambridge, Mass.: Association for Jewish Studies, 1978), 143–154.

45. See Tcherikover, 269–377.

46. See F. E. Peters, *The Harvest of Hellenism* (New York: Simon & Schuster, 1970), 446–479.

47. See E. Schürer, "Alexandria," *JE* 1, 361–366.

48. See H. St. John Thackeray, *The Septuagint and Jewish Worship* (London: H. Milford, 1921), and S. Jellicoe, *The Septuagint and Modern Study* (Oxford: Clarendon Press, 1968).

49. See H. A. Wolfson, *Philo* (Cambridge: Harvard University Press, 1968), 2 vols., for a detailed study of this synthesis.

50. S. Lieberman, *Greek in Jewish Palestine* (New York: P. Feldheim, 1965),

29–67; G. Mussies, "Greek in Palestine and the Diaspora," *The Jewish People in the First Century*, ed. Safrai and Stern, II, 1040–1064; Hengel, *Judaism and Hellenism* I, 58–65.

51. *Antiquities* XIII, 5:9.

52. Schürer (1891) II, ii, 29 f. On the priesthood and offerings, see ibid., II, 207–305.

53. Ibid II, 31–34.

54. On the Zadokites see L. Schiffman. *Halakhah at Qumran* (Leiden: E. J. Brill, 1975), 72–75; J. Liver, "Bene Sadok She-Be-Khat Midbar Yehudah," *Eretz Israel* 8 (1967), 71–81. Although the Hasmonean takeover of the priesthood resulted in the expulsion of the Zadokites, it is interesting that the Hasmonean family under John Hyrcanus eventually adopted the views of the Sadducean priests and aligned themselves with them politically (Schürer I [1973], 211–213).

55. *Antiquities* XIII, 10:6; Schürer (1891) II, ii, 34–38.

56. J. Neusner, "The Rabbinic Traditions about the Pharisees before A.D. 70: The Problem of Oral Transmission," *JJS* 22 (1971), 9 f., correctly points out that these traditions of the fathers are not to be identified with the Oral Law. On the other hand, we see these traditions as a step toward the development of a full-fledged Oral Torah concept.

57. Surveyed in Schürer (1891) II, ii, 35–38 and discussed in detail in Finkelstein. *Pharisees*, I, 101–144, II, 637–753. This discussion, however, tends to find socio-economic background for practically all differences. It must also be remembered that different approaches to legal exegesis of the Scriptures may have played a part.

58. L. Ginzberg, "Boethusians," *JE* 3, 284 f. remains the best summary.

59. Schürer (1891) II, ii, 19–22. He is probably correct that this name was first given to them by their adversaries. They seem from tannaitic sources to have called themselves *haverim*, "fellows" or "colleagues," on which see Schürer, pp. 22–24.

60. On the pre–70 C.E. Pharisees and the problems in dealing with the sources regarding them, see Neusner, *From Politics to Piety*, 1–95.

61. Finkelstein I, 73–81.

62. Cf. S. Baron, *A Social and Religious History of the Jews* II (New York, Columbia University Press, 1952), 37.

63. Neusner, *From Politics to Piety*, 91.

64. *Antiquities* XIII, 5:9. Cf. Schürer (1891) II, ii, 26.

65. So Schürer, loc. cit. following Wellhausen.

66. The little that is known about the Hasidim is conveniently brought together in K. Kohler, "Essenes," *JE* 5, 225, 227, and in "Hasidim," *EJ* 7, 1383–1388.

67. This is the import of M. Avot 1:1. See L. Finkelstein, *Ha-Perushim Ve-'Anshe Keneset Ha-Gedolah* (New York: Jewish Theological Seminary, 1950).

68. G. F. Moore, *Judaism* (New York: Schocken Books, 1971) I, 33, sees the Scribes as the successors to the Men of the Great Assembly and predecessors of the Rabbis, i.e. the Pharisees. Others saw the Soferim as the originators of that assembly (Y. D. Gilat, "Soferim," *EJ* 15, 79–81). Y. Kaufmann, *Toledot* IV, 481–5 takes the view that there never was a period of the Soferim. He sees the term *sofer* ("scribe") as a general professional term not denoting a class of teachers

of any specific period. Indeed, the entire concept of an era of Soferim may be the result of the tendency of the *Wissenschaft des Judentums* to see halakhic categories, in this case *divre soferim*, in historical terms. But of. B. Qiddushin 30a and P. Sheqalim 5:1.

69. Hengel, *Judaism and Hellenism* I, 218–247, takes the view that the Essenes, who according to him are identical with the Dead Sea sect, were greatly influenced by Hellenism.

70. See F. M. Cross, "The Early History of the Qumran Community," *New Directions in Biblical Archaeology*, ed. D. N. Freedman and J. C. Greenfield (Garden City, N.Y.: Doubleday, 1971), 70–89.

71. Schiffman, *Halakhah at Qumran*, 70–75.

72. On the settlements, see R. de Vaux, *Archaeology and the Dead Sea Scrolls*, 1–90.

73. For a catalogue of the texts, see above, n. 22. On the relationship of the scrolls to the settlement, see de Vaux, 95–102.

74. Schiffman, *Halakhah at Qumran*, 75 f.

75. Cf. ibid., 134–136.

76. H. Strack, *Introduction to the Talmud and Midrash* (New York: Harper & Row, 1965), 12–20; S. Lieberman, *Hellenism in Jewish Palestine* (New York: Jewish Theological Seminary, 1962), 93–99; and Neusner, "Rabbinic Traditions about the Pharisees before A.D. 70," 1–18.

77. But cf. J. Neusner, "The Written Tradition in the Pre-Rabbinic Period," *JSJ* 4 (1973), 56–65.

78. It is alleged by the post-talmudic scholion to *Megillat Ta'anit* that the Sadducees did have a written legal code, the *Sefer Gezerata'*. For this text, see H. Lichtenstein, "Die Fastenrolle: Eine Untersuchung zur jüdisch-hellenistischen Gerichte," *HUCA* 8–9 (1931–32), 331.

79. See above, n. 24.

80. *Antiquities* XIII, 5:9; Schürer (1891) II, ii, 191.

81. The etymologies are surveyed by Schürer, 190 f.

82. Cf. M. Mansoor, "Essenes," *EJ* 6, 901 f.

83. Schürer (1891) II, ii, 195 f., 200.

84. See above, n. 69.

85. Philo, *On the Contemplative Life*; K. Kohler, "Therapeutae," *JE* 12, 138 f.

86. For a survey see K. Kohler, "Essenes," *JE* 5, 225–227. There is no basis on which to connect these groups with the Essenes, except in the most general way.

87. This term, when used in the Bible to describe Israelites, clearly refers to some social or political group within the society of Israel during the First Temple period. Some scholars take the term to refer to some kind of legislative-judicial assembly, while others see it as denoting the free citizenry. For the various views, none of which can be conclusively proven, see S. Talmon, " 'Am Ha-'Ares," *'Ensiqlopedia Miqra'it* 6, 239–242. In tannaitic usage the term refers to the common people, but already in tannaitic sources, it begins to mean an unlearned Jew, a usage much more prominent in amoraic times and in medieval Jewish folklore.

88. Finkelstein, *Pharisees* II, 754–761. Contrast the less flattering view of A. Oppenheimer, "Am Ha-Arez, Second Temple and Mishnah," *EJ* 2, 833–36.

89. On the origins of the synagogue, see J. Guttmann, ed., *The Synagogue: Studies in Origins, Archaeology and Architecture* (New York: KTAV, 1975), 3–40. On prayer and the worship service, see I. Elbogen, *Ha-Tefillah Be-Yisra'el* (Tel Aviv: Dvir, 1972), 177–189.

90. "Pottery," *EJ* 13, 942. Cf. Smith, 61 f.

91. Some hesitations on both sides may be the cause of the reports of tension found in Rabbinic sources. For these, see Oppenheimer, above, n. 88.

92. *Antiquities* XVIII, 1:3.

93. R. de Vaux, *Ancient Israel* (New York, Toronto: McGraw-Hill, 1965) II, 331–344.

94. On the Josianic reformation, see Bright, 316–321, and E. W. Nicholson, *Deuteronomy and Tradition* (Philadephia: Fortress Press, 1967), 1–17.

95. Ezek. 44:6–16.

96. See Schiffman, *Halakhah at Qumran* 73–75, and J. Liver, *Hiqere Miqra' U-Megillot Midbar Yehudah* (Jerusalem: Mossad Bialik, 1971), 131–154.

97. Porton, *Archives from Elephantine*, 105–186.

98. A. Schalit, "Onias, Temple of," *EJ* 12, 1404 f.

99. *Antiquities* XI, 8:2, 4.

100. Coggins, 95–97.

101. F. M. Cross, "Papyri of the Fourth Century B.C. from Daliyeh," *New Directions in Biblical Archaeology*, 45–69.

102. Some have claimed that sacrifices were offered at Qumran by the Dead Sea sect, but this is most unlikely. See my Response to B. Bokser, "Philo's Description of Jewish Practices," *Center for Hermeneutical Studies*, Colloquy 30 (Berkeley, 1977), 20 f.

103. N. M. Sarna, "Bible, Canon, Text," *EJ* 4, 817. Sarna explains the term as coming from Sumerian into Semitic and then Greek usage, for a "reed, cane," and later "measuring rod."

104. The tripartite canon, as Sarna terms it, was known to Ben Sira (ca. 180 B.C.E.), his grandson who translated his work into Greek (ca. 132 B.C.E.), the author of 2 Maccabees, Josephus, and the New Testament (Sarna, 821). There is no evidence that this was disputed except by the Samaritans, on which see below.

105. See Sarna, 824f. Canonization of the *Ketuvim* is seen by him as a gradual process ending "well into the second century C.E." For this reason, "The widely held, although unsupported, view that the formal and final canonization of the *Ketuvim* occurred at the Synod of Jabneh (c. 100 C.E.) has to be considerably modified. More probably, decisions taken on that occasion came to be widely accepted and thus regarded as final in succeeding generations" (col. 825).

106. Origen, Jerome, and Pseudo-Tertullian (for the texts see Schürer [1891] II, ii, 34 f., n. 89).

107. Ibid., ii, 35.

108. After all, it was shared by all the sources mentioned in n. 104.

109. See Sarna, 825 f., on the Hellenistic canon, but contrast Coggins, 154, who follows G. W. Anderson. "Canonical and Non-Canonical," *The Cambridge History of the Bible* (Cambridge: University Press, 1970) I, 145–9, who sees the Torah as the extent of the Hellenistic Jewish canon of Alexandria.

110. See Coggins, 148–155. The Samaritan Book of Joshua is a medieval

Arabic text containing much legendary material. Although its author claims to have translated it from a Hebrew source, this cannot be adduced as evidence for the claim that the Samaritans had the biblical Book of Joshua. See A. Loewenstamm, "Samaritans, Language and Literature," *EJ* 14, 754.

111. Coggins, 148–155.

112. Cross, *Ancient Library*, 30–47, and the index of biblical passages in J. A. Fitzmyer, *The Dead Sea Scrolls: Major Publications and Tools for Study* (Missoula, Mont.: Scholars Press, 1975), 152–170.

113. See J. A. Sanders, "Cave 11 Surprises and the Question of Canon," *New Directions in Biblical Archaeology*, 113–130.

114. Cross, 163–194.

115. The absence of these variants in what are clearly the proto-Samaritan fragments from Qumran shows that these are late, tendentious readings. It is not possible that they are authentic.

116. E. Würthwein, *The Text of the Old Testament* (Oxford: Blackwell, 1957), 3–5. Cf. Coggins, 149 f.

117. Bright, 233 f.

118. Cf. S. Talmon, "Divergences in Calendar-Reckoning in Ephraim and Judah," *VT* 8 (1958), 48–74.

119. S. Talmon, "The Calendar Reckoning of the Sect from the Judean Desert," *Aspects of the Dead Sea Scrolls*, ed. C. Rabin and Y. Yadin (Jerusalem: Magnes Press, 1958), 162–199.

120. Ibid., 185–187.

121. The odd features of the Samaritan calendar seem to be the result of Byzantine and Islamic influence and need not be discussed here.

122. *Pesher Habakkuk* 11:4–9; cf. Talmon, *Aspects*, 167.

123. On urbanization in ancient Israel, see H. Reviv, "City," *EJ* 5, 583–590; E. Neufeld, "The Emergence of a Royal-Urban Society in Ancient Israel," *HUCA* 31 (1960), 31–53.

124. De Vaux, *Ancient Israel* I, 14 f.; S. Abramsky, "Rechabites," *EJ* 13, 1609–1611.

125. Abramsky, 1611.

126. B. 'Eruvin 21b.

127. Tcherikover, 90–116; Hengel I, 58–106; Lieberman, *Greek in Jewish Palestine*, 91–114.

128. Cf. Schürer (1891) II, ii, 39 f., for the Hellenism of the Sadducees.

129. Pharisaic support seems to have come from the plebeian classes in the city of Jerusalem, while the aristocrats aligned themselves with the Sadducees.

130. See "The Sect and its Opponents," in C. Rabin, *Qumran Studies* (Oxford: University Press, 1957), 53–70. Regardless of how we identify the sect's many opponents, described by the Dead Sea Scrolls in epithets, it is certain that they represented the Jerusalem establishment, priestly, Pharisaic, or both.

131. Most theories for the founding of the sect presume that the Qumranites withdrew at some time from Jerusalem due to a disagreement with the establishment there. See above, p. 15.

132. See *Rule of the Congregation* (1QSᵃ) 2:11–21, and my discussion of it in Response to B. Bokser, 24–26.

133. For the biblical attitude, see J. H. Tigay, "Drunkenness," *EJ* 6, 237 f.

On a possible wine cult in Palestine, see M. Smith, "On the Wine God in Palestine," *S. W. Baron Jubilee Volume*, ed. S. Lieberman and A. Hyman (New York: American Academy for Jewish Research, 1974), II, 815–829.

134. Rabin, *Qumran Studies*, 22–36; J. Licht, *Megillat Ha-Serakhim* (Jerusalem: Mossad Bialik, 1965), 10–13; Schiffman, *Halakhah at Qumran*, 90. See also M. Hengel, *Property and Riches in the Early Church* (Philadelphia: Fortress Press, 1974), although to some extent this work is aimed at pointing the way for modern Christians.

135. This is despite prophetic criticism of excesses and social divisions. See Hengel, *Property*, 12–19.

136. Schürer (1891) II, ii, 195–197.

137. See Acts 2:44, 4:32, and Hengel, *Property*, 31–34.

138. Philo, *Every Good Man Is Free*, sec. 76; Schürer II, ii, 192 f.

139. Josephus, *Life* 2 (Banus), Matt. 3:1–12, Mark 1:1–8, Luke 3:1–18, John 1:6–8, 19–28 (John the Baptist).

140. On these sites, see R. de Vaux, *Archaeology and the Dead Sea Scrolls*, 1–48, 61–83, and E.-M. Lapperousaz, *Qoumrân* (Paris: A. & J. Picard, 1976), 63–92.

141. S. Loewenstamm, "Mawet," *'Enṣiqlopedia Miqra'it* 4, 754–763; "She'ol," *'Enṣiqlopedia Miqra'it* 7, 454–7. Ossuaries and other forms of burial in caves should also be seen as below ground. Cf. E. Meyers, *Jewish Ossuaries: Reburial and Rebirth* (Rome: Biblical Institute Press, 1971).

142. J. Guttmann, *Philosophies of Judaism* (Garden City, N.Y.: Doubleday, 1966), 24 f.

143. *Wars* II, 8:14 (note the use of "Hades"); *Antiquities* XVIII, 1:4; Schürer (1891) II, ii, 13.

144. Ibid.

145. *Wars* II, 8:11; Schürer, 205. Josephus' account does give a gnostic tinge to the views of the Essenes, but this is probably the result of his attempt to appeal to his Hellenistic readers.

146. W. S. LaSor, *The Dead Sea Scrolls and the New Testament* (Grand Rapids, Mich.: Eerdmans, 1972), 93 f.; H. Ringgren, *The Faith of Qumran* (Philadelphia: Fortress Press, 1963), 148 f. Ringgren notes that only one doubtful passage would support the idea that the dead were to be resurrected for the final battle at the end of days. He notes that the sect seems to have known the Book of Daniel, which includes this teaching. Nonetheless, we should note that the Book of Daniel at Qumran was still not closed, and that some sections we have may not have been in their recension.

147. Ringgren, 149–151. Some passages have been taken by others to refer to immortality of the soul, but we interpret these to refer to Messianic bliss. Ringgren notes that Josephus' account of the Essene tenet of the immortality of the soul disagrees with the Qumran texts. If so, and if the two groups are to be identified, he notes the need to assume that Josephus modified his description in accord with his "Hellenizing tendency."

148. *Antiquities* XIII, 5:9, XVIII, 1:3; *Wars* II, 8:14.

149. Schürer (1891) II, ii, 14–17.

150. Ringgren, 52–55, 100–112.

151. See J. Liver," "Mashiah," *'Enṣiqlopedia Miqra'it* 5, 507–526, and J. Licht, "Yom 'Adonai," *'Enṣiqlopedia Miqra'it* 3, 593–595 for a survey of the sources.

152. For a thorough discussion, see R. H. Charles, *Eschatology* (New York: Schocken, 1963), 167–361.
153. A considerable literature exists on this question. See J. Liver, "The Doctrine of the Two Messiahs in Sectarian Literature in the Time of the Second Commonwealth," *HTR* 52 (1959), 149–85. For further bibliography see *Halakhah at Qumran*, 51, n. 202.
154. Schürer (1891) II, ii, 14; K. Kohler, "Sadducees," *JE* 10, 631.
155. For an enlightening view on Jesus within the context of Jewish Messianic movements, see W. D. Davies, "From Schweitzer to Scholem: Reflections on Sabbatai Svi," *JBL* 95 (1976), 529–558.
156. So Tcherikover throughout his discussion, 152–234.
157. Talmon, *Aspects*, 167.
158. Schürer (1973) I, 213 f.
159. Coggins, 114.
160. T. Ḥagigah 2:11–12.
161. Collected in Schürer (1891) II, ii, 5–8. Many other tannaitic sources of this kind can also be cited.
162. T. Rosh Ha-Shanah 1:15 and parallels cited by Lieberman, ad loc.
163. Ginzberg, "Boethusians," *JE* 6, 285.
164. Schürer (1973) I, 498.
165. Rabin, *Qumran Studies*, 1–21, describes the relationship of these purity laws to membership in the group.
166. See Rabin, loc. cit., and S. Lieberman, "The Discipline in the So-Called Dead Sea Manual of Discipline," *Texts and Studies* (New York: KTAV, 1974), 200–207.
167. Finkelstein, *Pharisees* I, 21–23 describes the exclusiveness of the priesthood in regard to marriage.
168. Neusner, *From Politics to Piety* 45–66, takes the view that Josephus' claims of Pharisaic popularity and control of the Temple only emerged as a bid to the Romans to support the Pharisees. In this he follows M. Smith, "Palestinian Judaism in the First Century," *Israel: Its Role in Civilization*, ed. M. Davis (New York: Harper & Row, 1956), 75 f.
169. See Bright, 323–339.
170. Tcherikover, 152–234.
171. *Antiquities* XVIII, 1:6.
172. D. M. Rhoads, *Israel in Revolution: 6–74 C.E.* (Philadelphia: Fortress Press, 1976), 111–122; M. Stern, "Zealots," *Encyclopaedia Judaica Yearbook* (Jerusalem: Keter, 1973), 134–140.
173. Rhoads, 97–110; Stern, 140–145.
174. Rhoads, 122–137, 140–148; Stern, 145–149.
175. *Wars* II, 20:4, III, 2:1.
176. Rhoads, 156; Stern, 150 n. 17.
177. *Every Good Man Is Free*, sec. 78.
178. So Stern, loc. cit.
179. But see Cross, *Ancient Library*, 20–25.
180. Rhoads, 156–158; de Vaux, *Archaeology*, 37–44; Y. Yadin, *Masada* (New York: Random House, 1966), 174.
181. See Rhoads, 150–159.

182. See A. J. Saldarini, "Johanan ben Zakkai's Escape from Jerusalem: Origin and Development of a Rabbinic Story," *JSJ* 6 (1975), 189–204.
183. Schürer (1973) I, 523–527.
184. Rhoads, 170–173.
185. B. Giṭṭin 55b–56a.
186. This is the import of M. 'Avot, chap. 1.
187. This theory is propounded by A. Geiger in numerous places. For a survey and bibliography see B. Revel, *The Karaite Halakah* (Philadelphia: Dropsie College, 1913), 9–14. For medieval sources espousing the same view, see ibid., 6–8.
188. N. Wieder, *The Judean Scrolls and Karaism* (London: East and West Library, 1962). But cf. L. Nemoy, "Karaites," *EJ* 10, 762 f., who rejects the possibility of any historical relationship.

SELECTED BIBLIOGRAPHY

Finkelstein, Louis. *The Pharisees*. Philadelphia: Jewish Publication Society, 1966.
Gaster, Moses. *The Samaritans*. London: Milford, 1925.
Lauterbach, Jacob Z. *Rabbinic Essays*. Cincinnati: Hebrew Union College Press, 1951.
Neusner, Jacob. *From Politics to Piety: The Emergence of Pharisaic Judaism*. Englewood Cliffs: Prentice Hall, 1973.
Rabin, Chaim. *Qumran Studies*. New York: Schocken Books, 1975.
Simon, Marcel. *Jewish Sects at the Time of Jesus*. Philadelphia: Fortress Press, 1967.
Tcherikover, Victor. *Hellenistic Civilization and the Jews*. Philadelphia: Jewish Publication Society, 1966.
Yadin, Yigael. *The Message of the Scrolls*, New York: Simon & Schuster, 1957.
Zeitlin, Solomon. *The Rise and Fall of the Judean State*, Vol. 1: 332–37 BCE; Vol. 2: 37 BCE—6CE; Vol. 3: 66CE—120CE. Philadelphia: Jewish Publication Society, 1962–1978.

Rabbanism and Karaism: The Contest for Supremacy

DANIEL J. LASKER
Ben Gurion University of the Negev, Beer Sheva

I

IN HIS MONUMENTAL WORK of theology and law, written in 937 C.E., the Karaite Jacob al-Qirqisani records a conversation he had with the Rabbanite Jacob ben Ephraim al-Shami. Qirqisani asks why it is that the Rabbanites, who at that time (as they are now) were the majority of the Jewish community, intermarried with the followers of the discredited pseudo-messiah Abu Isa al-Isfahani. The latter, Qirqisani claims, "attribute prophecy to men who had nothing to do with it" and, therefore, are virtually heretics. Ben Ephraim responds that the Rabbanites accept the Isunians, the followers of Abu Isa, "because they do not differ from us in the observance of holidays." Qirqisani, whose own Karaites were not acceptable to the Rabbanite majority, takes this answer to mean that "manifestation of (complete) unbelief is more pardonable than display of (petty) differences in the observance of holidays." In other words, Rabbanite Judaism can coexist with major doctrinal differences as long as they do not lead to substantial behavioral divergencies. It is not able to abide ritual changes which involve, for example, the existence of a different calendar. Theological heresy is pardonable; observance of Passover on a different date is not.[1]

In a way, Qirqisani is correct that this is somewhat illogical. After all, in most theological matters the Karaites and the Rabbanites shared identical views. Still, the Rabbanites preferred the doctrinally divergent Isunians, whose ritual changes were minor,

47

to the doctrinally acceptable Karaites, who had adopted a different calendar. We see, then, that the Rabbanite acceptance or rejection of a competing sect was not predicated upon logic, and, in general, we may conclude that reason plays only a minor role in the determination of which dissidents are tolerated by the majority.[2] Even more significant, we note from Qirqisani's report that calendrical changes are those which most sharply distinguish one sect of Judaism from another. From the earliest days of Jewish schism, which, Qirqisani claims, happened first in the days of Jeroboam ben Nabat, who divided the Israelite monarchy into two nations after the death of King Solomon, the calendar has been a major focus of these controversies.[3]

It is not necessary here to give all the details of the Rabbanite-Karaite dispute regarding the calendar. We may ask, however, why it is that the Karaites adopted their own calculations instead of going along with the prevalent Rabbanite system. The answer to this question has been the subject of much dispute, since the reason for the emergence of Karaism may well rest upon it. In investigating this issue, let us look first at the best-known Rabbanite explanation of the history of the sect and its founder, Anan ben David.

According to the Rabbanite source, which, ironically, is preserved only in a Karaite work, Anan, who lived in the second half of the eighth century, was in line to become the exilarch, or chief civil authority, of all Babylonian Jewry. Since, however, he was accused of lawlessness and lack of piety, his less learned but more humble brother Hananiah was chosen for this prestigious and powerful position. Out of jealousy, Anan gathered around him remnants of those sectarian groups which had flourished at the time of the Second Temple, namely Sadducees and Boethusians, and organized his own group with himself as exilarch.

This affair was discovered by the Muslim authorities, and Anan was put in prison and sentenced to death. In jail with him was a Muslim scholar, identified by other sources as Abu Ḥanifa al-Nuʿuman ibn Thabit,[4] who was likewise sentenced to death. The Muslim suggested that Anan bribe the viceroy into permitting him an audience with the caliph. At that meeting Anan could persuade the ruler that he did not claim to be the head of Judaism but was the leader of a different religion. Therefore, since he was not contesting his brother, whom the caliph had appointed exilarch, he was not, in effect, challenging the authority of the caliph. If Anan could entice his followers to support this assertion that they had their own religion, Abu Ḥanifa told him, his life would be spared. He was able to convince his supporters by claiming a vision from the prophet Elijah.

When he was received by the caliph, Anan is reported to have said: "The religion of my brother employs a calendar based upon calculation of the time of the new moon and intercalation of leap years by cycles, whereas mine depends upon actual observation of the new moon and intercalation regulated by the ripening of new grain." Since the caliph's religion likewise declared the new months on the basis of astronomical observation, Anan gained his favor and good will.[5] Thus, Karaism was founded.

The standard Rabbanite explanation of how Karaism began is, then, as follows: Anan was a crass opportunist who acted out of personal pique and desire for advancement. Changes in the calendar were made to curry favor with the ruling Muslims. Other differences were the result of Anan's attempt to demonstrate that his religion was not that of his brother, the caliph-appointed exilarch. Were it not for Anan's desire to avoid the death penalty, the family squabble would never have turned into a religious schism.

The Karaites, of course, tell a much different story of their origin. The true Judaism was always Karaism, but many schismatics, starting, as mentioned, with Jeroboam, and continuing through the Second Temple period and up to the present day with Rabbanites, perverted the truth. Anan merely restored the Jewish religion to its original biblical form. Ritual divergencies were the result not of Anan's opportunism, but of his return to the correct biblical way of life. Thus, the change in the calendrical system was mandated by the biblical text, which, in Anan's view, the Rabbanites had circumvented by their use of mathematical calculations. The conclusions Anan reached by his literal interpretation of the Scriptures were embodied in his *Book of Precepts (Sefer*

Ha-Mizvot), seen by his opponents as an attempt to replace the Talmud.[6] Anan, nevertheless, was aware that the Bible is amenable to varying interpretations, and he is said to have coined the motto of Karaism, "Search well in the Torah, and do not rely upon my opinion."[7]

Both the Rabbanite and the Karaite views of the founding of this sect are subject to critical inquiry. A number of scholars have questioned the historicity of the Rabbanite account because of its lateness and obvious bias.[8] On the other hand, in light of our extensive knowledge of the history of Rabbinic Judaism, the rewriting of history, so that the Rabbanites are the schismatics and the Karaites are the original exponents of Judaism, is not an acceptable explanation, either. Unfortunately, given the paucity of sources, it is likely that we will never know the whole story behind Anan's defection from Rabbanism and the reasons for the ritual changes he introduced into Judaism. We do know, however, that the processes he put into motion resulted in the formation of a new Jewish sect.

No matter what view we accept of Anan's motivations, we are still confronted by the question of his success. Even if we picture Anan as the basest of characters, as many Rabbanites were wont to do, that does not explain his ability to rally around himself enough supporters to give impetus to a sectarian movement which has now lasted over twelve hundred years. Modern Karaism is very different from Ananism, which, in its original form, lasted but a relatively short time.[9] Nevertheless, Karaism does go back to Anan and his original schism. It might be instructive, therefore, to look at Anan's teachings in their historical setting.

II

Rabbinic Judaism as we know it came about as a result of a long process which began even before the Bible was completed. It is based on the major presupposition that the laws of the Torah, incomplete as they are in their written form, are to be supplemented by an Oral Torah, whose authority is equal to that of the Written Torah. This Oral Torah was also given to Moses at

Sinai and was vouchsafed through its preservation by Joshua, the elders, the prophets, and, finally, the men of the Great Assembly.[10] The successors of the men of the Great Assembly eventually became known as the Rabbis, and it is their teachings which form the basis of the Jewish religion to this day. The two great literary-legal works of Rabbinic Jewry are the Mishnah, edited approximately 200 C.E., and the commentary on it, the Gemara, around 500 C.E., which together constitute the Talmud.[11]

It must be noted that as the Talmud was being developed, not all Jews agreed with its basic premise, namely, that there is a divine Oral Torah which has equal status with the Written Torah. During the Second Temple period, these dissenters were members of a number of different groups, the most prominent being the Sadducees and their allies the Boethusians, the Essenes, and the sect of the Dead Sea Scrolls (who may or may not have been Essenes). Those Jews who did believe in the Oral Torah were known as Pharisees and their leaders as the Rabbis. Their view of Jewish law, which became known as Rabbanism, eventually was triumphant. With the destruction of the Temple, apparently only the Pharisees remained as a functioning movement. If it were not for the Dead Sea Scrolls, we would have almost no literary remains of a non-Pharisaic Second Temple Jewish sect. As it is, most of our knowledge of the sectarian groups of that period comes from secondary, and often subjective and antagonistic, sources.[12]

Since the Pharisees emerged from the destruction of the Second Temple as the dominant, if not the only, organized Jewish movement, it is customary to think of Rabbinic Judaism as proceeding unhindered to the compilation of the Talmud and to total hegemony over the religious affairs of the Jewish people. We have little or no evidence of dissenters from the destruction of the Temple to around 700 C.E., and, therefore, it may very well be the case that the earlier sectarian movements did, more or less, disappear. Yet in the eighth, ninth, and tenth centuries, a large number of Jewish dissenting groups arose. From the fact that some of their divergent teachings are similar to those of the sectarians of the Second Temple period, it may be much more correct to assume that dissent in Judaism continued into the Diaspora. As noted, the Rabbanite account of the founding of Karaism made mention of residual Sadducees. Yet this dissent remained smoldering beneath the surface, waiting for an Anan to add sufficient new fuel to cause a major conflagration.[13]

There may be other reasons for Anan's success. Even if no undercurrents of sectarianism were left over from the Second Temple period, the completion of the Talmud did not necessarily imply that all Jews were contented with Rabbinic authority. The imposition of Rabbanism undoubtedly took a great deal of time and effort on the part of the Babylonian Jewish religious and secular leadership. Resentment of this process was strongest in those areas farthest away from the centers of Rabbinic Judaism, where local customs may well have predominated. Thus, most of the sectarian movements of this period seem to have been led by Jews living in Persia. Additional opposition to Babylonian hegemony was evident in the Land of Israel, which had traditionally been the center of Jewish life. Given, then, the possible residual antagonism to Pharisaism and the newly created resentment of the Babylonian academies, the receptivity to a figure like Anan is more readily understandable.[14]

Though our sources concerning Anan ben David's motives and background are not too reliable, and the reasons for his success not completely clear, the major outlines of his religious views are known. He taught that the ultimate source of Jewish law and practice must be a literal reading of the Bible. Thus, well-established Rabbinical observances, e.g., phylacteries and the prohibition of eating milk and meat together, were disregarded as not actually written in the Torah. On the other hand, interpreting too literally the biblical verse, "And they shall become as one flesh" (Gen. 2:24), Anan expanded the laws of incest so that one's relatives by marriage took on the status of blood relatives. This resulted in the catenary theory of incest *(rikkuv)*, whereby even one's distant relatives could not marry his spouse's distant relatives because they were now considered blood relatives with each other. Likewise, Anan's literal approach to the Bible turned the Sabbath into a gloomy day. The injunction against the use of fire led to the prohibition of any lights, especially the Rabbinically-ordained Sabbath lamps, which, though lit before the Sabbath, were intended to spread illumination after dark. Similarly, on the basis of other verses, circumcision, sexual intercourse, and leaving one's house except for going to the synagogue, were forbidden on the Sabbath. As noted, the method of determining the calendar was changed so that actual observation of the new moon and not mathematical calculation was the determining factor. Anan also revived the Sadducean practice of setting Shavuot (the Feast of Weeks) invariably on Sunday, understanding literally the biblical words "on the morrow of the Sabbath" (Lev. 23:15).[15]

From these few examples, it is clear that Anan's impetus was not antinomian. He was not determined somehow to make Jewish law easier, for many of his practices, e.g., an annual seventy-day fast based, perhaps, on the Muslim Ramadan, and his prohibition of Sabbath lights, were obviously more stringent than Rabbinic enactments. In fact, it may very well be that Anan had no desire to form his own religion, Rabbanite claims notwithstanding. Instead, he most likely was trying to institute internal reforms by competing with the laws of the Talmud. The use of Aramaic, the language of the Talmud but not of the Bible, in the writing of his *Book of Precepts* supports this conclusion.[16] It is also unclear whether his innovative legal decisions were original to him. They may simply have been a codification of existing regional or otherwise non-normative Jewish practices which were in vogue among the various anti-Rabbinic constituencies. No matter what his aim or his sources, Anan was successful in gathering around him enough dissenters to produce a flourishing sectarian movement, separate from the majority of Rabbanism. His apparent claim to the exilarchate, which implied Davidic descent, was no doubt helpful in his attempt to win followers.[17]

If it is true that Anan wished only for internal reform and not for a revolutionary schism, he was woefully mistaken as to his chances. There comes a time in the life of any religion that certain practices and scriptural interpretations become so completely entrenched that any attempt to dislodge them must result either in failure or in schism. One classical example will suffice. As noted, both Anan and the Sadducees believed that the biblically-ordained offering of the Omer should take place on a Sunday, i.e., "the morrow of the Sabbath," and, thus, Shavuot would always fall on a Sunday. It may be the case that the Sadducees and Anan understood the Bible correctly and the Omer should be offered on the first Sunday after the beginning of Passover and not on the second day of that holiday. If the Sadducees had emerged as the majority, no doubt Jews up until today would readily accept their interpretation as correct and the Pharisaic rendering as mistaken. Yet the Pharisees prevailed, and their view became authoritative. Once the Pharisaic-Sadducean dispute was settled in favor of Shavuot's being on different days of the week, that was the officially correct interpretation of Scripture, whether or not the Bible actually meant for this festival to be invariably on Sunday. If Anan wished to have Judaism adopt the Shavuot-on-Sunday policy, as biblically ordained, he was approximately seven hundred years too late. Whatever the Bible originally meant was no longer a relevant issue for Judaism in Anan's day. His failure to perceive that fact changed Anan from a reformer into a schismatic.[18]

III

The Ananites were at first only one among a number of Jewish sectarian groups who populated the Islamic empire in the eighth and ninth centuries. The two individuals who transformed Ananism into Karaism were Persian Jews, Benjamin al-Nahawandi (ca. 830–860) and Daniel al-Qumisi (end of 9th–beginning of 10th cent.). Al-Nahawandi, apparently the first to call the group Karaites (*Qara'im, B'nei Miqra*, those who follow Scripture), wrote his own *Book of Precepts (Sefer Ha-Mizvot)*, reversing a number of Anan's enactments. He believed, nevertheless, that individual interpretation of the Bible could legitimately lead to differences in practice. He also adopted a curious theology, asserting that God created an angel who, in turn, produced the world and was responsible for it.[19]

Daniel al-Qumisi was the first major figure of the Karaite period in the Land of Israel. This was a most productive era which lasted from about 870 to the capture of Jerusalem by the First Crusade in 1099. Al-Qumisi strongly encouraged his fellow Karaites to abandon the Diaspora and move to the Land of Israel. He argued quite vehemently against those who were waiting for the Messiah to facilitate the ingathering of exiles, and he claimed that laziness and greed, not theological considerations, prevented their emigration to Eretz Israel. Al-Qumisi is also famous for his opinion of Anan. Although at one time having referred to him as the "chief of learned men" (rosh ha-maskilim), al-Qumisi became disillusioned with the first Karaite's teachings and ended up calling him "the chief of fools" (rosh ha-kesilim).[20]

From this last statement, we see that there was a great deal of disagreement among the early Karaites. Relying upon the principle that each individual was equally capable of understanding the Bible and deriving from it the correct behavior, Karaism was in danger of deteriorating into a large number of small, ineffectual sectarian groupings. Qirqisani, who is our chief source of the history of such factionalism, records in great detail the divergent practices of the varying Karaite groups and distinguishes between Ananites, who continued in the ways of Anan, and the later Karaites.[21] It is at this point in the history of Karaism, namely at the beginning of the tenth century, that Saadia Gaon, the chief Rabbanite opponent of this dissenting sect, made his appearance.

Saadia (882–942) is a very problematical figure for the student of Karaism. The Rabbanites revered him as the savior of Judaism against this heretical menace. The Karaites saw in him their chief enemy, and practically every Karaite polemical work was directed against him. Yet, ironically, Saadia may be given credit for uniting Karaism into a cohesive group which finally realized that if it were to survive against Rabbanism, it must put aside internal differences. Thus, whereas the early tenth century was marked by the bickering recorded by Qirqisani, who wrote during Saadia's lifetime, soon thereafter such divisiveness came to an end. Therefore, Saadia may have been the catalyst which united the dissidents. It may be true, nonetheless, that Saadia is to be credited with arousing Rabbanism to the possible consequences of Karaism and, in that sense, should be seen as important in the eventual failure of that group.[22]

During the tenth and eleventh centuries, Karaism flourished and reached its greatest intellectual heights. Jacob al-Qirqisani has already been mentioned a number of times. His main work, *The Book of Lights and Watchtowers (Kitab al-Anwar wal-Maraqib)*, covers the whole scope of Karaite religious views and practices. There were quite a number of other outstanding figures in this period. Sahl ben Maṣliaḥ and Salmon ben Yeroḥam were both important anti-Rabbanite polemicists, who argued the Karaite cause very forcefully.[23] Yefet ben Ali, the leading Karaite exegete, wrote commentaries on every book of the Bible.[24] Joseph al-Baṣir and his student Yeshua ben Judah were philosophers and legalists who, among other things, contributed to the reform of the extreme Karaite position on incest.[25] During these centuries, Karaism became firmly established and its religious doctrines finally crystallized. We might now turn to a close analysis of the Karaite religion.

IV

Elijah Bashyatchi was the last great Karaite codifier. His major work, *The Mantle of Elijah (Aderet Eliyahu)*, remained unfinished at the author's death in 1490. In this work, Bashyatchi lists the following ten principles of Karaite Judaism:

1. The physical world was created.
2. It was created by a Creator who did not create Himself, but is eternal.
3. The Creator has no likeness and is unique in all respects.
4. He sent the prophet Moses.
5. He sent, along with Moses, His perfect Torah.
6. It is the duty of the believer to understand the original language of the Torah.
7. God inspired the other prophets.
8. God will resurrect humans on the day of judgment.

9. God requites each person according to his ways and the fruits of his deeds.

10. God has not forsaken the people of the Dispersion; rather they are suffering the Lord's punishment, and they should hope every day for His salvation at the hands of the Messiah, the descendant of David.[26]

A close examination of these principles, which are not significantly different from Rabbanite articles of faith, such as those proposed by Maimonides, will give us a better idea of the Karaite religion.

First and foremost, Karaites believe in an eternal, unique God who created the world. In their exposition of this belief, Karaites follow closely the Kalam, the Muslim system of philosophical theology. This is evident immediately when we see that creation is listed as the first principle, and the existence of God follows after that. This is in accord with the standard Kalamic method of proving the existence of God by first demonstrating that the world was created and, therefore, needs a creator.[27] The relationship between Karaism and Kalam is especially close, and all Karaite philosophy is more or less of the Kalamic type, as is that of their opponent Saadia. Unlike Rabbanite philosophy, which began as Kalam but moved on to Neoplatonism and Aristotelianism, Karaite philosophy remained loyal to its original form. Thus, Aaron ben Elijah (14th cent.), the last major Karaite philosopher, devotes his philosophical work, *The Tree of Life (Eẓ Ḥayyim)*, to a defense of Karaite Kalam against Maimonidean Aristotelianism. Despite the difference in approach, there is little in the Karaite doctrine of God which would be unacceptable to the Rabbanite philosopher. In fact, Saadia's major philosophical work, *Beliefs and Opinions (Ha-'Emunot ve-ha-De'ot)*, surprisingly has almost nothing to say about Karaism. It has been theorized that this is a result of the close affinity between Rabbanite and Karaite philosophy.[28]

There is, however, an element of Rabbanite theology which is missing in Karaism. There is virtually no mystical tendency in Karaite writings, and if there is any major disagreement between the God-concepts of each group, it is over this point. Karaites often bitterly criticized the Rabbanites for the anthropomorphisms of the Talmud and Midrash. Specifically mystical works, e.g., the *Shi'ur Qomah*, which figuratively describes the dimensions of God's body, were singled out as targets for attack. It should be noted that, of course, Rabbanite philosophers were just as adamantly opposed to the anthropomorphisms and physical descriptions of God which were in vogue among the mystics and common people.[29] The Karaites were distinct, however, in that they exhibited almost no anti-rationalistic tendencies.

Devoted as they were to the concept of absolute divine unity, a number of Karaites played an important part in anti-Christian polemics. Drawing upon the works of their Muslim colleagues, and adding their own innovative arguments, such Karaite philosophers as David al-Muqammiṣ (9th cent.), Qirqisani, and Joseph al-Baṣir devoted a large part of their discussions of God's unity to philosophical refutations of the Trinity. By so doing, they were forced to clarify their own position on the central philosophical issue of divine attributes. Their discussion of this topic was important in the general progress of Jewish philosophy.[30]

The last three of Bashyatchi's ten principles, namely resurrection of the dead, reward and punishment, and the Messiah, are all standard items of Jewish faith.[31] It is significant that the Karaites, who are so often called Sadducees by the Rabbanites, are strong believers in resurrection, a doctrine which the Sadducees rejected. As a result, the identification of the two groups is fiercely resented by the Karaites, who also consider the Sadducees to be heretics.[32] The Karaites differ among themselves as to the details of resurrection, e.g., when it will occur and who will be resurrected, but this is not surprising. The Rabbanites have the same internal arguments.[33]

One aspect of Karaite eschatology, namely, the doctrine of future reward and punishment, differs somewhat from Rabbanite views. Though there is no unanimity in Rabbinic sources, it appears that the Rabbis do not consider Hell as a place of eternal punishment. After the allotted time of retribution, the wicked will either be destroyed or ascend to heaven. The idea that the punishment of Hell would last forever, except perhaps for a very few terrible sinners, seems to be all but absent from Rabbinic theology.[34]

This is not the case in Karaism. Most Karaite authorities are united in their belief that the sinner's retribution in the world-to-come will be eternal. Though in some disagreement on the details of the punishment, e.g., whether it is physical or spiritual, on the basic issue of the infinite duration of the suffering, there seems to be little dissent among Karaite thinkers.[35]

A similar difference between Rabbinism and Karaism centers on the reaction of the righteous to the sufferings of the wicked. Though one can find an isolated passage in Rabbinic literature to the effect that the righteous in Paradise will delight in the sufferings of the wicked in Hell, this is by no means the generally accepted view. In Karaism, however, the situation is much different. Whether the wicked are to be punished by being devoured by maggots, fire, or sulphur, or by being crushed between the two sides of the Mount of Olives, watching the wicked suffer will be one of the pleasures of the righteous.[36]

It is interesting that Karaites held such doctrines about the afterlife, which were virtually absent in Rabbinic works. One could argue that as a despised and persecuted minority, the Karaites felt more keenly the disappointments of this world. Therefore, they looked forward to the pleasures of the afterlife, one of which would be enjoyment of the pains of their adversaries. Yet the Rabbanites lacked no persecution, and they generally did not adopt such beliefs about the next world. The Karaites may also have been influenced by Muslim concepts of reward and punishment. Nevertheless, the exact reason for the Karaite adoption of the doctrines of eternal punishment and the delight of the righteous in the sufferings of the wicked can only be the subject of speculation.[37]

It is when we move to the middle four of Bashyatchi's articles of faith, namely those that deal with prophecy and the Torah, that we see major differences with the Rabbanites. True, the latter agree with the principles of prophecy, the superiority of Moses to the other prophets, and the perfection of the Torah. On the other hand, even though the requirement that each believer learn Hebrew in order to understand the Bible is not on any Rabbanite list of principles, it is certainly not objectionable from their point of view. Nevertheless, if we analyze the doctrines of prophecy and revelation, we can discern the core of the Karaite-Rabbanite dispute.

While both the Rabbanites and Karaites believe the Torah to be perfect, the former, as mentioned, believe that there are two Torahs, one written and one oral. Jewish ritual, as practiced in the post-Rabbinic period, draws its authority not only from the Written Torah, but also from the Oral Torah. Thus, while some laws might be considered explicitly written in the Torah, and others known only through oral tradition, while still others are rabbinical ordinances, all are equally to be observed.

The Karaites fiercely disagree with the theory of two Torahs. The one written Torah itself is sufficient for the derivation of all laws. If a practice is to be considered acceptable, it must be *mi-de-'loraita* (from the Torah). Diversity of opinion among Karaites is to be expected because the Torah can be understood differently by different people.[38] Hence, it is the responsibility of every believer to be able to read the original biblical text in order to know what Judaism requires of him. Whereas the Rabbanite could depend upon postbiblical and even posttalmudic codes to inform him of his religious duties, the Karaite was enjoined to go back to the Bible. While it is true that many Karaites, starting with Anan and including Bashyatchi, wrote their own books of Jewish law, nevertheless, there was still an emphasis on the Karaite motto attributed to Anan: "Search well in the Torah, and do not rely upon my opinion."

This basic difference between the two theologies was the major issue discussed in the Rabbanite-Karaite debate. The former claimed that without the Oral Torah one would have no basis for biblical interpretation. Since the Karaites themselves disagreed as to the correct interpretation of the Bible, it is clear that the real meaning of the Scriptures is not self-evident. Reliable tradition is the only guarantee of correct exegesis. The Karaites, for their part, argued that "the Torah of the Lord is perfect" (Ps. 19:8).

There is no mention of an Oral Torah in the Bible. Even if some traditions are necessary, the Rabbinic Oral Torah is inadmissible because it contradicts the biblical text (as the Karaites interpret it). Therefore, Rabbinic Judaism is a corruption of biblical teachings and not its legitimate exponent.

Given this basic disagreement, it is not surprising that even though each group bases itself upon the Torah, the legal systems that developed are radically different. In this context, the following items might be mentioned. Rabbanites and Karaites have different dietary laws because they disagree on such issues as the method of slaughter of animals, which birds are prohibited, and whether the Bible prohibits all milk and meat together. As has been noted, the Karaite calendar, in its original form, was not based on mathematical calculations. New months were determined by actual observation, and the proclamation of leap years depended on the status of the crops. Now, even though Karaites have finally adopted a standard calendar,[39] the two groups often celebrate their holidays on different days. In addition, the Karaites object to the Rabbanite second day of festivals, the observance of Shavuot on varying days of the week, and the system which prevents Passover and Rosh Ha-Shanah from falling on certain days. They also do not celebrate the postbiblical holiday of Hannukkah.

A serious difference between Rabbanites and Karaites involves laws of marriage. Though Karaites after Yeshua ben Judah no longer hold the catenary theory of incest, namely that one's relatives by marriage take on the status of blood relatives, their laws of incest are still more stringent than those of the Rabbanites. Levirate marriage and its release, *ḥaliẓah*, though explicitly written in the Torah, were both severely modified and then abolished. Most significantly, Karaites have their own writ of divorce, which, since it differs from the Rabbinic mode, does not effectively divorce couples as far as the Rabbanites are concerned. Thus, the child of a remarried woman who had been divorced according to Karaite law would be considered illegitimate (a *mamzer*) and not marriageable in Rabbinic law. Though there are records of intermarriage over several centuries, eventually Rabbanites forbade such marriages on the presumption of general Karaite illegitimacy.[40]

Karaism and Rabbanism also divide on the nature of the liturgical services. Whereas most of the Rabbanite prayers are from the postbiblical period, the early Karaites insisted that all prayers must come from the Bible itself. Thus, there was a great emphasis on the Psalms, which, though they play an important part in the Rabbanite prayer book, are not central to that liturgy. In time, the Karaites began to realize that new compositions were necessary to express the full range of religious emotions. In addition, as in all Karaite matters, there was a great diversity of practice. Therefore, an authoritative Karaite prayer book, which included many nonbiblical sections, was eventually adopted for general use. In fact a number of Karaite blessings, e.g., that which is recited before eating bread, are identical with Rabbanite ones. Still, the Karaite services, consisting mostly of biblical passages, are very different from their Rabbanite counterparts.[41]

The Karaite reform of its liturgy is but one example of the tendency away from the strict literalism of Anan and his early followers. In fact, through the centuries, Karaism became closer and closer to Rabbanite Judaism. One important example is the use of Sabbath lamps. For the early Karaites, it was better to extinguish a fire on the Sabbath than to let it burn. Darkness was the Sabbath rule for Karaites. This was one of the most visible differences with the Rabbanites, who not only commanded the use of illumination, but also expressly said that it was a divine injunction. In the eleventh century, Yeshua ben Judah changed Karaite practice so that a burning fire should not be extinguished on the Sabbath. Finally, in the fifteenth century, the Bashyatchi family was instrumental in having Sabbath candle-lighting become mandatory under Karaite law. As the Karaites began to realize that they had no hope of overtaking Rabbanism, they moved much closer to its legal norms.[42]

The road back to Rabbanism is evident also in the Karaites' approach to their Jewish opponents. Whereas in earlier Karaite literature Rabbanite sources were quoted mostly as objects of attack, later authors adopted a much more respectful attitude. Outstanding Rabbanites, such as Judah Ha-Levi and Maimonides, are often cited as authorities in such later works. Even passages from the Talmud and Midrash are sometimes cited approvingly. Though a number of Rabbanite authors were influenced by Karaite writers and some reciprocated the Karaite attempt at rapprochement, this was not the general Rabbanite approach.[43]

V

Let us return somewhat to the history of the Karaites. After their center in the Land of Israel was destroyed by the First Crusade, the new capital of Karaism became the Byzantine empire. A number of outstanding figures emerged between the twelfth and sixteenth centuries. Judah Hadassi (mid-12th cent.) wrote a major work on Karaite theology and practice, summarizing much of the law and lore that had developed since the time of Anan.[44] Aaron ben Joseph (known as the Elder, second half of the 13th cent.) was responsible for organizing Karaite liturgy and also wrote a major commentary on the Bible.[45] Aaron ben Elijah (the Younger, died 1369) was known as the Karaite Maimonides for his works in philosophy, law, and exegesis.[46] Elijah Bashyatchi (late 15th cent.) has already been mentioned. His school of thought was perpetuated by his brother-in-law Caleb Afendopolo and his great-grandson, Moses Bashyatchi (16th cent.).[47]

The center of Karaite activity shifted in the seventeenth and eighteenth centuries to the Crimea and Lithuania. It is not necessary to list all the major figures of this period, but mention should be made of the first important Karaite author in Lithuania. Isaac of Troki (1533–1594) is best known for his anti-Christian polemic, *Faith Strengthened (Ḥizzuq Emunah)*, which was quite popular with Rabbanites.[48] In these European areas, Karaites were at first considered part of the general Jewish community by the secular, as well as by the rabbinical, authorities. When Lithuania and the Crimea were incorporated into Russia in the late eighteenth century, the legal status of the Karaites changed. Through various enactments in the course of the next century, Karaism came to be considered a religion totally separate from Judaism, and Karaites were relieved of many of the disabilities suffered by Rabbanite Jews and of their financial responsibilities to the general Jewish community. This policy was continued by the Nazis, who spared the Karaites from the extermination camps. Small Karaite communities continue to this day in parts of Russia and Poland, but they are almost completely isolated from the world Jewish community.[49]

There is also a Karaite community in Israel, which has its own separate religious authorities. With the help of the Israeli government, these Karaites have been able to reprint a number of their classical texts. Their small numbers, and their inability to intermarry with Rabbanites, makes it unlikely that Karaism will ever again become a major force in Jewish life. In sum, then, the history of Karaism from the twelfth century to the present has been marked by general numerical decline and intellectual stagnation, punctuated every so often by bursts of creativity and marked by dogged tenaciousness.

VI

Karaism's goal, from the time of Anan and perhaps even to this day, has been to be recognized as the correct Judaism and to capture the majority of the Jewish people. In its early days, it flowed as a mighty river, hoping to become the mainstream of Judaism. In time, however, Karaism's power receded, and it subsided to but a tributary of the sea of dominant Rabbanism. It is not unlikely that Karaism will eventually dry up completely.

In the light of this virtual demise after a long history of minority status, it is tempting to speak of the failure of Karaism. It might be useful, however, first to inquire what it means for a religion to fail. If it signifies that the religion attracted only a small following, then, compared to the whole population of the world, every religion is a failure. If we talk about relative numbers, e.g., Rabbanism always had at least x times the number of adherents and was, thus, x times as successful, then we would, in effect, be saying that might is right. On the other hand, Karaism has been a living force in the lives of its adherents, few as they may have been. It created a thoroughgoing legal system and a sophisticated theology. Though born in dissent and nurtured by polemical dispute, Karaism survived. In a sense, then, Karaism was not a failure but a success. Still, its relative success is limited, and we are justified in considering the reasons that prevented Karaism from becoming the major force in Judaism.

When discussing the Karaite-Rabbanite schism, it should be remembered that it was Karaism that split away from Rabbanism. Though it claimed to be the true, historical Judaism, most Jews recognized that the movement started by Anan was something new and revolutionary. Even if we assume that there were undercurrents of dissent to Pharisaism and Rabbanism which surfaced with Anan, these were never so strong as to pretend to sway the majority of the Jewish people. Despite its claims of antiquity, Anan's movement inevitably suffered in comparison to Rabbanism, whose continuity from Second Temple days was well documented. By renewing some of the battles that had been decided centuries before, e.g., the day of Shavuot, Anan just reinforced the notion that he was attempting to upset the well-established order. Karaism, thus, had the burden of overcoming Rabbanite charges of illegitimacy. It was never able to clear this hurdle.

There are other factors as well. Early Karaism may well have fed on popular unhappiness with the imposition of Rabbanism. Anan, however, did not lessen the burden of the legal system; if anything, Karaism was much stricter in its development of Jewish law. Perhaps if Anan had opted for the route of antinomianism, more followers would have marched on his path.[50] When Karaism finally began to adopt more lenient rulings that were closer to Rabbanism, the fate of the contest had already been decided.

Rabbanism also held an advantage over Karaism because of its flexibility. The development of Rabbinic Judaism over hundreds of years allowed it to respond to the stresses and strains of everyday life. Even if it is highly rigorous, the end-result takes into consideration popular ability to abide by its decisions and provides mechanisms for change.[51] The early Karaite legal system, however, sprung up, as it were, overnight without the leavening process that time adds to any code of laws. Thus, when Anan set out the catenary theory of incest, he had no way of knowing that it would eventually make marriage almost impossible for his followers. Likewise, the prohibition of having lights burning on Friday evenings might have been fine in theory; in practice, it made the Sabbath unnecessarily mournful. Eventually, Karaism reversed itself on these and other items, but only after prolonged internal struggles. Rabbinism, with a well-developed system of growth and change nurtured over centuries, was better able to deal with the practical needs of its adherents. Ironically, Karaism, which is more flexible than Rabbanism in theory, turned out to be more rigid in practice.

There may well be other reasons for the Karaite failure. Karaite theology, though very close to Rabbanite beliefs, insisted on an unmitigated rational view of God which did not allow for any mystical approaches. The masses, who were used to thinking of God in anthropomorphic terms, may not have been ready for the more reserved view of the Deity. They likewise were probably unable to accept the Karaite asceticism, which seemed to exclude any warmth and joy in religion. The Rabbanite idea of the joy of performing the commandments was missing in Karaism. A religion intended for the intellectual or ascetic few is unlikely to become a mass movement.

In retrospect, we can see that the seeds of Karaism's defeat may well have been sown from the very beginning. Despite Anan's reforming vigor, he lacked the vision necessary to realize that Rabbinic Judaism had already so firmly established itself that no major revisions would be tolerated. Mainstream Judaism would never become Karaism, so Karaism was destined to remain an outcast group which would eventually be considered almost a separate religion. The early Karaites, however, lacked the foresight to realize their fate. They created a parallel, competing system to Rabbanism, which, though doomed to perpetual minority status, remains an imposing edifice. Jewish history has been enriched by their efforts.

NOTES

1. See Ya°qūb al-Qiraisānī, *Kitāb al-Anwār Wal-Marāqib (The Book of Lights and Watchtowers)*, ed. Leon Nemoy (New York, 1939–43), I, 11, 2, in vol. 1 (1939), p. 52. For a translation, see Nemoy, "Al-Qirqisānī's Account of the Jewish Sects and Christianity," *Hebrew Union College Annual*, VII (1930), pp. 382–83. According to Qirqisani, the Isunians did differ from the Rabbanites in certain ritual matters, but not the calendar. As for Karaite-Rabbanite intermarriages, Qirqisani may be slightly misrepresenting the case; see below, n. 40.

2. One might compare a similar phenomenon today. A Jew who denies all facets of Jewish belief and even excludes himself from the Jewish community is still generally thought of as Jewish. On the other hand, the Jew who believes in God, the divinity of the Torah, the election of Israel, and other traditional beliefs, but also accepts Jesus as the messiah, is generally read out of the Jewish people.

3. The first monarch of the northern Kingdom of Israel, Jeroboam (928–907 B.C.E.) changed the date of Sukkot from the seventh month to the eighth month; see 1 Kings 12:32–33. In the Second Temple period, the Pharisees had a lunar-solar calendar (the standard reckoning to this day), but the Sadducees, the Dead Sea Sect, and the authors of the books of Jubilees and Enoch, followed solar calendars. These groups also disagreed on the setting of the date of Shavuot; cf. Jacob Licht, "The 364-Day Calendar," s.v. "Calendar," *Encyclopaedia Judaica*, V (1971), cols. 51–53. See also the internal rabbinic dispute over the calendar recorded in Mishnah Rosh Ha-Shanah 2:8–9, and the Saadia–Ben Meir controversy: cf. below n. 14. Most of the sects mentioned by Qirqisani were noted for some calendrical variations; cf. Nemoy, "Al-Qirqisānī's Account," pp. 362–64, 383–85, 389–90. On the importance of calendrical diversity, see Zvi Ankory, *Karaites in Byzantium* (New York, 1959), pp. 293–95.

4. Cf. Samuel Poznanski, "Anan et ses écrits," *Revue des études juives*, XLIV (1902), p. 167, n. 2. Abu Ḥanifa is thought to have died in 767. If Anan's fellow prisoner was Abu Ḥanifa, Karaism was most likely founded in 767.

5. This account is recorded by the Karaite Elijah ben Abraham in his *Ḥilluq Ha-Qara'im Ve-ha-Rabbanim*, in Simḥah Pinsker, *Lickute Kadmoniot* (Vienna, 1860), II, p. 103. English translations are provided by Nemoy in "Anan ben David: A Re-Appraisal of the Historical Data," *Semitic Studies in Memory of Immanuel Low* (Budapest, 1947), reprinted, Philip Birnbaum, *Karaite Studies* (New York, 1971), pp. 314–15; and in *Karaite Anthology* (New Haven, 1952), pp. 4–5. Pinsker and Poznanski, op. cit., p. 166, consider Saadia as the author of this anonymous story, but there is no proof for this contention. For a similar Rabbanite account of the origins of Karaism, cf. Abraham ibn Daud, *Sefer Ha-Qabbalah (The Book of Tradition)*, ed. Gerson D. Cohen (Philadelphia, 1967), pp. 37–38 (Heb.), 48–50 (Eng.).

6. Fragments of Anan's *Sefer Ha-Miẓvot* can be found in Abraham Harkavy, *Zikheron La-Rishonim* (St. Petersburg, 1903; reprinted, Jerusalem, 1969), pp. 3–172; and Solomon Schechter, *Documents of Jewish Sectaries*, II (Cambridge, 1910; reprinted, New York, 1970). The view that this work was intended to replace the Talmud is found in *Siddur Rav Amram Gaon* quoted by Poznanski, op. cit., XLV

(1902), p. 192. Nemoy provides translations in "Anan ben David," pp. 310–11, and *Karaite Anthology*, pp. 3–4.

7. Typical Karaite views of the sect's origin are recorded in Elijah ben Abraham's *Ḥilluq*, Pinsker, op. cit., pp. 99–106; Elijah Bashyatchi, *Aderet Eliyahu* (Israel, 1966), Introduction (unpaginated); Mordecai ben Nisan, *Dod Mordecai* (Israel, 1966), and Simhah Isaac Lutzki, *Oraḥ Ẓaddiqim*, ibid., pp. 79–119. Some scholars have doubted the authenticity of Anan's motto, *Ḥapisu be-oraita shappir ve-ʿal tishʿanu ʿal daʿati*, which appears first in the tenth century and is part Aramaic and part Hebrew. Cf. Salo W. Baron, *A Social and Religious History of the Jews*, V, (Phildelphia, 1957), pp. 389–90, n. 4; André Paul, *Écrits de Qumran et Sectes Juives aux Premiers Siècles de l'Islam. Recherches sur l'origine du Qaraïsme* (Paris, 1969), pp. 31–33.

8. This is especially the view of Nemoy; cf. "Anan ben David," and *Karaite Anthology*, pp. 3–8. Strong support for the Rabbanite account is provided by Baron, op. cit., pp. 210–11, 388–89. A compromise position on the question is held by Ankory, op. cit., pp. 14–16.

9. Qirqisani (10th cent.) already distinguishes between Ananites and Karaites; cf. op. cit., I, pp. 53–54, 60–64, and, especially, p. 59; trans. Nemoy, "Al-Qirqisānī's Account," pp. 383–86, 392–96, and, especially, p. 391.

10. Cf. Avot 1:1.

11. For literature on the Talmud, cf., e.g., Hermann L. Strack, *Introduction to the Talmud and Midrash* (Philadelphia, 1931); Z. H. Chajes, *The Student's Guide Through the Talmud* (New York, 1960); Baron, op. cit., II (Philadelphia, 1952), pp. 215–321.

12. For a discussion of the sectarian groups of the Second Temple, see the first chapter in this book. Many of the apocryphal and pseudipigraphical works represent non-Pharisaic traditions, but it is often unclear whether or not they belong to a particular sect. Other information about dissenting groups comes from the Talmud, Philo, Josephus, and some Church Fathers.

13. A number of contemporary scholars have argued strongly that there is a direct link between the Dead Sea sect and Karaism. Unfortunately, no explicit evidence has yet to be found to corroborate this theory. Cf., e.g., N. Wieder, *The Judean Scrolls and Karaism* (London, 1962); Paul, op. cit.; J. Heller and R. Nemoy, "Karaites," *Encyclopaedia Judaica*, X (1971), cols. 761–782; Lawrence H. Schiffman, *The Halakhah at Qumran* (Leiden, 1975), esp. pp. 134–35. An attempt to connect Karaite law with Philo's Judaism is made by Bernard Revel, "The Karaite Halakha," Birnbaum, op. cit., pp. 1–88. The relation between the Code of Damascus, found in the Cairo Geniza, and Karaism, is discussed by Louis Ginzberg, *An Unknown Jewish Sect* (New York, 1976), esp. pp. 144–54, 338–408, and Schechter, *Documents*, I, pp. 9–119. For a discussion of sects contemporary with Anan, see Qirqisani, *Al-Anwār*, I, pp. 3–64, and Nemoy, "Al Qirqisānī's Account." The existence of anti-Rabbanite sectarian groups prior to Anan may be reflected in Aḥai Gaon's *She'iltot;* cf. Chaim Tchernowitz, *Toldoth Ha-Poskim*, I (New York. 1946), pp. 62–69.

14. The existence of regional differences even among Rabbanites is corroborated by Qirqisani, ibid., pp. 48–51 (trans., pp. 377–82). Some scholars have theorized that Karaism is the direct result of regional resentment of Babylonian hegemony; cf. Ankori, op. cit., pp. 3–25. The competition between Babylonia

and the Land of Israel may have been the root cause of the Saadia–Ben Meir controversy over the calendar; see Henry Malter, *Saadia Gaon: His Life and Works* (Philadelphia, 1921), pp. 69–88, and H. J. Bornstein, "Maḥloqet Rav Saadia Gaon U-Ven Meir," in *Nahum Sokolow Jubilee Volume* (Warsaw, 1904, reprinted). Other historians have seen Karaism as a result of general Muslim sectarianism in the eight century; for a discussion, see I. Friedlaender, "Jewish-Arabic Studies," *Jewish Quarterly Review*, N.S. I (1910–11), pp. 183–215; II (1911–12), pp. 481–515; III (1912–13), 235–300. For a short overview of the various theories of Karaism's origin, see Nemoy, *Anthology*, pp. xii–xx.

15. For Anan's legal views, see his *Sefer Ha-Mizvot;* Qirqisani, op. cit., pp. 53–55 (trans., pp. 383–86); Baron, op. cit., pp. 210–22; Nemoy, *Anthology*, pp. 8–20. A study of Anan's work shows that he instituted not so much a literal interpretation of the Bible, but an exegetical system parallel to that of the Rabbanites. In many respects, Anan departs from the simple meaning of the text as much as his opponents.

16. Cf. Ankori, op. cit., p. 17; Nemoy, *Anthology*, p. 8.

17. Cf. Ankori, op. cit., pp. 14–16; Baron, op. cit., pp. 209–16.

18. A parallel situation can be seen in the Protestant Reformation. It may very well be that the earliest dissenters wished not to form separate churches but to institute changes in Christianity (i.e., Catholicism) based on divergent interpretations of the New Testament. Just as the real meaning of the Bible was irrelevant for Judaism in Anan's day, so, too, was the original intent of the New Testament irrelevant for Catholicism in Luther's day. Thus, given the enormity of the differences between himself and traditional Catholic interpretation, Luther could be only a schismatic, not a reformer.

19. Cf. Qirqisani, op. cit., I, pp. 55–56 (trans., pp. 386–87); Nemoy, *Anthology* pp. 21–29; Paul, op. cit., pp. 83–96; his *Sefer Ha-Mizvot* is found in Harkavy, op. cit., pp. 175–84. On the creator angel, see Harry A. Wolfson, "The Preexistent Angel of the Magharians and Al-Nahawandi," *Jewish Quarterly Review*, LI (1960–61), pp. 89–106.

20. For al-Qumisi's view of Anan, and criticism thereupon, see Qirqisani, op. cit., pp. 4–5 (trans., p. 321). For his doctrines see ibid., pp. 58–59 (trans., pp. 390–91); Nemoy, *Anthology*, pp, 30–41; Harkavy, op. cit., pp. 187–92; Paul, op. cit., pp. 97–113.

21. Op. cit., p. 59 (trans., p. 391); cf. pp. 59–64 (trans., pp. 392–96). A general discussion of early Karaism is provided by Baron, op. cit., pp. 222–32; cf. also Paul, op. cit., pp. 77–82.

22. For the traditional view of Saadia's triumph over Karaism, cf. Malter, op. cit., pp. 261–263. Saadia's polemical activities are chronicled in Poznanski, "The Anti-Karaite Writings of Saadiah Gaon," *Jewish Quarterly Review*, O.S., X (1897–98), pp. 238–76 (reprinted, Birnbaum, op. cit., pp. 89–127). Karaite reaction to Saadia is reported by idem, *The Karaite Literary Opponents of Saadia Gaon* (London, 1909; reprinted, Birnbaum, op. cit., pp. 131–234). Cf., also, Baron, op. cit., pp. 277–79; and Nemoy, *Anthology*, pp. xx–xxi.

23. See Nemoy, *Anthology*, pp. 69–82, 109–122. Salmon's anti-Saadia polemic, *The Book of the Wars of the Lord*, was edited by Israel Davidson (New York, 1934). Sahl's polemical *Epistle to Jacob ben Samuel* is found in Pinsker, op. cit., II, pp. 25–43.

70   *Rabbinism and Karaism*

24. Yefet has been called the Karaite Abraham ibn Ezra, yet most of his commentaries are still in manuscript; for the printed editions, cf. Ankori, op. cit., p. 483. See, also, Nemoy, *Anthology*, pp. 83–108.

25. See Isaac Husik, *A History of Mediaeval Jewish Philosophy* (Philadelphia, 1940), pp. 48–58; Julius Guttmann, *Philosophies of Judaism* (New York, 1964), pp. 88–94; P. F. Frankl, *Ein Mu'tazilitischer Kalam aus dem 10. Jahrhundert* (Vienna, 1872); Martin Schreiner, *Studien ueber Jeschuʿa ben Jehuda* (Berlin 1900); Nemoy, *Anthology*, pp. 123–132; I. Markon, *Meqorot Le-Qorot Dinei Nashim Va-ʿArayot Etzel Ha-Qaraʾim* (St. Petersburg, 1908). A review of this halcyon period in Karaism is provided by Baron, op. cit., pp. 233–40; cf. also Jacob Mann, *Texts and Studies in Jewish History and Literature*, II (Philadelphia, 1935), pp. 3–127.

26. Bashyatchi, op. cit., pp. 162–175; cf. Nemoy, *Anthology*, pp. 250–56. The first Karaite list of principles was composed by Judah Hadassi (ca. 1150): cf. Schechter, *Studies in Judaism*, First Series (Philadelphia, 1911), p. 160.

27. Cf. Saadia, *Beliefs and Opinions*, I–II; Maimonides, *Guide of the Perplexed*, I:73; Wolfson, *The Philosophy of the Kalam* (Cambridge, Mass., 1976); W. Montgomery Watt, *The Formative Period of Islamic Thought* (Edinburgh, 1973), esp. pp. 151–250; Shlomo Pines, *Beitraege zur Islamischen Atomenlehre* (Berlin, 1936). For Jewish Kalam, see Schreiner, *Der Kalam in der juedischen Literatur* (Berlin, 1895).

28. Cf. Poznanski, "Anti-Karaite Writings," *Karaite Studies*, p. 109; Baron, op. cit., p. 415, n. 80.

29. Qirqisani mentions *Shi'ur Qomah* explicitly in op. cit., pp. 15, 31 (trans., pp. 331, 350), while other anthropomorphisms are attacked on pp. 31–40 (trans., pp. 350–61); cf. Saul Lieberman, *Shkiin*, 2d ed. (Jerusalem, 1970), pp. 11–18. On *Shi'ur Qomah*, see Gershom Scholem, *Major Trends in Jewish Mysticism* (New York, 1954), pp. 63–67. Cf., also, Baron, op. cit., pp. 258–59.

30. Cf. the present author's *Jewish Philosophical Polemics Against Christianity in the Middle Ages* (New York, 1977), pp. 51–63; Nemoy, "The Attitude of the Early Karaites towards Christianity," *Salo W. Baron Jubilee Volume* (New York and London, 1975), II, pp. 697–716. It is not certain that al-Muqammiṣ was a Karaite.

31. In Maimonides' list of thirteen principles, these topics occupy articles 10–13. On Jewish dogmas in general, cf. Schechter, *Studies*, pp. 147–181.

32. Cf. Mann, op. cit., pp. 302–303; Mordecai ben Nisan, op. cit., pp. 20–31. On the other hand, see Qirqisani, *al-Anwār*, p. 11 (trans., p. 326), and Ibn Daud, op. cit., p. xxxvii. The Karaites are often called Sadducees in medieval Rabbanite literature.

33. Maimonides tries to sort out the various Rabbanite approaches in his introduction to Chapter Ten *(Ḥeleq)* of Mishnah Sanhedrin, which is also the source of his thirteen principles. Cf. Isidore Twersky, *A Maimonides Reader* (New York, 1972), pp. 401–23.

34. Cf. Tosefta Sanhedrin 13:5; B. Rosh Ha-Shanah 16b–17a; Yalkut Isaiah 429; B. Baba Metzia 586. On the other hand, Saadia, op. cit., IX:7.

35. See Qirqisani, op. cit., II (New York, 1940), pp. 246–53; David al-Muqammiṣ, quoted in Judah ben Barzilai, *Commentary on Sefer Yetzirah*, ed. S. J. Halberstam (Berlin, 1885), pp. 151–54; Yefet ben Ali, *A Commentary on the Book of Daniel by Jephet ibn 'Ali the Karaite*, ed. and trans., D. S. Margaliouth (Oxford, 1889), pp. 137–140 (Arabic), 75–76 (English); Bashyatchi, op. cit., p. 171.

36. The Rabbinic source is Leviticus Rabba 32:1; cf. David Kimḥi's commentary on Ps. 73:20, and Saadia, op. cit., IX:9. The Karaite view is found in Qirqisani, op. cit., pp. 234–35, and Yefet ben Ali, op. cit.

37. Many Christians also believed that the righteous would enjoy seeing the wicked suffer in the next world; cf. Thomas Aquinas, *Summa Theologiae*, Supplem. Q. 94.

38. Qirqisani, op. cit., I, pp. 63–64 (trans. p. 396).

39. Cf., eg., Mann, op. cit., pp. 468–550, and index, s. v. "Calendation"; Ankori, op. cit., 292–353.

40. It should be noted that the halakhic reason for prohibiting intermarriage stems from the problem of *mamzerut*, and not from calendrical divergencies as Qirqisani suggested. This prohibition of intermarriage is codified by Joseph Caro, *Bet Yosef* on *Tur*, Even Ha-'Ezer 4, end, quoting Samson of Sens, and by Moses Isserles, on *Shulḥan Arukh*, Even Ha-'Ezer 4:27. A lenient view, however, is propounded by David ibn Abi Zimra; cf. Solomon Freehof, *A Treasury of Responsa* (Philadelphia, 1963), pp. 122–27 (and for a modern, Reform view, see idem, *Current Reform Responsa* [Cincinnati, 1969], pp. 186–88). On the existence of Karaite-Rabbanite intermarriage, see Mann, op. cit., pp. 157–58, 160, 173, 177–80; Baron, op. cit., pp. 270–75. In response to Rabbanite marriage bans, Karaites reciprocated by prohibiting intermarriage. On the Karaite interpretation of levirate marriage, see Anan, op. cit., pp. 106–18, and Bashyatchi, op. cit., pp. 308–10.

41. Fragments of Anan's liturgy are found in Mann, "Anan's Liturgy and his Half-yearly Cycle of the Reading of the Law," *Journal of Jewish Lore and Philosophy*, I (1919), pp. 329–53, reprinted in *The Collected Articles of Jacob Mann* (Gedera, Israel, 1971) and in Birnbaum, op. cit., pp. 283–307. For the Karaite prayer book in use today, see *Siddur Ha-Tefilot Ke-Minhag Ha-Qara'im* (Vilna, 1891–92), 3 vols. Large sections are translated by Nemoy, *Anthology*, pp. 271–321.

42. Elijah Bashyatchi was probably most responsible for this rabbinizing trend in Karaism; cf. Ankori, "Bet Bashyatchi ve-Taqqanotav," in Bashyatchi, op. cit., pp. 1–16 (before main text). For a summary of Karaite religious practices, see Nemoy, *Anthology*, pp. xxiii–xxv; Baron, op. cit., pp. 240–251; Revel, op. cit.; and Ankori, *Byzantium*, pp. 204–251.

43. Cf., esp., Bashyatchi, Aaron ben Elijah, and Mordecai ben Nisan, op. cit., passim; Ankori, *Byzantium*, pp. 239–43. Among the Rabbanites who took lenient approaches were Maimonides, David ibn Abi Zimra, and Joseph Delmedigo. For anti-Karaite tendencies of Maimonides' *Mishnah Torah*, cf. Tchernowitz, op. cit., pp. 197–208.

44. His major work is *Eshkol Ha-Kofer* (Eupatoria, 1836; reprinted, Westmead, England, 1971); cf. Ankori, *Byzantium*, index, s.v.

45. Cf. Ankori, op. cit., bibliography and index, s.v.

46. His philosophical work is *Eẓ Ḥayyim*; partial translation in Moses Charner, *The Tree of Life by Aaron ben Elijah of Nicomedia* (New York). His legal work is *Gan 'Eden* (Eupatoria, 1866), and his commentary on the Torah is *Keter Torah* (Eupatoria, 1867). Cf. Nemoy, *Anthology*, pp. 170–195; Husik, op. cit., pp. 362–87. Ankori, op. cit., index, s.v.

47. Cf. Ankori, "Bet Bashyatchi." For the whole Byzantine period, see idem, *Byzantium*; Mann, *Texts and Studies*, pp. 285–550. For Karaism in Spain, cf. Ibn Daud, op. cit., pp. xlvi–l. For a Karaite chronology of Karaite scholars to the

middle of the fifteenth century, see David Ibn al-Hiti, *Chronicle*, in Nemoy, *Anthology*, pp. 230–35.

48. Cf. *Ḥizzuk Emunah*, ed. David Deutsch (Berlin, 1873); trans. by Moses Mocatto (London, 1850; reprinted, New York, 1970).

49. Present-day Polish Karaism and its own special dialect have become a subject of research for Polish scholars. Cf. Ananiasz Zajaczkowski, *Karaims in Poland* (Warsaw, 1961), esp. bibliography, pp. 109–114. If one did not know that the Karaites were a Jewish sect, he would never learn it from this publication. The author propounds the theory that the Karaites were originally Khazars who adopted an Old Testament religion; cf. Ankori, *Byzantium*, pp. 64–79. For the history of Karaites in Lithuania and Poland, see Mann, *Texts and Studies*, pp. 551–1407.

50. This may be inferred from the history of the only two relatively successful anti-Rabbinic schismatic groups, namely Christianity and Reform Judaism. An apparent reason for their attractiveness was their renunciation of Jewish law as a means of salvation. If Anan had similarly encouraged a release from talmudic legislation without replacing it with his own, more stringent, code, he might have won more followers. Of course, there were many other factors involved in the success of Christianity and Reform so any such conclusions must be approached with caution.

51. Though change in Rabbinic law is sometimes slow in coming and difficult to achieve, especially in the past few centuries, there is room for maneuvering inside the system. A popular instrument of reform in the Middle Ages was the *Taqqanah* (enactment). See, e.g., Louis Finkelstein, *Jewish Self-Government in the Middle Ages* (New York, 1924). New legal decisions, which were necessitated by changing conditions, were often embodied in the responsa literature.

SELECTED ENGLISH BIBLIOGRAPHY

Ankori, Zvi. *Karaites in Byzantium*. New York, 1959.

Baron, Salo W. *A Social and Religious History of the Jews*, V, pp. 209–85. Philadelphia, 1957.

Birnbaum, Philip. *Karaite Studies*. New York, 1971.

Mann, Jacob. *Collected Articles*, III. Gedera, Israel, 1971.

———. *Texts and Studies in Jewish History and Literature*, II. Philadelphia, 1935.

Nemoy, Leon. "Al-Qirqisānī's Account of the Jewish Sects and Christianity." *Hebrew Union College Annual*, VII (1930), pp. 317–97.

———. *Karaite Anthology*. New Haven, 1952.

Wieder, N. *The Judean Scrolls and Karaism*. London, 1962.

Faith and Reason: The Controversy Over Philosophy

RAPHAEL JOSPE
University of Denver

THE YEAR IS 1232; the place is Montpellier, in southern France. Solomon ben Abraham, assisted by his friends Jonah ben Abraham Gerundi and David ben Saul, has recently convinced the rabbis of France to impose the rabbinic ban, the *ḥerem*, upon anyone who studies philosophy, and specifically anyone who studies Maimonides' *Guide of the Perplexed*[1] and the *Book of Knowledge*.[2] Some months later, the Dominicans publicly burned these two books in the marketplace of Montpellier, with the approval of the papal legate, Cardinal Romanus, apparently after some Jews denounced them to the Church. These Jewish informers *(malshinim)* in turn had their tongues cut out by supporters of Maimonides.[3] The Church seems to have enjoyed the flames; ten years later twenty-four cartloads of volumes of the Talmud were burned by the Dominicans in the *place* in front of the Cathedral of Notre Dame in Paris.[4]

Although there is no direct link between these two burnings of Jewish books by the Church, many Jews widely regarded the two events as related. Maimonides' supporters, such as Hillel ben Samuel of Verona, as well one of Maimonides' chief opponents, Jonah Gerundi, who subsequently repented his opposition to philosophy and Maimonides and vowed to pay penance at the philosopher's grave near Tiberias, saw the burning of the Talmud as the inevitable consequence of, and even punishment for, the burning of Maimonides' works.

Almost seven hundred years later, at the opposite end of the spectrum of Jewish philosophy, the twentieth-century German-

Jewish philosopher Franz Rosenzweig wrote about his teacher and predecessor, the neo-Kantian philosopher Hermann Cohen:

> When Hermann Cohen was in Marburg, he once expounded the God-idea of his *Ethics* to an old Jew of that city. The Jew listened with reverent attention, but when Cohen was through, he asked: "And where is the *bore olam* (creator of the universe)?" Cohen had no answer to this and tears rose in his eyes.[5]

Here, then, are two events illustrating the tension between faith and reason in Judaism. In the Middle Ages it led Jews to pronounce bans of excommunication against each other, to inform on other Jews to the Church, and to resort to physical violence. Even in the twentieth century the problem seems not to have been resolved. The question remains: can faith and reason coexist in Judaism? Can we identify the historical God of Abraham with the rational God of Aristotle (to use Judah Ha-Levi's terms), without seriously violating the integrity of both concepts? As we philosophically refine our ideas about God, what happens to the personal God to whom humans relate? At what point is God replaced by the *idea* of God? In short, what is it about reason that threatens faith, and is this threat real and inherent in the very nature of both faith and reason, or is the threat merely imagined by those who fail to see the light of reason?

Defining Reason and Faith: Formal Process vs. Substantive Conclusion

Philosophy, a product of Greek civilization, is neither indigenous nor native to Judaism.[6] Reason, the use of the human intellect to understand and come to terms with natural reality, conceptualizes in certain logical categories and systematic lines of thought. As such, reason claims to be basically value-free: any two people, whatever else they may believe, and however else they may relate on an emotional level to reality, may proceed from common axiomatic assumptions to shared conclusions which are necessitated by logical and objective rules and principles. Granted that the axioms with which they begin are, by definition, unproven and therefore accepted, as it were, on faith, the rational mode of inquiry itself is objective. Reason is also inherently universal; it is available to any human being inasmuch as he or she is a human being, that is to say, an animal possessing intellect. Reason is thus not limited by, nor does it respect the limits of, any subgrouping of the human race, whether that grouping be religious, national, racial, or political.

Faith differs from reason in several significant ways. First, whereas the rational method can theoretically lead to any conclusion, faith is neither universal nor open-ended. It is not open-ended because it reverses the process of inquiry: one starts with the conclusion which, for one reason or another, is accepted as true and given. Any inquiry is, therefore, limited to understanding, explaining, or justifying that conclusion. The conclusion per se cannot be questioned. Second, unlike reason, faith is not universal. What is known rationally can potentially be known to any person, since all people, by virtue of having reason, can use their reason independently to arrive at the same conclusion. Indeed, if something can really be proved to be true, any reasonable person should accept it as true. However, in faith we assert something as true not because we have arrived at that conclusion at the end of a process of deduction which any person could follow, but rather because we believe it to be true despite the lack of conclusive evidence of its truth. Faith may therefore be conventional: other people may share our conviction that something is true despite our inability to prove it to be true. But since we cannot prove it to be true, their assent to its truth is not necessary, and they can just as rationally reject it. Therefore, while the phenomenon of faith may be universal, faith per se can at most be conventional. Third, reason claims to lead to *knowledge*. But faith leads only to *belief*, which lacks the certainty of rational proof or empirical evidence. In either case, one considers a proposition to be true. But with reason one can prove or verify that proposition, whereas a belief is asserted to be true despite the absence of conclusive proof or evidence.

The Phenomenon of Faith

Granted, then, that faith differs phenomenologically from reason, how have philosophers, who are committed to a rational explanation of phenomena, viewed faith? Even if faith itself is not a rational phenomenon, it should be possible to come to a rational understanding of the nature of that phenomenon.

Martin Buber (1878–1965) discusses two types of faith:

> There are two, and in the end, only two types of faith. To be sure, there are very many contents of faith, but we only know faith itself in two basic forms. Both can be understood from the simple data of our life: the one from the fact that I trust someone, without being able to offer sufficient reasons for my trust in him; the other, from the fact that, likewise without being able to give a sufficient reason, I acknowledge a thing to be true.[7]

Buber identifies the first type of faith—an attitude of trust—with Judaism, and the second type of faith—the assertion that something is true—with Christianity. In both cases, faith is an attitude that a person maintains despite the absence of conclusive proof that this attitude is justified.

Buber's distinction between the two types of faith is easily justified by comparing a passage in the Torah with a passage in the New Testament. In Numbers 20:12, after Moses struck a rock to produce water instead of speaking to it, "The Lord said to Moses and Aaron: Because you did not believe me (*he'emantem bi*) to sanctify me in the eyes of the children of Israel, therefore you will not bring this congregation to the land which I have given them." What can the word *emunah*, usually rendered as "faith" or "belief," mean in this context? Can we possibly argue that Moses, who spoke daily with God (or at least believed that he did), actually questioned the existence of God? When we refer to belief in God, we usually mean the affirmation that there is a God, that God exists. This can obviously not be the meaning of biblical *emunah*, which does not mean to *believe in God*, but rather to *believe God*, to trust God, to be faithful to him. *Emunah* in its biblical sense therefore does not mean "faith," but "faithfulness" or "fidelity," even as we use these terms in a marital context, where fidelity refers not to the existence of the partner, which is obvious and taken for granted, but to an attitude of trust toward the partner.[8] *Emunah* thus does not mean that the Jew and God affirm each other's existence—which is taken for granted and is regarded as obvious—but rather that God and man have a relationship of fidelity and a mutuality of trust; and it was this relationship and attitude that Moses failed to maintain.

The other type of faith, which Buber identifies with Christianity, refers to an affirmation of something as true, even though one may lack conclusive evidence of its truth. What is at stake in this type of faith is the facticity of a proposition. Does something exist, or does it not exist? Did something happen, or did it not in fact happen? In his Letter to the Corinthians, Paul puts it succinctly (1 Cor. 15:12–20):

> Now if Christ is preached as raised from the dead, how can some of you say that there is no resurrection of the dead? But if there is no resurrection of the dead, then Christ has not been raised; if Christ has not been raised, then our preaching is in vain and your faith is in vain. We are even found to be misrepresenting God, because we testified of God that he raised Christ, whom he did not raise. . . . If Christ has not been raised, your faith is futile, and you are still in your sins. . . . But in fact Christ has been raised from the dead . . .

For Paul, Christianity stands or falls on the factual truth of the account of the resurrection of Jesus. Pauline faith, then, is less an attitude of trust, in the biblical sense of *emunah*, than a Greek notion of the verification of a proposition.

This distinction became vital for Jewish philosophers because they had to come to grips with the Greek and Christian type of faith. The Greeks had developed a system of philosophy and science—which were largely synonymous until early modern times—which had to be understood and faced by any intelligent Jew. The system seemed incontrovertible, at least in general method if not in all of its specific conclusions, and the Jew had to confront its claims and come to terms with any apparent contradictions between the philosophic-scientific wisdom of the Greeks and the traditional wisdom, based on revelation, of the Jews.

But if Jews were to adopt the Greek philosophical method as a path to truth, that method had to make room for a specifically Jewish claim to truth, the claim of historic revelation. In other words, the challenge to the Jewish philosopher was not merely to justify philosophy within a Jewish context, but also to demonstrate that the rational method of philosophy could incorporate as true the historic prophetic revelation that the Jewish people claimed to possess. Philosophy as a method could be valid, but it had to accommodate the possibility that there is another source of truth, prophetic revelation. In short, for the Jewish philosopher, there was not one but two sources of truth.

The first of the medieval Jewish philosophers, Isaac ben Solomon Israeli (855–955, Egypt), although he discussed the phenomenon of prophecy,[9] clearly posited belief or opinion on a different level from true knowledge. In his *Book of Definitions*[10] Israeli gave four separate definitions of rational knowledge, and only one definition of "opinion."

> *Reason (nutq).* Reason is knowledge which attains the truth through deliberation and cognition.

> *Absolute knowledge (al-'ilm al-mursal).* The soul's perception of the truths of things which are the objects of knowledge.

> *True knowledge (al-'ilm al-ṣadiq).* True cognition confirmed by syllogism and established by demonstration.

> *Cognition (ma'rifa).* An established opinion which does not cease.

In each of these cases, the knowledge is purely rational. It is based on some form of demonstration or proof and, therefore, is true. But opinion or belief has no such evidence or certainty. Israeli simply says of opinion: *"Opinion (ra'y).* Belief in some thing." He thus distinguishes mere opinion, which seems to have no evidence to support it (as Buber also maintained is the case with faith), from true knowledge. Although Israeli certainly believed in the phenomenon of prophecy, his definition of opinion scarcely reflects serious philosophic consideration of the transmission of the message of revelation as truth.

Israeli's younger contemporary, Saadia ben Joseph (882–942), from Fayyum, Egypt, and Gaon (head of the academy) at Sura in Babylonia, did attempt explicitly to find a place for faith as a type of true knowledge in order to justify Jewish claims of possessing truth from a source other than reason, namely revelation.

In his great philosophical work, the *Book of Beliefs and Opinions*,[11] Saadia defines both belief *(i'tiqad, emunah)* and knowledge.

> It behooves us to explain what is meant by belief. We say that it is a notion that arises in the soul in regard to the actual character of anything that is apprehended. . . . Then the person becomes convinced of the truth of the notion he has thus acquired. . . . Now beliefs fall into two categories: true and false. A true belief consists in believing a thing to be as it really is. . . . A false belief, on the other hand, consists in believing a thing to be the opposite of what it actually is.[12]

Since a belief, according to this definition, can presumably be either true or false, depending on whether it corresponds to reality, there should be some way to verify belief to ascertain whether it is true. In fact, as we shall see, Saadia does provide a way to verify belief. Such verification may not be sufficient to be absolutely conclusive, in which case our belief, having been proven, would be knowledge and no longer belief; but the verification, even if not so absolutely conclusive as to constitute knowledge, can give us sufficient certainty or conviction to assert that the belief is true.

Saadia then discusses three types of knowledge *('ilm)*.[13]

> The first consists of the knowledge gained by direct observation *('ilm al-shahada; yedi'at ha-nir'eh)*. The second is composed of the intuition of the intellect *('ilm al-'aql; mada' ha-sekhel)*. The third comprises that knowledge which is inferred by logical necessity *('ilm ma dafa'at al-darara 'ilahu; yedi'at mah she-ha-hekhrah mevi' 'elav)*.

These three types of knowledge—empirical, rational, and deductive (combining rational and empirical)—are universal. But there is another, fourth type of knowledge, according to Saadia:[14]

> As for ourselves, the community of monotheists *(jama'ah al-muwahadin; qehal ha-meyahadim)*, we hold these three sources of

knowledge to be genuine. To them, however, we add a fourth source, which we have derived by means of the (other) three, and which has thus become for us a further principle. This (is to say, we believe in) the validity of authentic tradition *(al-khabr al-ṣadiq; ha-haggadah ha-ne'emenet)* . . . This type of knowledge . . . corroborates for us the validity of the first three sources of knowledge.

It is this fourth type of knowledge, authentic tradition, that is especially relevant to our discussion of faith or belief, because it is precisely in the area of tradition, or historical information, that we lack immediate and conclusive evidence, whether that evidence be rational, empirical, or deductive. How do we know that something that allegedly occurred in the past actually did occur? We are dealing here with historical events, which reason alone is incapable of verifying or refuting. We cannot determine rationally whether something did or did not happen; it is basically an empirical question. At the same time, since the event occurred in the past, we are also not able to verify it empirically, by the use of our senses. How, then, can we verify it? For Saadia, this is ultimately a question of belief.[15] We believe that something happened because we trust the testimony of the original witnesses, and we further trust the reliability of those who have transmitted the original testimony to us over the years. And here, the qualitative judgment that we must make about the report may be influenced by a quantitative factor. The more original witnesses there were, and the larger the number of people who have been involved in the process of transmitting the original testimony, the more likely we are to give credence to their report. Errors in the original testimony and in the process of transmitting it to us are less likely to occur when greater numbers of people are involved in that process. One individual, or a few individuals, may be mistaken about something; they may be deceived or tricked; or they may suffer the same illusion—or they may even agree deliberately to deceive for some reason. But it is not likely that any of these conditions which lead to error can be attributed to a large number of people. Therefore, the quality of the veracity of the report is directly affected by the quantity of people making the report.[16]

This view of Saadia's, which is accepted and developed by later Jewish philosophers such as Judah Ha-Levi and Moses Mendelssohn,[17] is crucial to Jewish religious philosophy, for it enables a rationalist philosopher to accept as true the claims of revelation made in the Torah and later Jewish tradition. It enables these philosophers to assert that whatever else we may wish to believe about God and how God relates to humans, the *fact* is that, at a given time in the history of the Jewish people, God revealed Himself to the people and their prophets. From this perspective, the revelation at Sinai is a fact, and whatever our theories may be, they must take this fact into account. We could conceivably argue, as Ha-Levi lets the king of the Khazars do,[18] that it is difficult to imagine that God would lower Himself by speaking, or relating, to mortal men. But from the point of view of Saadia and Ha-Levi, the incontrovertible fact is that God did reveal Himself to Israel, and that we know this fact through authentic tradition. Theory can be debated. The philosopher's goal is to provide a rational explanation of natural reality, and historical revelation is now assumed to be part of the reality which the philosopher must explain and with which he must come to terms.

The Inherent Potential Conflict of Faith and Reason

If the philosopher must come to terms with historical reality, just as the Jew must come to terms with philosophy, why is there, at least potentially, an inherent conflict between the claims of faith and the claims of reason?

Ultimately, the answer is simple. Each system—reason and faith—can be seen as inherently undermining and negating the authority and basic premises of the other.

Faith essentially negates the autonomy of reason. Reason, seeking to arrive at the truth by rational means, accepts no pre-set limitations as to what it may investigate or as to the conclusions at which it may arrive. The process of deduction alone verifies a proposition. If the process is valid the conclusion is verified, whether or not that conclusion agrees with our preconceived notions. In faith, however, we have an *a priori* commitment to a certain position as true (in this case, that God revealed Himself in a certain manner). How, then, can any conclusion different from our position be true? Since any conclusion is possible in philosophy or science, granted that the integrity of the method is ensured, faith, by insisting that only one conclusion is and can be true, negates the validity of the rational system itself.

Conversely, reason negates the autonomy of faith. If it is true that God revealed Himself to humans, it presumably follows that what God revealed is true and should be accepted merely by virtue of having been revealed. For the believer, it is sufficient to say that the fact is that this is what God revealed. But the philosopher threatens and undermines that faith when he insists on his prerogative to ask the question: Why? Why did God reveal Himself thus? How do we know what this means? Why should I accept something simply because I am told that it is true or that it is God's will? Rationally, I can only accept something as true if I can understand it and rationally affirm its truth. The rationalist thus subjects God's revelation to his own individual judgment; something is no longer true merely because God revealed it, but only because one can affirm it rationally.

The believer, then, subordinates his individual judgment to what he regards as a higher, and possibly objective, standard, the divine standard of revelation. The rationalist does the opposite: he subordinates revelation to his own individual judgment and questions the authenticity and revealed nature of anything which cannot pass his rational judgment.

The Relationship of Revelation to Reason

There are basically two ways of resolving the conflict between faith and reason. Each causes its own problems, and both are followed by various Jewish philosophers. The one way is to assert that whatever is revealed must be in harmony with reason, or even rational in content, and that revelation and reason arrive at the same truth by different means. The other way is to assert that what is revealed need not, and cannot be, rational in content, although one can still assert that nothing revealed can actually contradict reason.

Saadia Gaon followed the first way of resolving this problem, by identifying the content of revelation with rational truth. What is revealed is essentially rational.[19] Saadia recognized that this solution immediately raises another problem. If what is revealed is rational, why is revelation altogether necessary? Why does God have to reveal something that could be arrived at independently through the use of reason? His answer is twofold. First, rational conclusions are only arrived at after a long process of speculation. Revelation is thus, in effect, a shortcut in the rational process. We are given the rational conclusion in detail from the outset, that we may behave properly even before we would on our own arrive at those conclusions. Second, some people are never capable of arriving at the truth by themselves, and such people are given the truth through revelation, so they may obey God's commandments and thus merit reward.

But this leads us then to a further problem. Clearly, the Torah contains ideas and precepts which are rational in content, and which we might maintain even if they were not revealed, such as the prohibition of murder. But there are other ideas and precepts in the Torah which are not rationally self-evident, and which we would certainly not deduce rationally. Accordingly, Saadia divides the commandments of the Torah into two categories: rational commandments and traditional commandments.[20] Rational commandments (al-shari'ah al-'aqliyah; mizvot sikhliyot) are commandments the rationale of which is immediately evident: we would deduce them rationally even if they were not revealed. These commandments prevent people from harming each other, for instance, by murder, theft, or lying. The second type consists of traditional commandments (al-shari'ah al-sami'ah; mizvot shim'iyot), which derive their authority exclusively from having been revealed, for example the dietary laws, priesthood, and laws of purity. The fact that they are not clearly necessitated by reason, and are merely optional in rational terms, does not imply that they either contradict reason or have no purpose. They all serve a valid utilitarian purpose, even though that purpose is not necessarily rational or immediately evident.[21]

Since revelation thus includes not only rational laws but also laws which are not obviously rational, in effect the rationalist attitude of a believer that assumes that anything revealed must ultimately be rational, is itself an ultimate act of faith.

But while, following Saadia, we may thus rationalize commandments which are not clearly rational and maintain that they do not contradict reason, there are passages in Scripture that do present a problem from a rationalist perspective. Some verses in the Torah violate reason by anthropomorphic and anthropopathic references to God, by attributing to God human bodily or emotional qualities, such as verses that refer to "the right hand of the Lord," or to God as sitting on His throne, or as being angry with people, or as regretting and repenting an earlier action or decision. How can such references to God be acceptable from a rationalist point of view, which would deny that God has a body or any of the qualities of a body? If revelation is rational, what can these verses possibly mean?

Saadia maintains that Scripture is to be understood as literally true, in general, but that there are four conditions under which it must be taken figuratively, not literally. When a biblical verse contradicts what we know empirically, or contradicts reason, or contradicts another biblical passage, or contradicts authentic tradition, we are not only permitted but actually obligated to understand it figuratively, and not literally.[22] But the rationalists generally maintained a conservative and respectful attitude toward the literal text. In his *Introduction to the Torah*, the rationalist exegete Abraham ibn Ezra (Spain, 1089–1164) reaffirms Saadia's position. Where the text does not contradict reason or experience it is to be taken literally, and Ibn Ezra opposes what he regards as unnecessary allegorization by Christian exegetes.[23]

Medieval Jewish rationalist exegetes and philosophers were, of course, not the first Jews to approach Scripture allegorically. The first Jewish philosopher, Philo of Alexandria (ca. 20 B.C.E.–50 C.E.) had set the pattern for such rationalist allegorization, even though he did not directly influence the course of Jewish philosophy in the Middle Ages (since he wrote in Greek and the medieval philosophers lived in an Arabic environment). When Philo attempted to harmonize the teachings of Moses and Plato, he did so out of the sincere conviction that he was uncovering in the Torah an esoteric meaning that was not only true rationally, but also faithful to the text and the original intention of the author.

Allegorical interpretation among Jews was by no means limited to the rationalist camp. Long before the rise of medieval Jewish philosophy, the rabbis of the Talmud, for example, interpreted the Song of Songs as an allegory of the love between God (symbolized by the male lover) and Israel (symbolized by the female lover, with their kisses symbolizing the *miẓvot* which God gave to Israel).[24]

The most popular medieval Jewish Bible exegete, Rashi (1040–1105), who certainly was no rationalist philosopher, felt free to reproduce the talmudic interpretation of Exodus 33:23 (where God says to Moses: "You will see my back, but my face will not be seen") as meaning that God showed Moses the knot of his *tefillin (her'ahu qesher shel tefillin)*.[25] Such rabbinic homiletical interpretation *(derash)* certainly was at times as great a violation of the literal text *(peshat)* as was rationalist allegorization. It would seem, then, that what non-philosophical and anti-rationalist Jews regarded as threatening in rationalist allegorization was not the violation of *peshat* per se, since *derash* also violates *peshat*. But *derash* is a source for defining and deriving *halakhah* as well as Jewish ethics *(aggadah)* from the biblical text, whereas *remez* (figurative or allegorical interpretation) is not. *Derash*, even by violating the *peshat*, not only strengthened *halakhah* but made its derivation from biblical texts possible. *Remez*, however, was regarded as potentially dangerous, since it was based on non-Jewish philosophical considerations and could, its opponents feared, lead to rejection of the biblical text rather than its fulfillment, and to laxity in, or even abandonment of, traditional Jewish observance. The rationalists rarely, if ever, justified such fears for their Jewish observance, and in the case of such major rationalists as Maimonides and Saadia Gaon, whose contributions to rabbinic Judiasm could not be ignored, such fears would have been completely absurd. But the fact that the fears of the anti-rationalists were unwarranted did not reduce the fervor with which they held to their view.

The medieval rationalists, no less than Philo, did not consider their rationalization of Scripture to be artificial or reading foreign values into the Torah. They sincerely believed that the Torah not only was but had to be rationally explicable by the very fact that it was revealed. Maimonides[26] understood prophecy to be an inherently intellectual activity. Ibn Ezra sincerely insisted that reason is fundamental to the Torah: "The Torah was not given to one lacking reason . . . the angel between man and God is his intellect."[27] Since God revealed the Torah only to humans and not to other animals, we can only conclude that humans received revelation by virtue of that which distinguishes them from animals, namely reason. Consequently, the content of revelation must be rational and comprehensible to humans.

Ibn Ezra, therefore, also argued against the rabbinic view that God revealed both versions of the Ten Commandments simultaneously.[28] Even if God could miraculously have spoken two different sets of commandments simultaneously, what good would it have done? How could the people have understood it? If the people had heard two different things at the same time they would have understood neither.[29]

We thus see the following progression of ideas about the relationship between revelation and reason from a rationalist perspective, as typified by Saadia:

First, both revelation and reason are true sources of knowledge.

Second, revelation and reason must, therefore, possess the same content, since both are true. Accordingly, they can only differ in form or method.

Third, Scripture contains laws and commandments which are clearly rational, and which we would accept rationally even if they had not been revealed.

Fourth, we also find in Scripture laws and commandments which we are unable to understand or explain rationally. We believe that they serve a utilitarian purpose, but we are not always able to discover that purpose. In any event, these commandments, although they are not rationally necessary, at least do not contradict reason in any way.

Fifth, when we study Scripture we also find passages that are offensive from a rational perspective, if understood literally. Since both revelation and reason are true and, in fact, coincide in the Torah, such passages cannot possibly mean what they say, and must, therefore, be understood to have a true figurative meaning.

This, then, is the solution adapted by those philosophers who are committed to both faith and reason, revelation and philosophy. The two are in harmony, or even identical in content. Whenever revelation violates reason it obviously cannot be the true meaning of revelation. One can affirm that revelation is true only if one denies that it means what it literally says. It was this rationalist denial of the literal meaning of Scripture that later aroused vigorous opposition in the controversy over philosophy.

Revelation as Nonrational

The second way of resolving the problem of faith and reason is to assert that what is revealed is not, and indeed cannot be, rational in content, although one need not therefore admit that anything revealed can actually contradict reason. Revelation, by this method, is nonrational, neither rational nor irrational.

The dichotomy between revelation and rational truth emerges most sharply in Judah Ha-Levi's *Kuzari (Kitab al-Khazari)*, which he calls "The Proof and Demonstration in Defense of the Despised Faith." Ha-Levi questions the reliability of reason with regard to ultimate metaphysical truth. The inadequacy of reason is evidenced by the fact that rationalist philosophers have always been unable to come to agreement on basic principles or actions.[30] Furthermore, Ha-Levi argues, the simple historical fact is that there never was a prophet among the philosophers, and never a philosopher among the prophets. The phenomenon of prophecy was historically limited to the people of Israel and the land of Israel.

Consequently, Ha-Levi argues that the phenomenon of prophetic revelation cannot be attributed to reason, for if prophecy were a function of reason, it could have appeared among all men in different times and of different nations. But since prophetic revelation is historically unique to Israel, it must be a function of some faculty other than reason. Ha-Levi, therefore, developed a theory that the Jews possess a unique, divine faculty *('amr 'ilahi; 'inyan 'elohi)* which transcends reason, by which they are able to commune directly with God and to receive revelation.[31]

Since Ha-Levi denied the identity of revelation and reason (although revelation cannot contain anything contrary to reason)[32], he was freed from the forced attempts of rationalists like

Maimonides, for whom prophecy is basically the highest form of philosophy, to show that the ancient prophets of Israel were all philosophers. In this respect Ha-Levi was far more attuned to historical reality than was Maimonides. Ha-Levi was also freed from the need to demonstrate that all the *mizvot* serve some rational purpose, even if the purpose is not immediately evident. They can serve a divine purpose, of preparing Jews for prophecy or for activating their latent prophetic potential in the *'inyan 'elohi*.

The idea that revelation, while not rational in content, cannot contradict reason was further developed by later Jewish philosophers, in the context of philosophical polemics against Christianity in the fourteenth and fifteenth centuries.[33]

Ibn Rushd had suggested that religious truth could not be supported by rational speculation.[34] This led such thirteenth-century Latin Averroists at the University of Paris as Siger of Brabant[35] to the radical "double-truth" theory, that reason and revelation are two entirely autonomous and separate realms of truth. Something can be true in the one system, while not being true in the other system.[36] Isaac Albalag (Spain, 13th cent.) was "the first and for many years the only, Jewish philosopher to maintain the doctrine of the double truth."[37] For Albalag "the Torah was only a political document, and did not purport to teach the truth."[38]

Subsequently, Elijah del Medigo (Italy, ca. 1460–1497) also accepted this doctrine of the double-truth, and argued that "philosophy and religion are two different spheres and operate under different laws."[39] Religious truth is incapable of rational demonstration. The philosophers and masses alike must affirm the basic principles of religion and may not give them philosophic interpretation, which might result in heresy if the rational proof of a religious doctrine should fail.

Other Jewish philosophers, while they did not go so far as to adopt the double-truth theory, did recognize the nonrational aspects of revelation. But if revelation is nonrational, how can one distinguish rationally between the claims of Jewish faith and the claims of other faiths, such as Christianity?

For Joseph Albo (Spain, 1380–1435), faith is superior to reason and only faith can lead to salvation.[40] Albo distinguished between what he regarded as the nonrational nature of Jewish faith and the irrationality of Christian faith. Basing himself on Maimonides' notion that God cannot do something logically impossible, but that God can do something naturally impossible,[41] Albo argued that God has no power over things which are essentially impossible (nimna'ot qayyamot be-'azmam),[42] but God does have power over things which are merely impossible according to the laws of nature (nimna'ot 'eẓel ha-teva' bilvad)[43] but which are intellectually conceivable and logically possible.[44]

The Torah contains accounts of such nonrational phenomena as miracles. But such phenomena are only naturally impossible: they contradict the laws of nature as we know them, and not the laws of logic. But such Christian dogmas as the trinity and incarnation are logically absurd as well as naturally impossible. From this point of view of Albo and others,[45] Judaism may not be fully rational; but it is not irrational, as is the case with Christianity. Therefore, while they cannot employ philosophy to prove Judaism, they do employ it to disprove Christianity.[46] "Reason does not have to prove a religion true, but . . . religious truths may not be irrational."[47] Thus, for the Jewish Averroists, "reason cannot prove a religion, but it can disprove one."[48]

In modern times, the nonrational approach to revelation was followed by Moses Mendelssohn (Germany, 1729–1786). Revelation cannot contradict reason.[49] But revelation can also not convey rational truth. If the truth can be understood rationally, revelation is superfluous, as Saadia had recognized. Conversely, if something cannot be understood rationally, revelation cannot have any effect, as Ibn Ezra had maintained. Therefore, revealed religion (in the sense of religion as the truth) is a contradiction in terms. Accordingly, Judaism is not (and cannot be) revealed religion, but rather revealed law.[50] Saadia had understood revelation to be rational in content, and a shortcut to the truth and to proper behavior. Mendelssohn denied its rationality, but regarded revelation as serving a similar purpose: regulating people's conduct so that their actions might remind and teach them of the abstract truth. Their concrete actions, correctly guided, would then lead them to truth and felicity.[51]

The double-truth theory was, in a way, revived in the nineteenth century by Samson Raphael Hirsch (1808–1888), ideological spokesman for modern or Neo-Orthodoxy in Germany. Hirsch welcomed the study of science and secular subjects by Jews. He interpreted Avot 2:2, "*yafeh talmud torah 'im derekh 'erez*" ("It is proper to have the study of Torah along with a worldly involvement"), to mean that the Jew should involve himself in the modern world, in secular studies, science, and European culture, while remaining faithful to the world of traditional Judaism and the way of life prescribed by the Torah. But while Hirsch affirmed the need to pursue secular studies and science, he rejected the view of modern Jewish scholarship *(Wissenschaft des Judentums)* that Judaism itself, specifically the Torah, could be scientifically and historically analyzed. The Torah is the expression of divine revelation, and, therefore, it can be understood only from within, from a position of commitment, and not from without, from a position of detached and objective inquiry. That which is supranatural cannot be subject to natural law and investigation. Science is true—for the natural realm. Revelation is true—for the supranatural realm. Both realms are true, independently of each other, although neither is true in the terms of the other.

While thinkers such as Ha-Levi, the Averroists, Mendelssohn, and Hirsch, who negated any identity between faith and reason, were freed from the need to rationalize the obviously nonrational aspects of the Torah,[52] their own approach logically led to a double-truth position which entails its own problems. It is very convenient to assert that something can be true either in rational terms or in terms of faith or revelation, without attempting to reconcile the two realms of truth. But one is then left with two different sets of truth, thus destroying the consistency and unity of truth. If something can be true in the one system and not in the other, what can truth possibly mean? If there are two truths, there is no one, absolute truth.

These, then, are the options faced by the religious philosopher in Judaism, who has a commitment to both faith and reason as sources of and approaches to truth. Revelation and reason can be viewed either as identical in content though different in form, or as entirely separate and distinct types of truth. Both of these approaches lead to further problems. A potential conflict is inherent in the nature of both faith and reason.

The Controversy over Maimonides: The Historical Background

Why is it that the conflict of faith and reason erupted into a public controversy only at certain times? Theoretically, the problem is posed by any attempt at Jewish philosophy. Why did only certain philosophers, among them Maimonides, arouse such a bitter controversy, whereas others, such as Saadia, did not? There are several historical reasons for the outbreak of a controversy over philosophy already within the lifetime, but especially after the death, of Maimonides. In some cases, the controversy was more over Maimonides than over philosophy, in other cases, more over philosophy than Maimonides.

The controversy over philosophy and especially over Maimonides was, to a large extent, a result of anti-philosophical sentiment in the Church, which in turn affected Jews living in Christian countries.[53] After the Crusaders had captured Constantinople in 1204 (the year in which Maimonides died), the Greek works of Aristotle became directly accessible to Western Christians; they no longer had to rely on Latin translations of Greek texts made, often by Jews, from Arabic versions or Hebrew versions based on the Arabic translations from the Greek. The growing universities challenged the monasteries as centers of learning. While the traditional doctrines of the Church were being confronted by secular learning, the Church's orthodoxy was also being challenged in the thirteenth century by heresies, especially that of the Albigensians, a heretical group from Albi in southern France, who had begun in the eleventh century to interpret Scripture allegorically and who denied the literal interpretation of the miraculous events of Jesus' life and death that was central to Catholic dogma. This "heresy" spread especially among the upper classes.

The Church moved against both threats. Against the threat of

secular philosophy, the University of Paris in 1209 banned the study
of Arabic writings (which were philosophical and scientific). The
Synod of Paris in 1210 banned the public or private reading of
Aristotle's works on natural philosophy, as well as commentaries on
those works. In 1215, the Papal Legate instructed the University of
Paris to forbid the study of Aristotle's *Physics* and *Metaphysics*,
although he permitted the study of Aristotle's *Ethics*. Pope Innocent
III had launched the Albigensian Crusade, to eliminate the threat of
the Albigensian heresy, which he regarded as instigated by educated
Jews. A few years later, in 1231, Pope Gregory IX renewed the ban
on Aristotle and established the permanent Inquisition under the
Dominicans, with the aim of completely eradicating Albigen-
sianism.

In fact, there were certain parallels between the Albigensian
heretics in Christianity and the Jewish philosophers of the day, at
least as perceived by their opponents, in the Church and in the
Jewish community respectively. The Albigensians engaged in
rationalist allegorization of Scripture, especially with regard to the
miracles of Jesus' body and resurrection. The Jewish philosophers
engaged in rationalist allegorization of Scripture, expecially with
regard to anthropomorphisms, miracles, and the doctrine of resurrection. In the case of the Albigensians, their allegorization led to
antinomian attitudes, resulting in a laxity in morals. In the case of the
Jewish philosophers, their opponents claimed, perhaps with some
justification but certainly with great exaggeration, that their allegorization led them to antinomianism in ritual matters, with a resulting
laxity in observance of the *mizvot*. As Joseph Sarachek wrote in his
history of the controversy over faith and reason in Judaism,

> If these clashes in church and synagogue are not connected as cause and
> effect, they are at any rate analogous movements. The seeds of an
> alleged heresy were blowing in all directions. . . . it was not until the
> thirteenth century that the real conflicts over heresy in Christendom
> were fought and that the mood for ferreting out and punishing heresy
> was transferred to the Jewish fold.[54]

Rationalist and sectarian heresies produced turmoil not only in
the Church but in the Jewish community as well. According to

Salo Baron, the rationalist individualism of Karaism, which contributed to the rise of Jewish philosophy, threatened religious
authority.

> The constant growth of educated classes, the sharp sectarian con-
> troversies, and the increasing spread of and reverence for the works
> of the most representative Greek thinkers and scientists . . . and the
> new interrelated forces of individualism and the quest for scientific
> discovery, all these factors made questioning of accepted beliefs and
> practices a common phenomenon among all religious groups.[55]

Moreover, the Jewish community faced not only a confrontation
with ideologies—rationalist and Karaite—which challenged it internally, but also external pressure and hostility from the Church.
The Fourth Lateran Council of 1215, among its seventy canonical
decrees, promulgated four decrees specifically aimed at Jews.[56]
For example, in the Paris disputation of 1240, Donin of La
Rochelle, who had been excommunicated by his Jewish community for doubting the validity of the Talmud, and had then been
baptized, taking the Christian name Nicholas, denounced the
Talmud to Pope Gregory IX, charging that the Talmud distorts
the Bible, that the Jews regard the Talmud as more important
than the Bible, and that the Talmud abuses or insults Jesus and
Mary. Subsequently, in 1242, twenty-four cartloads of the Talmud were burned by the Dominicans in the *place* in front of the
Cathedral of Notre Dame.[57] But we cannot overlook internal
Jewish developments which led to a negative reaction to
philosophy. The great opposition to philosophy emerged among
Jews only after Maimonides' works had become known among
Jewish communities in Christian areas of Europe. The early works
of Jewish philosophy were written in Arabic and were only later
translated into Hebrew. Hence, the works of early philosophers
such as Saadia, Isaac Israeli, and Solomon ibn Gabirol, who wrote
in Arabic, remained largely unread in the lifetimes of their authors
or even later, in those Jewish communities which did not know
Arabic.

The situation was different in Maimonides' case. Because of his
great prestige, not as a philosopher but as the *nagid*, the political

and spiritual head of the Egyptian Jewish community, and as the author of the *Mishneh Torah*, which was written in Hebrew, his other works, including the *Guide of the Perplexed* (originally written in Arabic), quickly became available in Hebrew to philosophically untrained Jews who did not know Arabic.[58] Maimonides never intended the *Guide of the Perplexed* to be read by the masses. He wrote it only for those who were perplexed, that is to say, who had studied some philosophy and who were troubled by the apparent contradictions between the teachings of philosophy and the teachings of Judaism. The *Guide* could solve the problems of the perplexed Jewish philosopher, but it could only perplex Jews who were not philosophers. Like the *parah 'adumah*, the red heifer (Numbers 19), which could purify those who had been defiled, but would defile those who were pure and engaged in its preparation, the *Guide of the Perplexed* could only aid those who were already perplexed from their exposure to philosophy, but would endanger the beliefs of the observant Jews whose education was purely traditional and who had previously not been exposed to philosophy.

As Shem Tov ibn Falaquera (d. Spain, 1291) put it in his commentary to Maimonides' *Guide of the Perplexed*,[59] the *Guide* can help someone who is perplexed but will harm someone who has not studied philosophy, just as medicine, which can heal the sick, harms the healthy person.

It must be emphasized that Maimonides did not write the *Guide* to justify philosophy to Jews, but to justify Judaism to philosophers. It was the philosopher who needed convincing, not the traditionalist Jew.[60] Maimonides' proofs of the existence of God, for example, are based on the assumption that the world is eternal, not created.[61] This could only confuse and even upset a traditionalist, nonphilosophical Jew. How could Maimonides deny the doctrine of creation? The fact might easily evade him that Maimonides did not write proofs of God for him; he needed no such proofs. Maimonides' proofs were intended for a Jewish skeptic who doubted the traditional teachings of Judaism because of his exposure to philosophy. To reach such a philosopher, Maimonides had to argue with him in his own terms—in terms of the philosophy, in this case the doctrine of eternity—which he accepted. Maimonides based his proofs of God on an eternal universe not because he accepted eternity, but because his intended audience did. But this kind of distinction probably evaded many of his opponents. It was, thus, Maimonides' fame as a rabbi and not as a philosopher that brought his philosophical works to the attention of Jews in Christian areas, Jews who were unprepared and unable to meet the challenge of the philosophy, which Maimonides had never intended them to read in the first place.

The Controversy: During Maimonides' Lifetime

The controversy over philosophy can be divided into four periods. The first period was during Maimonides' lifetime; the second period was in the years 1230–1235; the third period was in the years 1288–1290; and the fourth period was in the years 1303–1306. In each period, different issues were prominent.

In the first period, Maimonides' lifetime, the controversy was not over philosophy as such or over Maimonides' philosophy in particular, since his *Guide of the Perplexed* was translated into Hebrew only at the very end of his life. In fact, during Maimonides' lifetime, there was less controversy over him than there was criticism of him in two major areas—criticism of his *Mishneh Torah*, and criticism of his attitude toward resurrection.[62]

The criticism of the *Mishneh Torah* focused on Maimonides' methodology in codifying Jewish law, but the halakhic criticism set the stage for philosophic criticism as well.[63]

One of the unique and controversial features of Maimonides' code is that the *Mishneh Torah*, in contradistinction to other codes of Jewish law, legislated beliefs as well as practices. Political law can at best serve the negative purpose of preventing people from harming each other, according to Maimonides. But divine law must also serve the positive purpose of perfecting people by bringing them to the truth. Hence, correct opinions, as well as proper actions, must be legislated.[64]

For instance, Maimonides categorized as a heretic *(min)* anyone who affirms that there is one God but that God has a body.[65] Maimonides later asserted that a person who believes in a corporeal

God is worse than an idolater.[66] Ravad (Rabbi Abraham ben David of Posquières) took strong exception to this, and wrote: "This is impossible. Why did he call such a person a heretic, when some who were greater and better than he followed this opinion, according to what they saw in the Bible and even more, according to what they saw in *aggadot* which corrupt opinions."[67]

During his lifetime Maimonides was also charged with failing to affirm the principle of resurrection. His discussion of the world-to-come *('olam ha-ba)* in the Mishneh Torah emphasizes the spiritual nature of the world to come, and rejects any notion of bodily immortality.[68] Ravad notes, "The words of this man seem close to one who says that there is no bodily resurrection of the dead, but only of the soul." Maimonides could easily refute the charge by referring to his *Thirteen Principles*, the last of which affirmed resurrection. But even there, Maimonides really did not commit himself to very much. He explained the concept of resurrection by referring loosely to a statement in the Talmud that the righteous, even in their death, are called living, and the wicked, even in their lives, are called dead.[69] Obviously, this is a far cry from asserting that the bodies of the dead are literally restored to life. In specific response to the charge that he denied resurrection, Maimonides wrote the *Treatise on Resurrection (Maqalah fi tehiyat ha-metim)*, in which he argued that the concept of resurrection *(tehiyat ha-metim)* is not to be confused with the world-to-come *('olam ha-ba)*, which refers only to the immortality of the human soul, and ultimately only to the survival of the intellect. Nor should resurrection be confused with the Messianic era *(yemot ha-mashiah)*, which Maimonides interpreted in purely naturalistic and political terms, as the restoration of the Jews to sovereignty in Israel. Resurrection, Maimonides argued in his *Treatise*, is a miracle, not something natural, and therefore did not merit discussion in his other works, which dealt with natural phenomena. Nor was resurrection—a possibility for the distant future—mentioned in the Torah, which was intended to legislate correct actions, and to provide people with a more immediate incentive than the remote possibility of resurrection. As a miracle, resurrection would be effected by God, not by a human such as the Messiah. But what Maimonides is really arguing for is not resurrection itself but the possibility of resurrection. To deny the possibility of resurrection is to deny that miracles (such as resurrection) are possible. In a world which is eternal, as Aristotle had posited, miracles are impossible, since the world eternally functions by unchanging necessity. But in a world which is created by God in accordance with will and purpose, there is no such mechanical necessity, and the possibility of miracles exists.[70] Therefore, to deny the possibility of resurrection is to deny the possibility of miracles, which, in turn, entails the denial of creation. And if the world was not created, then there can have been no revelation (which is also an expression of divine will rather than necessity), in which case the authority of the Torah collapses.[71]

Nevertheless, despite his inclusion of resurrection among the *Thirteen Principles*, and his statements in his *Treatise on Resurrection*, Maimonides clearly tried as hard as possible to interpret resurrection loosely or even metaphorically and to emphasize the possibility of resurrection rather than resurrection itself. In short, on the question of resurrection, "Maimonides affirmed even as he squirmed."[72]

This stage of the controversy ended with Maimonides' death. The question of resurrection was ultimately unresolved. As for the criticism of the *Mishneh Torah*, it was incorporated into the text of the *Mishneh Torah* by the inclusion of critical glosses *(hasagot)* in editions of the code.

The Controversy: Stage II (1230–1235)

Maimonides' *Guide of the Perplexed (Dalalat al-Ḥa'irin; Moreh Nevukhim)* was translated from the original Arabic into Hebrew twice, first by Samuel ibn Tibbon in 1204 at the request of Provençal Jews, and shortly thereafter, in a freer but less accurate translation, by the poet Judah al-Ḥarizi. Later it was also translated into Latin.[73] The *Guide*, which had been written explicitly only for philosophically trained Jews, thus became quickly accessible to Jews in Christian areas and even to the Christians. The Jewish reaction in the southern French areas of Languedoc and Provence was often vehemently negative, especially in Montpellier.

It is unlikely that Maimonides could have conceived of the trouble his works would arouse. In the words of Heinrich Graetz,

Maimonides "aimed at unifying Judaism, and produced divisions; he had sought to give it transparent clearness and general simplicity, and only caused misunderstanding and complication."[74] But Maimonides had not, of course, intended his philosophical works to reach the audiences they did, precisely because of the danger inherent in them. Yet, despite the fact that the controversy over Maimonidean philosophy reached levels of mutual excommunication and physical violence between 1230 and 1235, "it must be emphasized that in the conflict the opposing sides stayed within the fold of Judaism. The conflict did not reach the stage of a secession or a schism."[75]

Although Maimonides himself was recognized even by his opponents to be above personal reproach, since his piety and observance of Jewish law could not possibly be questioned, it seems there were Jews who justified a laxity in their own observance by figurative interpretation of Scripture, including its legal portions. These Jews justified their laxity in observance by quoting Maimonides' figurative interpretation of Scripture in the *Guide of the Perplexed.* Maimonides had given a historical interpretation to many commandments in the Torah. He maintained, for instance, that the sacrificial cult was, in effect, a concession to the primitive and immature condition of the Israelites who came out of Egyptian slavery, and that the cult was restricted to Jerusalem in order to abolish all nonessential sacrifices.[76] He also suggested that various practices were enacted in reaction to pagan customs.[77] Such a historically relativistic interpretation of commandments did not imply that Maimonides advocated the abrogation of these commandments once their original historical setting was no longer relevant. But historical relativism could easily lead others to abandon the practices (as happened in modern times with the Reform movement). Therefore, while the opponents of philosophy recognized that such a great Jew as Maimonides could safely engage in philosophy without endangering Jewish observance, they feared that the pursuit of philosophy by lesser scholars and authorities might endanger their fidelity to the law. In the words of Julius Guttmann,

Even the opponents of philosophy did not wish to impugn Maimonides himself, but only the abuses to which his teaching had lent itself; they objected to the popularization of philosophy, which bred confusion in the souls of the young, and wished to prohibit the study of philosophy and the sciences to those who had not yet reached a mature age. A more extreme group sought to deny science any place at all in Jewish life.[78]

In accordance with these views, Solomon ben Abraham of Montpellier, together with David ben Saul and Jonah ben Abraham Gerundi, sought to ban the study of philosophy in general, and specifically that of Maimonides' *Guide of the Perplexed* and the *Sefer Ha-Mada'*.

Solomon ben Abraham seems to have been a literalist, who took even the anthropomorphic references in the Bible and Talmud literally, and understood the concept of the world-to-come in physical terms, although his associate David ben Saul seems to have denied anthropomorphisms.[79] But, like Ravad before him, David ben Saul, while personally rejecting anthropomorphic and corporealist beliefs, apparently also rejected in principle Maimonides' philosophical attempt to require all Jews to adhere to a more philosophically acceptable and spiritualized set of beliefs.

In any event, Solomon ben Abraham and his associates David ben Saul and Jonah Gerundi convinced the rabbis in northern France in 1232 to ban the study of philosophy and of Maimonides' philosophical works, the *Guide* and the *Book of Knowledge*. In August of that year, these three anti-philosophical agitators were in turn counter-banned in Aragon by supporters of Maimonides' philosophy. This led, subsequently, to the denunciation of Maimonides' works to the Church and the burning of his books in the marketplace of Montpellier.[80]

It is not clear which Jews were responsible for denouncing Maimonides' works to the Church. David Kimḥi, who was traveling around in order to gather support for Maimonides, but who was not in Montpellier at the time, claimed that Solomon ben Abraham, David ben Saul, and Jonah Gerundi were the parties guilty of informing to the Franciscans, the Dominicans, and Cardinal Romanus. But if it is true that the tongues of the informers were cut out, as reported by the brothers Judah and Abraham ibn Hisdah of Barcelona, it would seem that these three agitators against philosophy could not have been the informers, since they continued to occupy positions of communal leadership as rabbis.[81]

A moderate position was taken by Rabbi Moses ben Naḥman (Nahmanides), who was a relative of Jonah Gerundi. He opposed the counter-ban of Aragon against Solomon ben Abraham, David ben Saul, and Jonah Gerundi, but he also urged the French rabbis to reconsider their original ban on Maimonides' philosophical works, or at least to moderate it by permitting the study of the *Book of Knowledge.* He argued that the ban was in any event unenforceable, and would merely lead to divisiveness among the Jewish people, since Maimonides was not only respected but even revered by Jews in the South and the East, and especially in Yemen. Nahmanides defended Maimonides by arguing that he had written his philosophy not for the Jews of France but for the Jews of the South, who were confronting the challenges of philosophy and Karaism and, therefore, needed a philosophical explanation and defense of Judaism. Maimonides had thus saved many Jews who were ignorant of Judaism and lax in their observance of Jewish law because of their exposure to the wisdom of the Greeks.[82] Nahmanides wanted, above all, to preserve the unity of Israel. Although he opposed Maimonides, he had great respect for him. In Silver's apt expression, for Nahmanides "Maimonides was the context of the quarrel, not its content."[83]

But what were Nahmanides' grounds for opposing philosophy if not Maimonides himself? A literalist like Solomon ben Abraham of Montpellier could oppose rationalist allegorization of Scripture in the name of preserving the integrity of the *peshat.* But Nahmanides himself was a mystic, not a literalist.[84]

The thirteenth century, which saw so much opposition to philosophy, also saw the great growth of Jewish mysticism, the Kabbalah, culminating toward the end of the century in the publication of the *Zohar.* According to Gershom Scholem, philosophy and mysticism initially developed together and influenced each other.[85] The mystics often used, or misused, philosophical terminology with which they were familiar, having studied Jewish philosophy. But as Scholem points out, once the Kabbalah became established as an independent discipline, it broke with philosophy and consciously began to oppose it.[86] Both the philosophers and the mystics referred to esoteric doctrines in the Torah as *sitrei torah*, secrets of the Torah. But philosophy engaged in abstract allegory, whereas the mystics sought a concrete symbol. Allegory itself, according to the Scholem, has no independent existence, and merely expresses the truth in abstract terms. But in mysticism, the symbol itself exists, and retains its original form. Scholem also points out that Jewish philosophy never came to grips with the *halakhah*, Jewish law, or with prayer.

We have seen how the rationalist interpretation of revelation and the *mizvot* is often forced and artificial—an attempt to rationalize what is clearly nonrational. Nor could philosophy take seriously the talmudic *aggadot*, with the exception of *aggadot* which deal with obvious ethical questions. But the Kabbalah relates positively to Jewish law and gives the *mizvot* and prayer a deeper meaning for their adherents. It also continues the process of *aggadah*. Indeed, the *Zohar* is written in the form of an aggadic *midrash* on the Torah.

In short, both philosophy and mysticism find esoteric meaning in Scripture for those who have the intelligence and sensitivity to understand it. But in philosophy, the rationalist allegory *(remez)* teaches a level of meaning that is independent of the literal text and could just as easily have been taught without the imagery of that particular text, while in mysticism the literal level is retained, as symbolic of the esoteric truth. That truth does not exist independently of its symbol; it is symbolized by it—the symbol itself is essential. Like *derash*, mystical interpretation *(sod)* thus enhances and reinforces the *peshat*, whereas *remez* may render it superfluous or may be embarrassed by its anthropomorphisms.

Moreover, by its very name, Kabbalah purports to be tradition, not something alien to Judaism, but the truest and most authentic form of Judaism.[87] But philosophy was obviously alien, deriving from Greek, rather than Jewish, culture, and indeed, never got rid of its Greek name.[88] There is no Hebrew word for philosophy, although the philosophers generally regarded it as *ḥokhmah*, wisdom.

The question of the validity of Jewish philosophy was not resolved theoretically, but practically, in this period; and the arguments on both sides remained essentially unanswered. The burning of the Talmud in Paris in 1242 was such an overwhelming tragedy that it completely eclipsed the actual philosophical issues, and opposition to philosophy simply collapsed. Jonah ben Abraham Gerundi repented his earlier opposition to Maimonides, and vowed to make penance at Maimonides' grave near Tiberias. His relative Nahmanides was forced into exile shortly after his public disputation with Pablo Christiani and emigrated to Israel.

The Controversy: Stage III (1288–1290)

The third stage in the controversy over philosophy and Maimonides differs sharply from the previous stage. Whereas the events of 1230–1235 took place largely in southern France, in Jewish communities within a Christian environment, most of the controversy at the end of the thirteenth century took place in the Near East. Solomon Petit, a mystic anti-rationalist, first agitated against Maimonides in northern France and Germany, where he received support in his attempts to ban Maimonides' *Guide* and *Book of Knowledge*. But in 1288, Petit emigrated to Akko, where he taught Kabbalah.[89] There he continued to agitate against Maimonides and to urge the burning of Maimonides' works, especially the *Guide*. But Petit met with failure. He himself was banned no less than four times, and was also opposed by Maimonides' grandson in Egypt, David ben Abraham ben Maimonides.[90]

Earlier in the century, where there had been bans and counterbans, the anti-rationalists had a great deal of support in Jewish communities in Christian environs which were hostile to philosophy. But in the Arabic environment of the East, philosophy was widespread, and the harmony of faith and reason, as well as the legitimacy of Jewish philosophy, were widely accepted. While the bans against Petit in the East succeeded, the bans against philosophy in the West had failed, and a philosophic literature specifically aiming at promoting the harmony of faith and reason and at popularizing philosophy began to emerge in the West. Hillel ban Samuel of Verona (1220–1295) popularized philosophy in Italy by giving public lectures on Maimonides' *Guide*.[91] In Spain, Shem Tov ibn Falaquera (b. between 1223 and 1228; d. after 1291) was writing prolific works on philosophy and translating Arabic philosophic texts into Hebrew, to ensure that philosophy would become the possession of the entire Jewish people and not merely the elitist occupation of the intelligentsia who read Arabic.

Convinced of the harmony of faith and reason, Falaquera saw his great task as supporting the process of consolidation of philosophy in Judaism at a time when philosophy and Maimonides were under attack. Unlike the works of Maimonides, who wrote for an intellectual elite, most of Falaquera's works sought to raise the cultural level of the Jewish people. Therefore, it is, perhaps, precisely such a personality as Falaquera who can best indicate the extent to which philosophy succeeded in finding a home in Judaism. The pioneering philosophical efforts of earlier luminaries only attained an enduring impact on the course of Jewish history and on the religious life of the Jewish people though the consolidation of those efforts at the hands of Jewish philosophers like Falaquera. Their contribution is no less important for the fact that their light may often have been a reflected one.

Falaquera became directly involved in the controversy aroused by Solomon Petit's agitation in the East. His last known work, *Mikhtav 'al Devar Ha-Moreh* (a "Letter Concerning the *Guide*"), is a defense of Maimonides, in which Falaquera mocks Maimonides' opponents in a poem:

> I wonder about those who differ with Moses (i.e., Maimonides),
> How they don't remember the punishment of Korah.
> He is a true teacher, and his word
> Is like fire; their word is like ice.[92]

Playing on Solomon Petit's name, Falaquera referred to him as *peti* (a fool). He argued that Maimonides was compelled to write the *Guide* because of widespread corporealist beliefs among the Jews, even among great rabbis. But such people, wrong as they are, are

not the perplexed for whom Maimonides wrote his *Guide*. No
wonder that Maimonides was misunderstood—after all, even the
Torah had been misunderstood by *minim* (sectarians). The masses
of Jews in the Torah rebelled against God and Moses; no wonder
they rebel against the Moses of this day.

The opponents of philosophy, Falaquera suggested, glorified in
their ignorance of science and philosophy. But there is no glory in
ignorance. The rabbis of the Talmud were great in both Torah
and science, and they knew "how to respond to an Apiqoros,"[93]
i.e., they knew how to respond to a philosopher in his own terms.

Falaquera questioned whether anyone "in these lands," who does
not know Arabic, can truly understand the *Guide*. They were
dependent on Hebrew translations, which are faulty, and they are
therefore likely to misunderstand Maimonides' true meaning.

In an earlier work,[94] Falaquera had defended the harmony
between the Torah and philosophy.[95] He did not claim that
philosophy is infallible, but took the moderate position of accepting from philosophy only that which is true and agrees with
religion. He "eats the pomegranate and discards the peel."[96] Like
Saadia,[97] Falaquera argued that what one knows through reason is
stronger than what one knows through religion alone, since if
one's tradition is challenged, one will not be able to defend it. The
Torah transcends reason, and therefore anything which contradicts it must be rejected. But those conclusions of the
philosophers which contradict the Torah are themselves positions
which have not been conclusively demonstrated.[98] Whatever is
truly and conclusively demonstrated cannot contradict the Torah.
To deny the validity of the speculative method because of some
mistaken conclusions of the philosophers is like denying water to a
thirsty person, so that he dies of thirst, just because some people
have drowned in water.[99]

Falaquera also argued that it is wrong to maintain that the truth
can be learned only from Jewish sources, and to reject the truth
because it is derived from non-Jews. The truth is universal; all
nations have access to the truth through philosophy and science;[100] as one takes honey from a bee, so one should accept the
truth from any source.[101] Maimonides had prefaced his work on

ethics and psychology, the *Shemonah Peraqim*, with the statement: "Listen to the truth from whoever says it."[102] Falaquera repeatedly and eloquently expounded on this theme.

> It is impossible for a person to know by himself everything that he needs, as the ancients said on this. There is no difference if these ancients are of our faith or not. When the speculation is true and perfect of any deficiency, we do not take notice if they are of our faith or not.[103]

> Many of the common folk who are empty and devoid of wisdom (find it) very difficult, when an author brings a proof from the words of non-Jewish philosophers, and they regard their words as worthless. They say that it is not proper to accept them. These ignorant fools never remember, nor understand, nor do they ever consider, that it is proper to accept the truth from any person, even if he is less than oneself or from another nation. . . . It is not proper to look at the speaker but rather at what is said.[104]

> He should listen to the truth from the one who says it, and he should not look at the speaker but rather at the truth of what he says.[105]

The Controversy: Stage IV (1303–1306)

The fourth and final flare-up of the controversy over philosophy took place in the early fourteenth century, primarily in northern Spain, southern France, and Provence. In this case, however, the controversy was not over Maimonides but over the principle of the legitimacy of philosophy within the framework of Judaism.[106] Abba Mari ben Moses Ha-Yarḥi, also known as Don Astrue of Lunel,[107] complained to Solomon ben Abraham Adret of Barcelona about the excessive and sometimes extreme rationalist allegorization of biblical narratives in which some of the philosophers had engaged. After the expulsion of the Jews from France in 1306, which ended this stage of the controversy, Abba Mari collected the letters and pamphlets written by both sides in the controversy, and published them in a book, *Minḥat Qena'ot*,[108] which serves to this day as the basic source book and history of the controversy. Abba Mari charged that the philosophers treated historical figures in the Bible purely symbolically, at the expense of their historicity; that they regarded Plato and

Aristotle, rather than the Torah, as the criteria of truth; that they rejected miracles and divine revelation; and that, therefore, philosophy was leading to laxity or even nonobservance of the *miẓvot*. Although these charges were rejected by such rationalists as Menaḥem ben Solomon Meiri and Yedaiah ben Abraham Bedershi ha-Penini, they were, to a certain extent, accurate.[109] Jacob ben Abba Mari Anatoli (1194–1296), the son-in-law of Samuel ibn Tibbon (who had translated the *Guide* into Hebrew), for example, in his book *Malmad Ha-Talmidim*,[110] interpreted the patriarchs and matriarchs allegorically, rather than historically. Abraham and Sarah symbolized form and matter; Lot and his wife symbolized the intellect and the body; Isaac symbolized the active soul, and his wife Rebecca the intelligent soul; Leah symbolized the perceptive soul, and her sons the five senses; Leah's daughter Deena represented sensations induced by imagination; Joseph symbolized practical reason, while Benjamin symbolized theoretical reason; the seven-branched *menorah* (candelabrum) represented the seven planets, and the twelve tribes symbolized the twelve constellations; the *urim* and *tumim* of the high priest represented the astrolabe. Anatoli also gave rationalist interpretations to the commandments, which he divided into three classes: the highest *miẓvot* are those which deal with belief in the existence and unity of God and loving God by proper conduct; the second class of *miẓvot*, such as those concerning *tefillin*, *ẓiẓit*, and *mezuzah*, remind people of the first class; and the third class are those occasional duties which are necessary to restore a person's moral and intellectual equilibrium, such as commandments concerning fasting or blowing the *shofar*.

The anti-rationalists claimed that such views could only lead to laxity in observance. If the Torah is true only on a symbolic level, the *miẓvot* might also be interpreted purely symbolically, at the expense of their actual observance, since their observance is based on the literal text. Nevertheless, their attacks on individual rationalists, such as Levi ben Abraham ben Ḥayyim of Vilefranche (who seems to have been the immediate cause of the outburst), were unwarranted, since such persons did not in fact go beyond Maimonides' views or give up strict observance of the law despite their radical allegorization.[111]

Whatever the accuracy of the anti-rationalists' claims that philosophy led to laxity in observance, they were correct in pointing out the violence which free and radical allegorization did to the literal text of the Bible. Solomon Adret succeeded in having the community of Barcelona place a ban on philosophy in 1305. But this ban was more moderate than earlier bans had been; it prohibited allegorization of Scripture as well as the study of science by anyone under the age of twenty-five; but the study of medicine and of the works of Jewish philosophers was exempted from the ban.

Nevertheless, despite its relative moderation the Barcelona ban was strongly rejected by many Jews, such as Jacob ben Makhir ibn Tibbon and Menaḥem ben Solomon Meiri, who opposed Adret and issued a counter-ban. They argued that the ban was unenforceable, and that the prohibition of the study of non-Jewish philosophy made it impossible to understand Maimonides' philosophy, the study of which was permitted.

Yedaiah ben Abraham Bedershi Ha-Penini wrote a "Letter of Apology" *(Ketav Hitnaẓlut)* to Adret, summing up the pros and cons of the conflict and urging him to repeal the Barcelona ban. If the ban did not forbid medicine, the cure of the body, why did it forbid philosophy, the cure of the soul?[112] Granted that the rationalists might possibly be wrong in being too open and public in their theories; but they were not heretics worthy of being banned. Bedershi documented the history of Jewish rationalist literature from the time of Saadia on. He regarded Jewish philosophy as valid, and in any event, as not so widespread as to pose any danger.

The Barcelona ban of 1305, like those which came before it, proved ineffective. According to Sarachek:

> The Jews could not condemn or brand any disbeliever in their midst as a heretic with the same effect that the Church did it through the Pope or the Church synods. The Jews had no such centralized organization, and no final authorities. The thing that came nearest to the Church's heresy laws was the ban. The ban was not very effective, for despite the impressive ceremony that attended its proclamation, it was often local, temporary and personal.[113]

This last great controversy over Jewish philosophy in the Middle Ages ended, as did the one of a generation or two before, without a theoretical resolution of the problem. It was terminated by the expulsion of the Jews from France on July 22, 1306, by King Philip IV, and their expulsion from Montpellier in October of that year. The greater external threat totally eclipsed any potential internal threat from philosophy. As a result, "it was the progressives who spoke the last word in the controversy."[114]

But the rationalists spoke the last word only in one sense— practically, not theoretically. The rationalists won because their opponents failed to make it impossible for Jews to engage in philosophy and to interpret Judaism freely and rationally. In this sense, as long as a Jew could engage in free thought, without other Jews attempting to force him to accept their beliefs, the rationalists won. Freedom of conscience and inquiry was upheld. Philosophy could become popularized among Jews and an inalienable aspect of Judaism.

The paradox in the history of Jewish philosophy was, however, that philosophy could only succeed in finding a home in Judaism if it was consolidated by the popularizing efforts of such philosophers as Falaquera. But the same popularization that ensured philosophy a home in Judaism also gave rise to opposition to philosophy among the people.

From a practical perspective, as we study the history of ideological struggles in Judaism, we see that only those movements which maintained that Judaism is flexible, capable of adopting foreign wisdom and adapting to life's needs, survived and ultimately shaped the course that Judaism was to take in its evolution. The Pharisees survived; the Sadducees did not. The medieval Rabbanite Jews, who maintained the oral traditions of the Pharisees, survived, while the literalist Karaites have, for all practical purposes, disappeared. The rationalists succeeded in demonstrating that it is impossible to restrict Judaism to the confines of a spiritual and intellectual ghetto, to shackle the free minds of Jews in the name of Judaism.

But the underlying theoretical question remained, and has yet to be solved: how do we reconcile two sources of truth, reason and revelation? The reconciliation of faith and reason is the task of the

Jewish philosopher. The assumption that faith and reason can be reconciled, that they are in harmony or even identical with each other, is the faith of the rationalist.

NOTES

1. *Guide of the Perplexed* (Arabic: *Dalalat al-Ḥa'irin;* Hebrew: *Moreh Nevukhim*). Two complete English translations of the *Guide* are available, by Shlomo Pines (University of Chicago, 1963) and by M. Friedlander (with notes, New York: Hebrew Publishing Co., 1904, and without notes, Dover paperbacks, 1956). Also see the selections in Isadore Twersky, *A Maimonides Reader* (New York: Behrman House, 1972) and in Lenn Evan Goodman, *Rambam: Readings in the Philosophy of Moses Maimonides* (New York: Viking, 1976).

2. *Sefer Ha-Mada'*, the first section of Maimonides' code of Jewish law *(Mishneh Torah*, also known as the *Yad Hazakah). Cf. The Code of Maimonides* (Yale University Press).

3. There is some disagreement among historians as to whether the burning of Maimonides' works took place in 1232 or 1233, and whether it occurred in Montpellier or in Paris, which was the site of the burning of the Talmud in 1242. See Sarachek, *Faith and Reason*, pp. 86–87; Baron, *Social and Religious History of the Jews*, vol. IX, chap. 38; Graetz, *History of the Jews*, vol. III, chap. 16. Silver *(Maimonidean Criticism and the Maimonidean Controversy*, chap. 9) argues that the informers cannot have been Solomon ben Abraham of Montpellier and his associates, because they continued to serve in communal office as rabbis, scholars, and preachers, which would not have been possible had they been known to be informers, as charged by David Kimḥi. The report of the punishment inflicted on the informers is given by the brothers Judah and Abraham ibn Ḥisdah in Barcelona (Silver, p. 153).

4. Baron, *Social and Religious History of the Jews*, vol. IX, chap. 38, lists the date as June, 1242.

5. Franz Rosenzweig, in *Judah Ha-Levi*, pp. 190–191, quoted by Nahum Glatzer, *Franz Rosenzweig: His Life and Thought*, p. 282.

6. For example, the treatment of ethics in Judaism differed radically from the Greek approach to the subject. In the case of the Greeks, Aristotle could inquire systematically and analytically into the nature of "the good" in his *Nicomachean Ethics*. Aristotle did not deal with what is good in a substantive sense, but with the criteria for determining that something is good in a formal sense; namely, as that at which all things aim *(Nicomachean Ethics* I, 1, 1094a), as resulting from habit (ibid. II, 1, 1103a), and as the mean between the vices of excess and deficiency (ibid. II, 6, 1106b). Similarly, Plato did not define justice substantively as this or that set of actions, but formally as a harmonious relationship of the three classes of society, analogous to the balanced interaction of the three faculties of the individual soul *(Republic*, 4, 427–434, 441–444). This is all in sharp contrast to biblical ethics. The prophets were uninterested in the analytical criteria for defining the good and justice. They demanded concrete just and ethical behavior: "He has told you, man, what is good, and what the Lord

requires of you: only to do justice, to love kindness, and to walk humbly with your God" (Micah 6:8). Rabbinic ethics (cf. Pirkei Avot) similarly emphasize specific concrete actions rather than analytical and systematic inquiry into the good.

7. Martin Buber, *Two Types of Faith*, trans. N. Goldhawk (New York: Harper, 1961), Foreword, p. 7. A similar point is made by Moses Mendelssohn, that *emunah* means "trust" (Mendelssohn, *Jerusalem and Other Jewish Writings*, trans. and ed. Alfred Jospe [New York, 1969], p. 71).

8. It is precisely in this sense that the term *emunah* is used in the *Amidah*, in which God is described as *mekayyem emunato li-shenei 'afar*, fulfilling his fidelity to mortals. *Emunah* is thus often attributed to God. For example, cf. Psalm 92:3.

9. See Alexander Altmann and Samuel Miklos Stern, *Isaac Israeli* (Oxford, 1958), pt. II, chap. 8, pp. 209 ff., on "The Role of Prophecy."

10. Ibid., pp. 53–54.

11. *Book of Beliefs and Opinions* (Arabic: *Kitab al-Amanat wal-I'tiqadat*; Hebrew: *Sefer Emunot ve-De'ot*). A complete English translation was published by Samuel Rosenblatt (New Haven: Yale University Press, 1948). An abridged translation was published by Alexander Altmann in *Three Jewish Philosophers* (New York: Harper, 1965). English references are to the Rosenblatt translation.

12. Saadia, *Emunot Ve-De'ot*, Introduction, #4 (English ed. p. 14; Arabic and Hebrew ed. by Joseph Kapah, pp. 11 ff.).

13. Saadia, *Emunot Ve-De'ot*, Introduction, #5 (English ed. p. 16; Arabic and Hebrew ed. p. 14). See Harry Wolfson's discussion of this in "The Double Faith Theory in Clement, Saadia, Averroes, and St. Thomas, and Its Origin in Aristotle and the Stoics," *Jewish Quarterly Review*, vol. 33 (1942), pp. 213–264.

14. Saadia, *Emunot Ve-De'ot*, Introduction, #5 (English ed. p. 18, Arabic and Hebrew ed. p. 15).

15. Cf. Mendelssohn, *Jerusalem*, p. 98: "As historical truths, they must, because of their very nature, be accepted on faith. Authority alone can provide evidence of their historicity."

16. Saadia, *Emunot Ve-De'ot*, Introduction, #6 (English ed., pp. 29–30; Arabic and Hebrew ed., pp. 26–27).

17. Ha-Levi, *Kuzari* 1:25, 48, 83–88; Mendelssohn, *Jerusalem*, pp. 98, 104, and "Letter to Charles Bonnet" in *Jerusalem and other Jewish Writings*, p. 132.

18. Ha-Levi, *Kuzari* 1:8.

19. Since revelation is essentially rational, miracles cannot actually verify the content of revelation, but can only support the people's appreciation of the fact of revelation. Cf. *Emunot Ve-De'ot*, Introduction, #6 (English ed., pp. 31–32; Arabic and Hebrew ed., pp. 27–28). Saadia states that we do not believe in Moses because of the miracles he performed, but because he first called on us to do what is inherently proper. The commandments were intrinsically good, and were not good merely in virtue of having been revealed (cf. *Emunot Ve-De'ot* 3:8; English ed., pp. 163–164; Arabic and Hebrew ed., pp. 136–137). Similarly, in his "Letter to Charles Bonnet" (in *Jerusalem and Other Jewish Writings*, ed. Alfred Jospe, p. 131), Moses Mendelssohn argued that miracles can support only that which is inherently true, since false prophets could also perform what people regarded as miracles, and since the miraculous claims of Judaism, Christianity, and Islam are often mutually contradictory.

20. Saadia, *Emunot Ve-De'ot* 3:2 (English ed., pp. 141–145; Arabic and Hebrew ed., pp. 119–122). Maimonides, *Shemonah Peraqim* (Eight Chapters), chap. 6, refers to this categorization of the commandments by Saadia and implicitly accepts it.

21. For example, Saddia suggests that the priesthood was necessary to provide teachers and moral examples for the rest of the nation. The dietary laws prevented the attribution of divinity to animals, since one would not worship an animal which one uses for food. The laws of sexual purity prevented sexual excess. Maimonides (*Guide of the Perplexed* 3:26) argued that in some cases, such as the specification of a certain animal for a sacrifice, the law may be arbitrary. It was necessary that some animal be specified, but others could conceivably have been chosen. Maimonides also argues that all laws have some reason, but that in some cases we are ignorant of it.

22. Saadia, *Emunot Ve-De'ot* 5:8 and 7:2.

23. Abraham ibn Ezra, *Haqdamat Ha-Torah*. He discusses this in the context of the third of five ways of approaching the biblical text. The third way (which in some texts is explicitly referred to as the "uncircumcised," i.e. Christians) finds esoteric or allegorical meaning (*sod*) everywhere in Scripture. Since Ibn Ezra is referring here to unnecessary Christian allegorization, it was not necessary for him to discuss at this point Saadia's other two conditions for nonliteral interpretation, i.e. when the passage contradicts another biblical verse or authentic (i.e. rabbinic) tradition. Cf. Saadia, *Emunot Ve-De'ot* 7:4 (English ed., pp. 272–273; Arabic and Hebrew ed., pp. 226–228).

24. Midrash Rabba on Song of Songs 1:2.

25. Rashi on Exodus 33:23. Rashi is quoting the statement by Rabbi Ḥina bar Bizna in Talmud, Berakhot 7a.

26. *Guide of the Perplexed* 2:32, 36–38.

27. Ibn Ezra, *Haqdamat Ha-Torah*, in his discussion of the third way of approaching Scripture (i.e. that of the Christian allegorists), "*Ki lo nitnah ha-torah la-'asher 'ein da'at lo. Veha-mal'akh bein 'adam u-vein 'elohav hu sikhlo.*"

28. Cf. Exodus, chap. 20, Deuteronomy, chap. 5.

29. Ibn Ezra on Exodus 20:1. Rashi accepts this rabbinic view of simultaneous revelation of both versions, mentioned in Talmud, Shevu'ot 20b: "*zakhor ve-shamor be-dibbur eḥad ne'emru*" ("Remember" [the Sabbath] and "Observe" [the Sabbath] were said as one word"). This view is reflected in the first stanza of the Sabbath poem *Lekha Dodi Likrat Kalah*, by Solomon Alkabetz, 16th century.

30. Ha-Levi, *Kuzari* 1:13. Cf. 2:14, 4:13.

31. Ibid. 1:31–43.

32. Ibid 1:67, 89.

33. See Daniel J. Lasker's discussion of this in *Jewish Philosophical Polemics Against Christianity in the Middle Ages* (New York, 1977), especially chaps. 3 and 8, and cf. Lasker's "Averroist Trends in Jewish-Christian Polemics in the Late Middle Ages" (Conference of the Association for Jewish Studies, 1977).

34. Cf. Lasker, *Jewish Philosophical Polemics*, p. 33.

35. Cf. A. Hyman and J. Walsh, *Philosophy in the Middle Ages* (New York, 1967), pp. 450–451.

36. "The conclusions reached by the most radical Christian Averroists, those who maintained the double-truth theory, are absent in Averroes' works" (Lasker,

"Averroist Trends," p. 18, n. 2). "For Averroes, the deepest sense of revelation necessarily agreed with the ideas of philosophy, and the philosopher was justified in so interpreting the contents of revelation that they would harmonize with the .esults of philosophic reflection. He did not recognize any limits to this freedom, as long as the conclusions of philosophy showed that the concept of revelation was a genuine possibility. The masses were to remain bound to the literal meaning of revelation" (Guttmann, *Philosophies of Judaism*, p. 258).

37. Guttmann, *Philosophies of Judaism*, p. 200. Cf. Georges Vajda, *Isaac Albalag* (Paris, 1960). Also cf. Lasker, *Jewish Philosophical Polemics*, p. 185, n. 55.

38. Guttmann, *Philosophies of Judaism*, p. 245.

39. Elijah del Medigo, *Beḥinat Ha-Dat*, pp. 11 ff. Cf. Guttmann, *Philosophies of Judaism*, pp. 258–259, and Lasker, "Averroistic Trends," p. 4. Del Medigo translated Averroes from Hebrew to Latin. According to Guttmann, Del Medigo learned the double-truth theory from the Christian Averroists and not from his predecessor Albalag.

40. Albo, *Sefer Ha-'Iqqarim* 1:24.

41. Cf. *Guide of the Perplexed* 1:73, 3:15.

42. For example, God cannot make the part greater than the whole or the side of a square greater than its diagonal.

43. For example, the resurrection of the dead.

44. Albo, *Sefer Ha-'Iqqarim* 1:22. Cf. Lasker, *Jewish Philosophical Polemics*, pp. 28–35.

45. See Lasker's discussion in *Jewish Philosophical Polemics*, chap. 3, as well as in "Averroist Trends."

46. Lasker, *Jewish Philosophical Polemics*, p. 34.

47. Lasker, "Averroist Trends," p. 8.

48. Ibid., p. 16.

49. Mendelssohn, "Letter to Karl-Wilhelm, Hereditary Prince of Braunschweig-Wolfenbüttel," in *Jerusalem and Other Jewish Writings*, ed. Alfred Jospe, pp. 123 ff.

50. Mendelssohn, *Jerusalem*, pp. 61, 69–71.

51. Ibid., p. 90.

52. For Maimonides, (*Guide of the Perplexed* 3:25), if we say that divine commandments need not serve any rational purpose, we have rendered God's commandments futile (*hevel*) or frivolous (*sehoq*), which is absurd. (A futile action is one which aims at no real end, while a frivolous action is one which aims at a lowly, base, or silly end.)

53. On the controversy and its historical background, see Joseph Sarachek, *Faith and Reason* (New York, 1955), chap. 1; D. J. Silver, *Maimonidean Criticism and the Maimonidean Controversy* (Leiden, 1965), chaps. 1–2; Haim Hillel Ben-Sasson, "Maimonidean Controversy," in *Encyclopaedia Judaica*, vol. 11, cols. 745–754; Salo Baron, *Social and Religious History of the Jews*, vol. VIII, chap. 34, "Faith and Reason," and vol. IX, chaps. 15–18; Y. Baer, *Toledot Ha-Yehudim Bi-Sefarad Ha-Noẓrit* [History of the Jews in Christian Spain] (Tel Aviv, 1965), chap. 2; Julius Guttmann, *Philosophies of Judaism*, "The Struggle Against Philosophy in the Hundred Years After Maimonides," pp. 183–208; Isaac Husik, *History of Mediaeval Jewish Philosophy*, pp. 304–311; Colette Sirat, *Hagut Pilosofit Bi-Yemei Ha-*

Beinayim [Jewish Philosophical Thought in the Middle Ages] (Jerusalem, 1975), pp. 292–299.

54. Sarachek; *Faith and Reason*, pp. 9–10. There may have been some contact between Jewish anti-Christian polemicists and anti-Catholic Christians. According to Lasker, (*Jewish Philosophical Polemics*, p. 164), "the anonymous author of *Vikuaḥ Radaq* used specifically Catharist arguments against the Catholics (and Catholic arguments against the Catharists), while Joseph ben Shem Tov referred to those who did not believe in transubstantiation and were, therefore, considered heretics. It appears, then, that the Jews, as the main target of Christian polemics, were aware of the position of other groups which also incurred orthodox wrath." Cf. Louis I. Newman, *Jewish Influence on Christian Reform Movements* (New York, 1925).

55. Baron, *Social and Religious History of the Jews*, vol. 8, chap. 34, pp. 57–58.

56. These decrees restricted Jewish banking activities (usury), required Jews to pay tithes on their property and a tax at Easter, forbade Christian rulers from bestowing public office on Jews, and required Jews to wear distinctive clothing to set them apart visibly from Christians.

57. Whereas in Paris in 1240 the Talmud was charged with blasphemy, in the Barcelona disputation of 1263 the apostate Pablo Christiani attempted to convince Nahmanides that the Talmud proves that Jesus is the Messiah. Nahmanides countered that Jews are only obligated to believe in the Bible and to accept as binding the halakhic portions of the Talmud, but that *aggadot* are not binding. See Nahmanides' account of the disputation in *Kitvei Ramban*, ed. C. Chavel (Jerusalem, 1963), vol. 1, pp. 300 ff.

58. "Undoubtedly, Maimonides' fame as a Talmudic author facilitated the success of his philosophic work" (Guttmann, *Philosophies of Judaism*, p. 183). This fame, of course, also made him a greater target for attack.

59. Shem Tov been Joseph ibn Falaquera, *Moreh ha-Moreh*, pp. 5–6, in *Sheloshah Qadmonei Mefarshei Ha-Moreh*.

60. Maimonides, *Guide of the Perplexed*, Introduction.

61. Ibid., 2:Introduction, 2:1.

62. Silver, *Maimonidean Criticism and the Maimonidean Controversy*, pp. 70 ff. See Isadore Twersky, "Beginnings of *Mishneh Torah* Criticism," in Alexander Altmann (ed.), *Biblical and Other Studies* (Harvard, 1963), pp. 161–182; Isadore Twersky, "Some Non-Halakic Aspects of the *Mishneh Torah*," in Alexander Altmann (ed.), *Jewish Medieval and Renaissance Studies*, (Harvard, 1967), pp. 95–118. Also see Joshua Finkel, "Maimonides' Treatise on Resurrection: A Comparative Study," in Salo Baron (ed.), *Essays on Maimonides: An Octocentennial Volume*, pp. 93–121.

63. See Isadore Twersky, "Beginnings of *Mishneh Torah* Criticism," pp. 161–182. Maimonides' critics pointed out his failure to cite his sources in the code. For instance, Ravad (Rabbi Abraham ben David of Posquières), in his critical gloss *(hasagah)* to the Introduction to the Code, asserted that Maimonides "has abandoned the method of all the authors who preceded him, because they brought proof for their words, and cited their sources. . . . But this way, I do not know why I should disregard my tradition and my proof for the sake of this author's book." Maimonides also offended many scholars by asserting, in the

Introduction, that "a person should study the written Torah first, and then read this (book), and thereby know the entire oral Torah, so that he will not need to read any other book between them." Criticism of the Code also reflected local custom *(minhag)*, which sometimes differed from Maimonides' practice.

64. The first of the fourteen sections of the *Mishneh Torah* is *Sefer Ha-Mada'* (Book of Knowledge), and contains what Maimonides considered to be "true opinions" obligatory for all Jews. Maimonides also legislated "true opinions" in his *Sefer Ha-Mizvot* (Book of Commandments) and in his famous "Thirteen Principles" (in his *Commentary on the Mishnah*, Sanhedrin, chap. 10), which he concludes by stating: "When a person affirms all these principles, and his belief in them is true, he enters the community of Israel, and it is obligatory to love him. . . . But when a person doubts one of these principles, he has left the community and denied the fundamental principle . . . and it is obligatory to hate and destroy him."

65. *Mishneh Torah*, *Sefer Mada'*, Hilkhot Teshuvah 3:7.

66. *Guide of the Perplexed* 1:36.

67. Ravad, *hasagah* (gloss) to Hilkhot Teshuvah 3:7. Ravad himself did not affirm any corporeal notions about God, but he rejected the view that such belief constitutes heresy or that Maimonides had the right to make such a determination.

68. *Sefer Mada'*, Hilkhot Teshuvah 8:2. Maimonides maintained an equally spiritualized notion of the world to come in his *Commentary on the Mishnah* (Sanhedrin 10), leading to his formulation of the Thirteen Principles (cf. Arthur Hyman, "Maimonides' Thirteen Principles," in *Jewish Medieval and Renaissance Studies*, ed. Alexander Altmann, pp. 119–144.)

69. Talmud, Berakhot 18a.

70. Cf. *Guide of the Perplexed* 2:19, 21, 23.

71. Cf. *Guide of the Perplexed* 2:25. It should be emphasized that in a Jewish context, nothing more than the *possibility* of resurrection need be discussed. One can affirm resurrection as possible without affirming it as factual, i.e. as having ever occurred. But this is in sharp contrast to Paul's statement in I Corinthians 15 that the truth of Christianity rests on the facticity of resurrection.

72. Silver, *Maimonidean Criticism and the Maimonidean Controversy*, p. 116.

73. The Ibn Tibbon version was translated into Latin by Johannes Buxtorf, (Basel, 1629), and the Al-Harizi edition by Augustinius Justinianus, (Paris, 1520). Cf. M. Friedlaender, trans., *Guide of the Perplexed*, (New York, 1885), vol. 3, pp. xv–xvii, and "Maimonides, Moses," in *Encyclopaedia Judaica*, vol. 11, col. 780.

74. Graetz, *History of the Jews*, vol. III, chap. 16, pp. 546–547.

75. Sarachek, *Faith and Reason*, pp. 78–79.

76. *Guide of the Perplexed* 3:32.

77. Ibid. 3:37, 46.

78. Guttmann, *Philosophies of Judaism*, pp. 186–187.

79. This is according to the testimony of Maimonides' son in his *Sefer Milhamot Adonai*, written in 1235 after the burning of Maimonides' books. Cf. Silver, *Maimonidean Criticism and the Maimonidean Controversy*, pp. 160–162. On Abraham ben Maimonides, see S. D. Goitein, "Abraham Maimonides and His Pietist

Circle," in *Jewish Medieval and Renaissance Studies*, ed. Alexander Altmann, pp. 145–164.

80. According to Graetz (*History of the Jews*, vol. III, chap. 16, p. 542), "the Dominicans may have feared that the fire of the Maimunist heresy might have set their own houses ablaze." The Church had banned the study of philosophy, and in 1210 the Dominicans had burned Aristotle's *Physics* and *Metaphysics*. "The suppression of Maimonides' allegedly heretical writings was a victory for the Church policy. . . . The scholastics refer at times to the Jewish heresies" (Sarachek, *Faith and Reason*, p. 87).

81. Silver, *Maimonidean Criticism and the Maimonidean Controversy*, pp. 150–154.

82. See '*Iggeret Ha-Ramban* in *Qovez Teshuvot Ha-Rambam* and '*Iggerot Qena'ot*, pp. 8 ff. Also see Sarachek, *Faith and Reason*, chap. 10; Silver, *Maimonidean Criticism and the Maimonidean Controversy*, pp. 170 ff.; Graetz, *History of the Jews*, vol. III, chap. 16, p. 534; H. H. Ben-Sasson, "Maimonidean Controversy," in *Encyclopaedia Judaica*, vol. II, cols. 749–754; Baer, *Toledot Ha-Yehudim Bi-Sefarad Ha-Nozrit*, chap. 2, pp. 56–64.

83. Silver, *Maimonidean Criticism and the Maimonidean Controversy*, p. 173.

84. In his disputation with the apostate Pablo Christiani (Barcelona, 1263), Nahmanides argued that the *aggadot* of the Talmud are not binding, and need not be taken literally.

85. Gershom Scholem, *Major Trends in Jewish Mysticism* (New York, 1965), chap. 1.

86. For instance, the philosophical doctrine of God's creation of the world out of nothing or nonbeing became transformed into the mystical concept of creation out of no-thing, by a process of emanation from God which is "no-thing."

87. Therefore, many of the major works of the Kabbalah were pseudepigraphical. The *Sefer Yezirah* was ascribed to, and commonly taken as really written by, Abraham. The *Zohar* was ascribed to the talmudic rabbi Shim'on bar Yohai.

88. Cf. Sarachek, *Faith and Reason*, p. 133.

89. Many of Petit's students had been students of Nahmanides after his emigration to Israel.

90. Petit was banned by the exilarch David ben Samuel of Mosul in 1288, by the *ga'on* Samuel ben David in Baghdad in 1289, by the exilarch Yishai ben Hezekiah in Damascus in 1291, and again by the community of Safed in 1291 (cf. Graetz, *History of the Jews*, vol. III, chap. 18, and Sarachek, *Faith and Reason*, chap. 13).

91. Cf. Sarachek, *Faith and Reason*, chap. 14.

92. Falaquera, *Mikhtav 'al Devar Ha-Moreh*, in Abba Mari Ha-Yarhi, *Minhat Qena'ot*, ed. Mordecai Bisliches (Pressburg, 1838; reprinted in Jerusalem, 1968), pp. 182–185.

93. The reference is to Avot 2:14, "know what you should respond to an Apiqoros."

94. '*Iggeret Ha-Vikuah Be-Ve'ur Ha-Haskamah Asher Bein Ha-Torah veha-Hokhmah* [Treatise on the Disputation, Explaining the Harmony Between the Torah and Philosophy], ed. Adolf Jellinek (Vienna, 1875; reprinted in Jerusalem, 1970).

95. Falaquera, '*Iggeret Ha-Vikuah*, p. 1; *Sefer Ha-Ma'alot*, p. 48. Falaquera refers to philosophy and the Torah as twins. Earlier, Abraham ibn Da'ud, in his

Emunah Ramah [Exalted Faith], p. 2, had referred to a person "holding in his two hands two lights; in his right hand, the light of religion, and in his left hand, the light of philosophy."

96. This is a reference to the statement in Talmud, Hagigah 15b, "Rabbi Meir found a pomegranate. He ate its contents and discarded its peel."

97. Saadia, *Emunot Ve-De'ot*, Introduction, #6.

98. Falaquera, *Sefer Ha-Mevaqqesh*, p. 73; *De'ot Ha-Pilosofim*, Introduction to bk. 11, p. 470.

99. Falaquera, *Sefer Ha-Ma'alot*, pp. 74–75.

100. Ibid., p. 75.

101. Falaquera, *Batei Hanhagat Ha-Nefesh*, p. 72.

102. Maimonides, *Shemonah Peraqim*, Introduction (ed. Joseph Gorfinkle, *The Eight Chapters of Maimonides on Ethics* [New York, 1912, 1966]), Arabic and Hebrew text p. 6, English, p. 36.

103. Falaquera, *'Iggeret Ha-Vikuah*, p. 13.

104. Falaquera, *Sefer Ha-Ma'alot*, pp. 11–12.

105. Falaquera, *De'ot Ha-Pilosofim*, Introduction, p. 12.

106. Saracheck, *Faith and Reason*, chap. 16, p. 167.

107. The name "Yarhi" (lunar) may be derived from his native city of Lunel. Cf. Michael Friedlaender and Kaufmann Kohler, "Abba Mari ben Moses ben Joseph Don Astruc of Lunel," in *Jewish Encyclopedia*, vol. 1, pp. 33 ff., and Jacob Freimann, "Astruc, Abba Mari ben Moses ben Joseph of Lunel," in *Encyclopaedia Judaica*, vol. 3, cols. 807–808.

108. *Minhat Qena'ot* [The Offering of Jealousy], ed. Mordcai Bisliches (Pressburg, 1838; reprinted in Jerusalem, 1968). The title of the book is taken from Numbers 5:25.

109. Cf. Sirat, *Hagut Pilosofit Bi-Yemei Ha-Beinayim*, pp. 292–299. Also see A. S. Halkin, "Yedaiah Bedershi's Apology," in A. Altmann (ed.), *Jewish Medieval and Renaissance Studies*, pp. 165–184.

110. *Malmad Ha- Talmidim* [A Goad to Scholars] (Lyck, 1866). Cf. Saracheck, *Faith and Reason*, chap. 16, pp. 173–179.

111. Saracheck, *Faith and Reason*, chap. 17. Also see A. S. Halkin, "Why Was Levi ben Hayyim Hounded," *Proceedings of the American Academy for Jewish Research*, vol. 34 (1966), pp. 65–76, and Guttmann, *Philosophies of Judaism*, p. 187.

112. See above, n. 109, and also Saracheck, *Faith and Reason*, chap. 23.

113. Saracheck, *Faith and Reason*, p. 182.

114. Saracheck, *Faith and Reason*, p. 262.

SELECTED BIBLIOGRAPHY

Altmann, Alexander, ed. *Biblical and Other Studies*. Cambridge: Harvard University Press, 1963.

―――, ed. *Jewish Medieval and Renaissance Studies*. Cambridge: Harvard University Press, 1967.

Baer, I. F. *Toledot Ha-Yehudim Bi-Sefarad Ha-Nozrit* [A History of the Jews in Christian Spain], chap. 2, pp. 45–64. Tel Aviv: Am Oved, 1965.

Baron, Salo W. *A Social and Religious History of the Jews*, vol. VIII, chap. 34, "Faith and Reason"; vol. IX, chap. 38, "Stubborn Dissenter." New York: Columbia University Press, 1958–65.

Ben-Sasson, Haim Hillel. "Maimonidean Controversy." In *Encyclopaedia Judaica*, vol. 11, cols. 745–754.

Graetz, Henrich. *History of the Jews*, vol. III, chaps. 14–18. Philadephia: Jewish Publication Society, 1894.

Guttmann, Julius. *Philosophies of Judaism*. New York: Holt, Rinehart, & Winston, 1964.

Husik, Isaac. *A History of Mediaeval Jewish Philosophy*. New York: Atheneum, 1969.

Lasker, Daniel. *Jewish Philosophical Polemics Against Christianity in the Middle Ages*. New York: KTAV, 1977.

Sarachek, Joseph. *Faith and Reason: The Conflict Over the Rationalism of Maimonides*. New York: Hermon, 1970.

Silver, Daniel Jeremy. *Maimonidean Criticism and the Maimonidean Controversy: 1180–1240*. Leiden: Brill, 1965.

Sirat, Colette. *Hagut Pilosofit Bi-Yemei Ha-Beinayim* [Jewish Philosophical Thought in the Middle Ages]. Jerusalem: Keter, 1975.

Wolfson, Harry A. "The Double Faith Theory in Clement, Saadia, Averroes, and St. Thomas, and Its Origin in Aristotle and the Stoics." *Jewish Quarterly Review*, vol. 33 (1942), pp. 213–264.

Hasidism and Its Opponents

SAMUEL H. DRESNER
Moriah Congregation
Deerfield, Illinois

THIS ESSAY is a contribution toward an understanding of the conflict between Hasidism and its opponents, from the Hasidic point of view. Its substance is the examination of two doctrines that early Hasidism promulgated which were central to the dissension. Its method is: (1) to justify the selection of these two doctrines for examination through the testimony of a unique document; (2) to describe both the conditions which gave rise to the emergence of Hasidism and the salutary effects of its victory, as exemplified by the substitution of joy for despair; (3) to argue that this victory and transformation of values was in large measure due to two Hasidic doctrines, which are then taken up for analysis.[1]

I. R. Shneur Zalman's Letter

What moved the most noted rabbinic figure of his time, the Gaon, Elijah of Vilna, to declare Hasidism to be a heretical sect and issue a ban of excommunication against its followers? Surely he must have questioned what authority the Hasidim had for the changes in custom and ritual which they introduced, such as adopting the Sefardic liturgical rite over the accustomed Ashkenazic one, the establishment of separate houses of worship, and the introduction of a new form of *shehitah* (ritual slaughter); as well having been angered by the rumors which reached him that the study of Torah had been deemphasized in favor of ecstatic prayer which itself was sometimes delayed beyond the prescribed hours. But, according to the testimony of a letter we possess by no less a figure than

Rabbi Shneur Zalman of Ladi, the foremost philosopher of the Hasidic movement and the one most directly involved in controversy with the Gaon, the latter questioned more seriously the conceptual basis of the new movement: particularly its doctrines (1) that God was literally "in all things," and (2) that man's task was to redeem the holy sparks which had fallen into the *kelipot*, the husks of evil. The doctrine of the *Shekhinah*, or the Divine Indwelling, is, of course, common to rabbinic literature. Midrash Exodus Rabba 1.9, for example, explains God's speaking out of the burning bush to mean that "there is no place in which the Divine Presence is not to be found, even the bush."[2] The Gaon, however, preferred to interpret such passages figuratively. The teaching that God was literally to be found everywhere, even in mundane matter, smacked of pantheism; while the doctrine of the holy sparks which were scattered through all creation at the "breaking of the vessels" and had to be redeemed even if it meant man's descent into evil, seemed to ring with Sabbatean overtones. Particularly suspect were these themes since they emerged from the early Hasidic settlements in Volynia and Podolia, the very areas in which the Sabbatean-Frankists had labored. All this is attested to in Rabbi Shneur Zalman's highly informative letter, printed toward the end of the book *Mezaref la-'Avodah* (Konigsberg, 1851),[3] which he writes to his friends in Vilna.

In this remarkable letter, Rabbi Shneur Zalman, both a distinguished legalist and a mystic, writing after the publication of his book *Likutei Amarim* in Tevet 1797, and before the death of the Vilna Gaon in 1798, described his role in the controversy. He speaks of the Gaon with great respect, calling him "Hasid," as he was in fact commonly referred to, not, of course, as a member of the Hasidic community but as noted for his "piety," and forbids the Hasidim from retaliating against those who burned a Hasidic book in Vilna. He tells how he failed in his attempt to meet and reason with the Gaon. He recounts the Gaon's opposition to Hasidic teachings that God is to be found everywhere, even in the lowliest forms of creation, and that the scattered divine sparks must be redeemed by man wherever they may be found. These doctrines, he explains, derive from the teaching of Rabbi Isaac

Luria, which the Gaon rejects in favor of the earlier philosophy of the *Zohar*. Sensing danger in such teachings, which in one version had indeed led to the apocalyptic hysteria of pressing for the end that culminated in the catastrophe of Shabbetai Tzvi and the demonic Jacob Frank, the Gaon considered them rank heresy and the cause for the public burning of a Hasidic book—*Toledot Ya'akov Yosef* or *Zava'at ha-Rivash*—in Vilna. God's presence in all things is understood by the Gaon not literally, as with Shneur Zalman, but figuratively, as extending God's providence to "all of His creation."

An abridgment of the letter follows:

> . . . I had hoped to bring the dispute with our opponents to a satisfactory conclusion, for surely there is no greater *mizvah* than establishing peace among Jews—but what could we have done that we did not in fact do? Surely, we are innocent before God and Israel.
>
> With prior notice, we went to the house of the Gaon and Hasid [Elijah of Vilna], long may he live, that we might remove his censures from us. But he [the Gaon of Vilna] twice shut the door upon us, departed from the city, and remained away until the day we left, as the elders of your city know. From there we went to Shklov, again to seek a debate. And again we failed. There they acted improperly to us, reneging upon the promise not to mistreat us. But seeing that they could not refute us, they resorted to violence, purporting to rely on the authority of the Gaon and Hasid, long may he prosper.
>
> We judged him in the scale of merit. The issue after all had been resolved in his mind without a shadow of a doubt, for he had arrived at a verdict on the testimony of what seemed to him to be trustworthy witnesses. For example, one of our teachings was reported to him and interpreted by the notorious *provocateur* [R. Avigdor, the main adversary of R. Shneur Zalman]. Perchance he misquoted it somewhat, for even a minor change in language may alter a teaching to mean something totally different. It certainly could not have occurred to him [the Gaon] that [the Hasidic leaders] might be in possession of the divine word of God revealed by Elijah [the Prophet] through which they interpreted the holy *Zohar* in a manner which may have eluded him.

Nothing has been heard from him [the Gaon] of late to indicate that he has retreated from his position of former days, or that any doubt has now arisen in his mind that perchance he had been in error. Though I possess answers to all their [the Mitnagdim's] concerns, they have rejected these answers, as we have personally witnessed in Shklov. Now, therefore, why should I toil in vain? For the dictum of our Sages of blessed memory is well known, that "just as it is a *mizvah* to say a thing that will be heeded, so it is a mizvah to refrain from saying a thing that will not be heeded." Especially after the many evil deeds which have been perpetrated against our Hasidic fellowship in the province of Lithuania and Little Russia on the basis of the expressed opinion of the Gaon and Hasid. I have seen with my own eyes a letter written by one of his disciples in Vilna in the name of his teacher containing things which I do not wish to put in writing out of respect for the Torah. In the province of Lithuania none would dare to maintain an opinion contrary to that of the Gaon and Hasid and declare openly that he erred, God forbid. Only in distant countries, such as Turkey, Italy, most of Germany, Greater Poland, and Minor Poland (Galicia) [would this be possible.]

I would welcome [a discussion] in matters of faith. According to a report from his disciples in our provinces, it is precisely in this area that the Gaon and Hasid found objections to [my] book Likutei Amarim *and other similar works. The teachings that God "fills the world" and that "there is no place void of Him" are interpreted [by us] in a literal sense, whereas in his esteemed opinion it is pure heresy to hold that God, blessed be He, is to be found in the mundane matters of our world, and it is for this reason, according to your esteemed letter, that the book* [Toledot Yaakov Yosef or Zava'at ha-Rivash] *was burned. For they [the Gaon and his disciples] explain the passages—"the whole earth is full of His glory," etc.—in a figurative manner, as referring to Divine Providence [namely, that God watches over each aspect of creation and not just creation as a whole]. Would that I might present our case to him, so as to remove from ourselves all his philosophical censures.* [Italics mine, S.H.D.]

If, however, he should find it hard to withdraw from the path to which he has been accustomed for so long, and should my words not be accepted by him, then let his greatness be matched by his modesty, by explaining fully all his objections to this belief in a document written by one who is close to him and signed by himself; and I will respond to all his objections, also over the signature and seal of my own hand. Both letters would then be copied and sent to all the great sages of Israel, both near and far, to express their opinion thereon. For Israel has not been forsaken by God, and there will be found many with a perfect knowledge of the Torah and with an impartial mind. Then the majority opinion will prevail, and peace will be established in Israel.

As for the teaching regarding the "elevation of the sparks" from the *kelipot*, etc., as explicated in the book *Likutei Amarim* and others, this doctrine, and the process of sublimation, were first mentioned in the Lurianic Kabbalah and not by previous Kabbalists, nor [are they found] explicitly in the holy *Zohar*. We know that the Gaon and Hasid, long may he live, does not accept the tradition of the ARI, of blessed memory, in its entirety, but only a small portion of it; moreover, the writings [of the ARI] have been defectively transcribed.

As for the burning of the book [*Toledot Yaakov Yosef* or *Zava'at ha-Rivash*], it is not for you to take up the cause of the Ba'al Shem Tov, of saintly memory, and to provoke strife, God forbid. This is not the way in which God delights. Consider a precedent: Who was greater than the Moses of his time, Moses Maimonides, of blessed memory, who in his country, Spain, rose to such high repute, that while he was yet alive they added to the words of the *Kaddish* prayer, "May His kingdom come in your lifetime, . . . *and in the life of our master, Moshe,* and in the life of all the House of Israel," etc., for they esteemed his holiness and piety. Nevertheless, in distant lands he was considered a heretic, and his books were publicly burned, by order of those who were wise in their own eyes, and objected to what he had written. It did not occur to them to ascribe it to their own lack of understanding of his sacred words, as was subsequently clarified by Nachmanides and Rabbi David Kimchi, of blessed memory. However, with the passing of time, their hatred disappeared, the truth became evident and all Israel recognized that Moses was true and his teaching was true. So may it be with us, speedily, in our time. Amen.

It is with the theoretical aspect of Hasidic teaching—the immanence of God, and serving Him through the corporeal world—which this essay will concentrate upon, rather than the challenge of Hasidism to the social structures of the time or the question of authority for the changes it introduced in Jewish rite and custom.

For it would seem, at least from Rabbi Shneur Zalman's letter, that the essence of the disagreement with the Gaon was not only social or halakhic but theological. Because of the limitations of space, I shall deal with these concerns principally from the Hasidic point of view.

II. Sweet Medicine

R. Nahman of Horodenki, one of that remarkable circle which gathered around the Ba'al Shem Tov (BeSHT), the founder of Hasidism, in the first part of the eighteenth century, was the earliest of the group to go up to the Holy Land. He had not yet become a disciple of the Besht and was troubled over whether he should remain in the Holy Land or return to sit at the master's feet. One morning found him gone. The words that suddenly sent him packing for home he reported hearing in a dream: "Many doctors heal with bitter medicine; but the doctor who heals with sweet medicine is to be preferred!"[4]

What did the dream mean? Who was sick? Who were the doctors? And what were the medicines that were being prescribed?

The patient was East European Jewry, which by the mid-eighteenth century had fallen gravely ill. The doctors were the religious leaders of the time. The standard remedy prescribed by the rabbinic establishment was bitter medicine. The people were not responding.

The mood was one of gloomy asceticism. Strict observance of the law and punishment for failure to do so, prolonged fasting, penitence, self-flagellation, fear, and superstition combined to provide an atmosphere of sullen solemnity. "There is no land," writes one eighteenth-century observer, "where the Jews are so much given to mystical fantasies, devil-haunting and exorcism of spirits, as they are in Poland."[5] A custom which expressed the spirit of the age was for Jews to rise up from their beds at midnight, dress in sackcloth, put ashes on their heads, sit upon the earth, and bewail the destruction of the Temple and the misery of the exile.

They had good reason to mourn—not alone for the glory of the ancient Temple of Jerusalem, which lay in ruins, but as well for the splendor of Polish Jewry, which, at its zenith, was perhaps unparalleled among post-talmudic Jewish communities.

That zenith can be located between the years 1500 and 1648. Although Jews had lived in Eastern Europe as long as they had in the West—the settlement along the Black Sea going back as far as two thousand years, while the Khazar Kingdom in the Crimea stretched from the eighth to the twelfth century—West European Jews first fled eastward in large numbers following the massacres of the German and French Jewish communities during the Crusades of the eleventh and twelfth centuries, and especially later during the holocaust that accompanied the Black Death (1348–1349), since it coincided with a generous invitation to immigrate offered by Casimir the Great of Poland (1333–1370). By the sixteenth century the Jews had benefited from the economic prosperity they had helped to bring, were accepted on various levels in a society where anti-Semitism was kept in check by the nobles and the king, and possessed a largely autonomous community structure in the form of the individual *Kahals* or Councils, and the great *Va'ad Arba' ha-Arazot*, Council of the Four Lands. The *Va'ad* and the *Kahals* ostensibly served the Poles as the central taxing agency for their Jewish population, but in fact provided the latter with the opportunity to develop a remarkable structure of order and authority which constituted what the Poles called "a government within a government."

Most worthy of note, however, was the flourishing of the inner life of Polish Jewry. "There was scarcely a house in the whole Kingdom of Poland," writes Rabbi Nathan Hannover, "where the Torah was not studied, and where either the head of the house or his son-in-law, or the yeshivah student boarding with him, was not an expert in Jewish learning: frequently all of these could be found under one roof." He goes on to describe the care with which the yeshivah curricula were structured, how they were generously funded and carefully supervised by the *Kahals* and ultimately by the Council of Four Lands. To appreciate the high level of talmudic learning that was achieved, it is enough to review how many of the classic commentaries to the Talmud or other basic rabbinic or moralistic works emerged from this period. The best known of these have become such hallmarks as to have had their names reduced to an abbreviated form familiar to students of Jewish literature. Thus—*ReMA* (Rabbi Moses Isserles, 1520–1572), *ReSHal* (Rabbi Solomon Luria of Posen, 1510–1573), *Levush* (Rabbi Mordecai Jaffe, d. 1612), *MaHaRaM* (Rabbi Meir of Lublin, 1554–1616), *MaHaRSHA* (Rabbi Samuel Edels, d. 1631), *TaZ* (Rabbi David Halevi, 1586–1667), *SHaKH* (Rabbi Sabbatai Cohen, 1621–1662), and the *SHeLAH* (Rabbi Isaiah Horovitz, ca. 1555–1630).[6]

The period of decline of Polish Jewry—1648–1772—was marked by three catastrophic events: (1) the Chmielnicki pogroms (1648–1649), (2) the false Messiahs Shabbetai Zevi (1625–1676) and Jacob Frank 1726–1791), and (3) the deteriorating political conditions which led to the triple partition of Poland (1772–1796) between Russia, Prussia, and Austria. The carnage wrought by Chmielnicki's horde of Greek Orthodox Ukrainian peasants and Cossacks laid waste much of Ukrainian Jewry, and the sweeping invasions by the Russians and Swedes which followed, as well as the hatred of the Poles themselves, brought terrible suffering to the Jewish communities of East Europe. Dubnow estimates the death-toll between 100,000 and 200,000, with some 700 communities destroyed or pillaged. In the throes of the chaotic despair which followed these massacres, a tragic hope was sown in many despairing hearts—the faith in the false Messiah, Shabbetai Zevi. While the shock of the latter's eventual conversion to Islam led most of the faithful to return, devotees fervently loyal to the imposter still persisted. The passion of some whose memories of the shattered dream had not abated was kindled once again by the demonic Jacob Frank, who drove the antinomian sect to the extreme of reveling in sin. Even with the conversion to Catholicism of Frank and many of his admirers, after promoting two public disputations between the rabbis and the Church—the first an attack on the Talmud as an anti-Christian book, which led to its public burning, and the second an assault on the Jews as consumers of Christian blood, which led to an epidemic of blood-libel accusations and terrible suffering—some underground followers yet clung to their unholy faith. Furthermore, there remained a body of teachings—derived from Lurianic Kabbalah—that was both extremely dangerous and strangely attractive, and which repudiated the legal as well as the moral foundations of Judaism.

The Chmielnicki pogroms, the Messianic heresies, and the surrounding unrest led to the rapid and tragic decline of Polish Jewry. Politically, the grand structure of the Council of Four Lands was abolished in 1764; economically, Jews were torn from their former livelihoods, often homeless and penniless; socially, an outburst of anti-Semitism struck them from peasant, priest, and noble alike, with torture and pogroms accompanying a vicious and seemingly unending series of blood libels; spiritually, learning declined in disastrous fashion, ignorance abounded, superstition increased, as well as friction between and within the Jewish communities. Contemporary Polish documents point to growing incidents of conversion and flight.

How did the prevailing leadership treat the ailing community? With bitter medicine. The rabbis retrenched: huddling over the Talmud, they closed their doors ever tighter, while the people were neglected. The method of study, characterized by hairsplitting dialectics, *pilpul* and *ḥiluk*, led more often to contests of mental superiority than enlightenment, and was, in any case, reserved for the scholars alone. "The Synagogue sermons of that period which have come down to us in various collections consist of a long string of Haggadic and Kabbalistic quotations . . . the preachers were evidently less anxious to instruct their audience than to exhibit their enormous erudition in theological literature."[7] Penitence and fasting were prescribed. Vivid pictures of punishment in the next world, gruesome stories concerning the torture of sinners in hell, the transmigration of souls, and the exploits of demons, were thought to keep man from sin. The devil was felt to be crouching at every door. The Frankists were excommunicated and the study of Kabbalah forbidden to anyone under forty years of age. Fear prevailed, a "gloomy asceticism," an atmosphere of strictness and melancholy.

One indication of how pervading must have been the mood of

despair in the time of the Besht is found in his assertion that while other human failings are capable of sublimation—for "God dwells with the people in the midst of their impurities" (Lev. 16:16)—melancholy is an exception. "I heard from my master [the Besht] that it is not possible [for the Ẓaddik] to join to God one who is in a state of *'aẓvut* [melancholy] . . ."[8]

R. Naḥman of Horodenka, whose dream of the doctor with the "sweet medicine" had driven him from the Holy Land back across the sea to learn the "wisdom of the Besht,"[9] explained his vision by a well-known talmudic tale.

R. Shim'on bar Yoḥai, the mystic sage and alleged author of the *Zohar*, was condemned to death by the Roman authorities. To escape their wrath, he and his son fled to a cave, where they were confined for twelve years, nourished only by a carob tree and a well of water which miraculously presented themselves. Separated from the daily pursuits of society, they gave themselves over to prayer, Torah study, and mystic speculation.

> After twelve years, Elijah the prophet appeared at the mouth of the cave and announced: "Who will inform the son of Yoḥai that the Emperor is dead and his decree annulled?" R. Shimon and his son came forth. But when they saw farmers tilling the soil, R. Shimon bewailed: "Lo! They neglect eternal things for those of the moment!" And so scorching was the wrath of R. Shimon and his son that wherever they cast their eyes a fire devoured it. Until a heavenly voice rang forth: "Have you come to destroy My world? Return to your cave!"[10]

In this striking legend, R. Naḥman found a parallel to the contemporary predicament. Locked in the seclusion of the house of study, many of the rabbis—like R. Shi'mon bar Yoḥai—grew intolerant of the needs of the people, did not comprehend their situation, and met their shortcomings with anger and rebuke. Providence itself rejected this approach. "Through fasting, afflicting oneself in other ways, and unrelieved study," observed R. Nahman,

> one falls into a melancholy of the spirit, and is led to condemn those who fail to conduct themselves in a similar fashion, because they

seem to be 'neglecting eternal things,' . . . as in the story of R. Shimon bar Yoḥai and his son, who emerged from the cave [only to wither the fields with the fire of their anger against the farmers who took time from study and prayer to till the soil]. Until a heavenly voice was heard: "Have you come to destroy My world? Return to your cave!" . . .

This is healing by means of bitter medicine. [11]

The conflict between doctors prescribing sweet and bitter medicines had a long history, R. Nahman reminds us. In talmudic times they were represented by two schools of thought—those of Shamai and Hillel. The school of Shamai which, like R. Shimon bar Yoḥai, followed the way of "rigor," was uncompromising, harsh, and final; while the school of Hillel, which followed the way of "compassion," was patient, forebearing, and understanding. R. Nahman called for a return to the path of Hillel, [12] and this he found in the "wisdom" of the Besht.

Outwardly, all seemed well. The structure of rabbinic Judaism appeared quite intact: Torah was studied; the commandments were observed; Jews followed the ritual pattern of their fathers. A closer look, however, afforded a different impression. Something was missing—the flame which gave life to all else. Jewish living had become stale. The Sabbath was routine, prayer a repetition of what had been said yesterday. Only a shell remained of the vibrant, healthy community of previous generations, a shell whose outer features belied a growing inner decay which, if left unimpeded, threatened to bring down the entire structure of Polish Jewry. The following parable describes the way the early Hasidic leaders diagnosed the situation.

An apprentice blacksmith, after he had learned his trade from the master, made a list for himself of how he must go about his craft. How he should pump the bellows, secure the anvil, and wield the hammer. He omitted nothing. When he went to work at the king's palace, however, he discovered to his dismay that he could not perform his duties, and was dismissed. He had forgotten to note one thing—perhaps because it was so obvious—that first he must ignite a spark to kindle the fire. He had to return to his master, who reminded him of the first principle which he had forgotten. [13]

What had been forgotten was what was self-evident: that all the commandments existed only that one might draw near to the Lord. A relearning of the "first principle," a return to the Master, was called for.

East European Jewry was ailing. The bitter pill offered by the rabbinic leaders had not healed the patient. They waited for the sweet medicine of the Besht.

"What is the essence of serving the Lord?" the Baal Shem Tov was asked. "We know that in olden times 'men of deeds' fasted from one Sabbath to the next. You have done away with this, however, saying that one who afflicts his flesh must render accounts as a sinner, for he has afflicted his soul. So tell us, then, what is the essence of serving the Lord?"

The Baal Shem replied: "I believe that one should strive to attain three loves: *the love of God, the love of Israel, and the love of Torah*—it is not necessary to mortify the flesh."[14]

"The Besht banished melancholy and uncovered the ineffable delight in being a Jew," wrote Abraham Heschel. The people "fell in love with the Lord and felt 'such sweet yearning for God that it was unbearable.' " They began to know the infinite delight in fulfilling the *mizvah* of welcoming the stranger to one's home, of putting on *talit* and *tefillin*. They discovered intimations of paradise in this world: while singing a *nigun*, studying Torah, or keeping the Sabbath. The Besht argued that the evil impulse should be fought "with the flames of ecstasy rather than with fasting or mortification."[15]

A passage from the so-called *Last Testament of the Ba'al Shem Tov* illustrates the power of the new teaching: both its manifest appeal for an age marked by sobriety and rigidity, as well as the vigorous opposition it engendered.

There are times when the *Yezer ha-Ra* (evil impulse) deceives one into believing that he has committed a serious transgression, though he may have merely violated the strict interpretation of the law (ḥumrah). . . . The intent of the Yeẓer ha-Ra is to reduce one to a state of melancholy, since by virtue of melancholy one's service to God is impaired. Be aware of the Yeẓer ha-Ra's intention to deceive you and confront him thus:

"I shall ignore this ḥumrah you speak of, for I am aware of your intention to deceive me by impairing my service to God. Even had I committed a minor infraction of the law, however, I know that God will prefer that I ignore the ḥumrah rather than allow my service to Him be tainted with melancholy. To the contrary, my service to God will be joyous. God will not be harsh with me, should I disregard the ḥumrah, seeing that my purpose is to serve Him with complete constancy and devotion, [which melancholy would prevent]."

When serving God, let a man not pay excessive attention to details. For it is the intent of the Yeẓer ha-Ra to so frighten one, should he fail to fulfill every requirement [of the law], that he lapse into melancholy and be prevented from the proper service of God. [Further,] even should one stumble into actual transgression let him not be crushed by despair, lest his service of God be annulled. Rather let him grieve over his sin and then turn to God in joy, since he truly regrets his actions and has resolved never to return to such foolishness. [Or] even should one know that he has failed to fulfil a certain requirement [of the law] because of certain obstacles, let him grieve not but be aware that the Creator, Who looks into the heart, knows that what he had every intention to do, he was unable to fulfill. And let him strive to rejoice in the Creator.

The verse: "It is time to work for the Lord; they have made void thy law" (Ps. 119:126) [may be interpreted to mean that "to work for the Lord" implies, under certain circumstances, making "void the law," that is,] there are occasions when doing a miẓvah, may involve a trace of transgression. Should the Yeẓer ha-Ra seek to prevent one from performing such a miẓvah, ignore him. . . . For if it is one's desire to give pleasure to God, then the Yeẓer will depart when he performs this precept. However, whether or not to perform such a miẓvah is a matter for scrupulous consideration.

In sum, all that I have written contains important principles. . . .[16]

From this passage we perceive the prevailing mood in which

man was measured almost solely by his observance of the law. But the law as it was expounded in eighteenth-century Poland was not identical with the law of Hillel or Rabbi Akiba of talmudic times. The piety of each generation expressed itself by adding restriction upon restriction, *ḥumrah* upon *ḥumrah*, until only the learned could thread their way through the maze. What of the Jew who stumbled or could not find his way? Often the law was open to interpretation, either leniently *(kulah)* or strictly *(ḥumrah)*. Piety had become synonymous with doing the *ḥumrah*. Reflecting the admonitions of the scholars, one of the preachers' favorite subjects was sin through failure to keep the fine points of the law, which led some to tremble lest their efforts be of no avail. Woe to such a one! The devil was ever waiting to plunge him into the cauldron of fire and brimstone.

The Besht responded to this situation by shifting the ground of the argument. The devil, he suggested, had found a more subtle way of deceiving the Jew. By enticing him to grieve over every failure to keep every detail of every law, so that even the slightest transgression required severe penitence, he would be brought to melancholy, and melancholy would prevent him from truly serving God. The Besht identified melancholy *('aẓvut)* as central to the spiritual malaise of the times. Highly desirable though it may have been to keep this or that minor commandment or to possess a comprehensive mastery of the law, in the eyes of the early Hasidic masters these were not the crucial issues. They preferred to treat what they believed lay at the heart of the matter, the dangerous mood of fear and despair. Therefore the Besht spoke of the devil's *(Yeẓer ha-Ra)* endeavoring not simply to prevent one from keeping a certain *ḥumrah*, but attacking what undergirded the entire enterprise of miẓvot, the joyous love of God. Be not misled by the *Yeẓer ha-Ra*, the Besht warned: strive for the highest: if you fail, heartfelt repentance will atone. Above all, do not give way to despair.

In the twenty-eighth chapter of Deuteronomy, Moses compiles a frightful catalogue of curses which will befall the people after his death should they fail to keep the way of the Lord. "Of all the people's sins which were responsible for these maledictions," writes a later Hasidic teacher, "the Torah lists only one: 'All these curses shall come upon you . . . 'because thou servest not the Lord with joyfulness and with gladness of heart' (Deut. 28:47). From this we may deduce that it [*not serving the Lord with joy*] is the *most serious of all transgressions!*"[17]

What is the power of joy?

Joy can achieve heavenly things, esoteric and mysterious. It can bring about the *yiḥud*, "the blissful union of the rhythms of divine existence in one great melody of God . . . the steady contact of God with the worlds of creation."[18] For heartfelt joy bursts all bounds. It has the power to advance, to repair, to make whole. Melancholy is a retreat, a weakening of the divine claim that "He saw all that He created and it was good." Melancholy flaws the service of the Lord, because it is devisive, turning back the movement toward unity which surges through the universe. For God's oneness is not only a oneness in essence but a striving to be one with His creation. Man's task is to aid in the effort to restore the original wholeness which marked our world before the "breaking of the vessels" of creation: a wholeness between God and His *Shekhinah*, between man and God, between man and man, and within man. Melancholy and joy are polar forces in this process, impeding or advancing God's kingdom. The following textual exposition, complex but typical, is by R. Yaakov Yosef, friend of R. Naḥman of Horodenka, and the source of most of his teachings.

I have heard from the learned scholar, R. Naḥman of Horodenka, that when in the Land of Israel he dreamed that while there are doctors who heal with bitter medicine, the doctors who heal with sweet medicine are to be preferred. By this he meant that, through afflicting oneself, one becomes bitter, cruel, intolerant, and the reverse contrariwise. . . .

I would add [an exposition on the following verse: "Sarah died in Kiryat Arba, which is called Hebron. And Abraham mourned for Sarah and wept for her. . . . Abraham took another wife . . . and Abraham begot Isaac" (Gen. 23:2, 25:1, 19).]

"Sarah died in Kiryat Arba, which is called Hebron. And Abraham mourned for Sarah and wept for her." . . . Affliction and tears bring on melancholy, which is "death," that is, the husks of evil *(kelipot)* which rend asunder the four letters of the Divine Name, YHWH. [This is what is meant by saying that Sarah "died] in Kiryat *Arba*" (Hebrew = "the city of *four*"). [In other words, melancholy (= "death") divides the Divine Name into its four letters (*Kiryat Arba* = "city of four"). But *Kiryat Arba* (= "city of four") "is called *Hebron*" (Hebrew = *"joined together."*) [That is, the Name, now separated by melancholy,] must be made whole again.

Therefore it further says that "Abraham took another wife" (Gen. 25:1), to unite the letters of the Name through joy . . . which is the quality of "compassion." . . . Thus we come to understand the verse, "And Abraham begot Yiẓhak" (Gen. 25:15) . . . that is, begot "laughter" (= Hebrew *ẓehok*), for joy is the healing which sweet medicine yields.[19]

Another example of the heavenly things that the power of joy can help to bring about is from a folk tale which is set against the prevailing power of penitence in the popular as well as the sophisticated mind, namely, the merit of fasting, the reward for self-abnegation and bitter remorse. According to the Hasidic teaching, the reverse becomes the case. Stories are now told not of what tears could produce—"Tears are a dreadful evil . . . only tears that flow from joy are acceptable."[20]—but, to the contrary, of what joy could bring about. In the following episode we note the contrast between the older mystical tradition, severe, complex, and reserved for the select, as against the free outpouring of the people's rejoicing.

Once, on the evening after Yom Kippur (the Day of Atonement, the moon was hidden behind the clouds so that the Ba'al Shem could not say the Blessing for the New Moon. Divining that a delay in fulfilling this *miẓvah* directly after Yom Kippur might bode ill for Israel, he grew apprehensive and gathered all his inner strength toward bringing forth the moon. To no avail. Despite his power of worship, each time he inquired whether the moon had appeared, he was told that the clouds had become even thicker.

The Besht's Hasidim, however, knowing nothing of these matters, had gathered in the front rooms of his house and began to dance, for this was their way of celebrating the atonement for the sins of the past year which the Besht's service, much as the high priest in the

Temple of old, had achieved. As their ecstasy mounted, they entered the very room of the Ba'al Shem, seized hold of their master, and drew him into their circle with a fervor that mounted ever higher. During this holy dance, it was suddenly announced that the moon had appeared, and everyone rushed outside to recite the Blessing.

The Ba'al Shem remarked that what he failed to bring to pass through his power of prayer, the Hasidim had achieved through joy alone.[21]

Joy can achieve things both heavenly and human. It is a necessary ingredient not only for *yiḥud* but also for *devekut*, man's cleaving to God, an attachment of the divine within to the divine beyond, which is a constant goal of all human service. (The concept of *devekut* will be treated more fully later.) The Besht's successor, R. Dov Ber, the Maggid of Mezritch, observed that while "one should conduct oneself in joy at all times, but especially when cleaving to the Lord, for *without joy one cannot cleave to the Lord, may He be blessed.*"[22]

Lastly, joy has the power to affect the purely human, man himself and his relation to his fellow man.

The Ba'al Shem was fond of telling the talmudic anecdote of Rabbi Beroka who, coming upon Elijah the Prophet in the marketplace, inquired whether anyone there was worthy of the world-to-come. "No," said Elijah at first, and then pointed to two men who were passing. "These two, they have a share in the world-to-come." "What is your trade?" asked Rabbi Beroka. "We are jesters," they replied. "When we see someone depressed, we cheer him up."[23] There were times when to "banish melancholy" became so vital a need that all those who lent a hand to this effort were seen as engaging in holy work. That was the Besht's view of his own age. It was for this reason that the talmudic tale about R. Shim'on bar Yoḥai, which we have already mentioned, was often recounted in the name of the Besht and his circle. R. Shim'on bar Yoḥai, it will be remembered, was remonstrated for his anger when he emerged from the cave and saw the people at work instead of engaged in study or worship. Similarly the Besht criticized the intolerance of some of the contemporary scholars.

The Besht argued that what was needed to heal the prevailing spiritual infirmity was compassion and patience. One of the "three loves" which the Besht said "one should strive to attain" was the "love of Israel," of all Israel, sinner and saint, wise and ignorant. Joy, stifled by harshness, could be released through love.

The meaning of joy according to the Besht was, first and foremost, what it had always been: "joy in doing the *miẓvah.*" The Jews knew that they were commanded to fulfill the commandments, but there were those who had forgotten *how* to fulfill them. Some prayed only because they had prayed the day before and kept the Sabbath only because their fathers had kept it, as if doing God's will were a chore; others were so meticulous in doing the law that they began to police others to be certain that they were equally meticulous and, if not, to remind them of their shortcomings. The mood was sober in the one case and somber in the other.

The talmudic admonition, that "the *Shekhinah* does not dwell amidst sadness or lethargy but only where there is joy in fulfilling the *miẓvah*,"[24] had been mislaid. It was the Besht who recovered it. The Hasidim began to argue that "just as a hungry man eats with ardor to nourish his body, so must one perform the *miẓvah* with joy to nourish the soul,"[25] and quoted an older mystical source that perhaps one receives a greater reward for the *simḥah* with which one performs it than for the *miẓvah* itself!

Joy rouses the heavens, for "from the stirring below comes the stirring above." Therefore, taught the Besht, "know that the marvelous quality of joy should not be wasted on frivolity but directed to doing the *miẓvah*, as Scripture says, 'Serve the Lord with joy.' But even then one must take care lest, when one performs a *miẓvah* publicly, his joy not be diluted by vainglory. . . . Thus it is written, 'And the fire on the altar burned *within*' (Lev. 6:5), That is to say, one need not reveal the flames of fire which are glowing on the altar of joyous service to God and through which we cleave to Him. Let the joy of one's heart remain within."[26]

The Ba'al Shem thought of the Jew's relationship to God as a romance, and it disturbed him to see how many rituals had become routine rather than rapturous acts, exercises in repetition rather than gestures of surprise—a hand without a heart. Faith was fire, not sediment. Did not a pillar of fire serve as a guide when the people Israel roamed in the wilderness? And fire was the beginning of light. . . . Obedience to God in carrying out His commandments is fundamental to existence. The Ba'al Shem, however, thought that obedience without passion, conformity without spontaniety was but a skeleton, dry, meager, lifeless. A Jew should serve God with ardor. It was necessary, vital, to have fire in the soul. Far from resembling an iceberg or a glacier, one's inner life is a hotbed of sinful desires, occasionally mixed with cruelty and self-destructive passion—a hotbed that can be purged only with Holy fire. When we face temptations, our power of will grows weak and all reasonable restraints break down. It is then that the ability to be aflame with the thought of God and His love may burn out lowly desires and give our will new strength.[27]

While formerly joyous *miẓvot* were performed perfunctorily, now even sad *miẓvot* were transformed by joy. The Besht was said to have rejoiced when he heard the reason why one who led the services on Yom Kippur recited the *Al Ḥet*—the confession of sins—with a happy melody: "The lowliest servant of the king, when he sweeps away the dirt from the court, sings a merry tune as he works, for to clean away the filth is to gladden the king!" The annual memorial of the death of a Ẓaddik, the *Yahrtzeit*, formerly a solemn day prescribed for fasting and remorse, was transformed into a *Hillula*, a time of rejoicing to God in gratitude for having given the world that holy man. The statement of the rabbi of Apt that were he to have the power, he would abolish all the fast days except for the Ninth of Av, commemorating the destruction of the Temple, "for who could eat then," and the Tenth of Tishri, the Day of Atonement, "for who needs to eat then," was typical of the new joyous affirmation of life.

The joy the Besht brought to his followers was not only a demanding, exalted joy—the joy of *yiḥud*, uniting the mysterious Name, the joy of *devekut*, entering into the Divine embrace, or even the joy of doing the *miẓvah* with all one's heart. Joy can be still more pervasive, more elementary, open to even the simplest

Jew. This view received classic expression by another Hasidic sage.

> Sadness is no sin. But the melancholy which sadness can bring no sin can equal. . . . When I speak of the need for *simḥah*, for joy, I do not refer to *simḥah shel miẓvah*, the joy in doing a *miẓvah*, for not everyone can achieve such a lofty rung. But just to banish sadness. To put it simply: not to rejoice in being a Jew is an affront to Heaven. It is a sign that one's ear has never heard the blessing in the morning service ". . . *shelo 'asani goy!*"
>
> *Atzves is dokh keyn averah. Ober dem timtum ha-lev vos atzves fershtelt ken nit farshtein di grubste averah. Vos mir shmeusen az men broykht simha, maynen mir nit simha shel mitzva, varum simha shel mitzve is dokh a madrega. Ken men nit farlangen az yeder Yid zol zein a baal madrega! Nor mir maynen: nit keyn atzves. Poshet: a Yid vos geyt nit arum mit simha mit dem vos er is a Yid, is a kofui tova dem himmel! Es is a simon az er hot keynmal nit derhert di berokho; "shelo osoni goy!"*[28]

The simple lesson of rejoicing in being a Jew is what R. Moshe Leib of Sassov learned when he visited the great Rabbi Elimelekh, and was asked to expound Torah. Moshe Leib read the verse which said that God passed over the houses of the Israelites to smite the Egyptians, and explained: "This cannot possibly mean that God 'passes over a certain place,' because 'there is no place where He is not.' But it means that when He passed through the Egyptians' houses and saw the corruption of their souls, and then came to a house full of piety and goodness, He was overjoyed and cried: 'A Jew lives here!' " When Rabbi Elimelekh heard this explanation, he jumped on the table, danced upon it, and sang over and over: "A Jew lives here! A Jew lives here!"

The power of joy reaches the heavens and penetrates the heart of man, is exalted and common, esoteric and everyday. So too the meaning of joy. Bound to the most recondite acts of the most select, it is the inheritance of the unlearned as well; turning the heart of man to man, it opens the way to the divine, giving wings to prayer, wonder to words, and the strength to lift up the heavens, for "the stirring below causes a stirring above."

The struggle against melancholy was a tidal wave in the history of the Hasidic movement, flowing through the generations that followed even until our own day. "All of Hasidism," said R. Aaron of Kaidenov, "revolves around two poles: humility and joy."[29] While some of the other characteristics of early Hasidism disappeared in time, the centrality of joy has remained a constant. An example is that of the great-grandson of the Ba'al Shem, R. Naḥman of Bratslav, one of the major figures in Hasidic thought. He taught that melancholy leads to "shame," "suffering," "sickness," "disaster," and "separation from God." To remove melancholy, he counseled one to "look upon the face of a *Zaddik*," "hear a *Zaddik* sing," "listen to stories," "for seeing, hearing, and smelling revive the spirit." A "remedy for melancholy is compassion." Joy enables "the heart to open" and "the mind to penetrate." "Doing the *mizvah* with joy brings one strength and the sense of God's presence, God's grace and salvation."[30] Within the *shtiebels* (prayer-houses) of the Bratslav Hasidim one always found on the wall the insignia: *"Gevald Yiden! Zeit zikh nit mi-yeush!"* ("O Jews! Do not give way to despair!"). Even during the Holocaust, in their *shtibels* in the Warsaw ghetto, for example, or in the first of their books printed in Europe after the war, these words were prominently displayed.

> The Ba'al Shem Tov revived the ancient biblical spirit of joy . . .
> an intrinsic, unique quality of Jewish spirituality frequently stressed
> in biblical and post-biblical literature. Normally, the attitudes in
> accord with religious existence all over the world are humility,
> contrition, obedience, sorrow, remorse. Joy is not a theological cate-
> gory in the teachings of most religions and is never discussed in the
> handbooks of theology. Those who are overwhelmed by a spiritual
> solemnity and are unable to forget that faith lives in a constant state
> of tension between ignominious death and eternal life find it difficult
> to comprehend the Jewish conception. Even with Judaism the
> teaching that joy lies at the very heart of worship, that it is a
> prerequisite for piety, is a scandal to the dullards and a stumbling
> block to the bigot. And yet a sense of humor is also a necessary
> ingredient of Jewish faith. Under the impact of exile and persecu-
> tions throughout the generations, the Jewish experience of gladness
> and delight was reduced to sorrow and grief. A spirit of moroseness

hung over the people. The constant admonitions of Hasidic pioneers against the people's gloom and melancholy prove how sullen and depressed the prevailing mood must have been.

The Baal Shem proclaimed joy to be the very heart of religious living, the essence of faith, greater than all other religious virtues . . .

The joy which marked the life of the Hasid—joy in living in God's world, in doing God's will, in studying God's word, in being one of God's people—was nourished by *hitlahavut*, ecstasy, exaltation, or, more literally, "being ablaze" with love of God.

> A hasid prays, studies and lives in exaltation. One can see the fire in his every feature, his speech, his bearing. When he hears an inspiring word, he gives himself up to ecstasy. . . . His soul shines. It is suffused with light. . . . Exaltation may last an hour, but its flower, joy, the jewel that wins the hearts of all men, lasts forever. The garnered fervors of great moments can flare forth again and again. In the new light that came from the Ba'al Shem's fire, the pressures of daily life no longer encumbered. People made of sighs and tears were remade into people of awe and joy.[31]

R. Naḥman of Horodenka's startling dream which he experienced in the Land of Israel, that "many doctors heal with bitter medicine but the doctor who heals with sweet medicine is to be preferred," frustrated his desire to settle in the Holy Land and sent him packing into the exile to search out the "wisdom of the Besht." That eighteenth-century Polish Jewry was ailing was clear to R. Naḥman. Clear to him also were the kinds of medicines available. The old and "bitter" and the new and "sweet." While he appreciated that "both were necessary,"[32] it was the elixir of the Besht which would best heal the malady of the time. For, R. Naḥman said, "in imbibing the 'sweet medicine,' the patient does not suffer but feels pleasure. . . . The main thing is to rid oneself of despair and hold fast to joy."[33] And, indeed, the remedy of the Besht proved more effective than those of the contemporary rabbinic leaders, as the ardent response of the people testified.

The healing which the Besht intended indeed transpired. The

ailing patient recovered. The transformation which he labored for became a reality for countless numbers. Many writers tried to express what this new sense of joyous affirmation of life, which the Besht and his circle of disciples promulgated through their teaching, meant for the people. We quote one.

> The spirit of our life, the holy of holies, Rabbi Israel Ba'al Shem Tov, and his holy disciples have illumined our lives. Until his time the principal manner of serving God was through fasting, affliction, and contending with evil. This way, however, is . . . difficult, treacherous, and suitable only for the elite. And because our transgressions were numerous, we grew faint. Indeed, many were drowning in sin, God forbid, because they refused to take upon themselves the rigors of serving the Lord in that fashion.
>
> Therefore God took mercy upon us by sending a holy angel from heaven, the light of Israel, to kindle the hearts of the people toward their Father in Heaven. And the fiery sparks that came from his mouth scattered in many directions so that his disciples and the disciples of his disciples have numbered in the hundreds and thousands, and they wrote countless treatises in various styles describing how one might correctly serve the Lord with love and awe. And all this . . . came about so that it would be easier for a Jew who truly wanted to serve the Lord. And then, of itself, evil will fall away.[34]

We have attempted to identify one major consequence of the Besht's teaching as the victory of "joy" and the defeat of sadness unto despair. But this fact alone, while important, does not tell us enough. What was it in the message of the Besht which kindled so rapturous a spirit that sadness could be swept aside? After all, the prevailing conditions of the gentile environment had not altered. Poverty remained as bitter as before. Helplessness was still the Jew's political predicament. Hatred was felt not less from their neighbors. Neither Church doctrine nor the foibles of the kings and nobles were upended. So why joy instead of sadness? How had the intrigue of the *Yezer ha-Ra*, so expert at exploiting apprehension, been rendered helpless? What was so powerful in the

new teaching which could overcome the foul conditions of contemporary Jewish existence? What were the ingredients of the
magic elixir which brought such robust health to the desperately
ailing? In analyzing more closely the "sweet medicine" of the Ba'al
Shem, we shall see that it had the power to "banish melancholy
and uncover the ineffable delight in being a Jew," because the
Besht knew and taught: that *God is in all things*, and that *God can be
served through all things*.

III. God Is Everywhere

Born in 1700, the Besht began his work in 1736 or thereabouts
and died in 1760. His teachings were not immediately accepted.
To the contrary, he and his successors were challenged along
every step of the way. Yet by 1772 the Hasidic movement had
grown powerful enough to warrant a ban against its spread, issued
by no less a personage than the Vilna Gaon himself, and by 1800
a large percentage of Polish-Galician-Ukrainian Jewry—in many
communities a majority—had become followers of the Besht.
How is this phenomenal success to be explained? The following
parable purports to do so:

The king of Poland had died. Since the king was not simply
born to his position, nobles from all over the country gathered to
nominate and elect the new sovereign; and since the king need not
be a Pole, princes from various lands, all in search of the crown,
sent their representatives to Poland. Each sang the praises of his
candidate: "My lord is the wisest," "my lord is the wealthiest,"
"my lord is the grandest," "my lord is the kindest." This went on
for days but no decision was reached. At last one representative,
wiser than the rest, decided he would return home and bring his
candidate, the prince himself, to the people, and say: "Here he is,
look at him, see how grand he is." That prince was elected king.

"So it is," said a Hasidic master, "that Rabbi Shim'on bar
Yoḥai wrote his wondrous book, the holy *Zohar*, in which he
expounded the glory of God; and later the ARI [Rabbi Yiẓḥak
Luria] explored so marvelously the mysteries of the Kabbalah.
Their wisdom, however, was, alas, reserved for the erudite few.

Until the Ba'al Shem Tov came and revealed the Lord to all men, teaching that there is no movement, no garment in which the Divine is not hidden, for 'there is no place void of Him.' He showed us how to cleave to the Lord through all our deeds, even in ordinary conversation and everyday actions. In this manner did the Besht bring the King of Kings, the Holy One, before our very eyes."[35]

"Many Jews talked about God," Abraham Heschel observed, "but it was the Besht and his followers who brought God to the people. And this is perhaps the best answer to the question of how to explain the unbelievable impact these men had in such a short span of time."[36]

After seven years of seclusion high up in the Carpathian Mountains amidst those fields and forests he so loved to wander in since his childhood, the Ba'al Shem Tov burst upon the stage of history with a shocking cry—"*Altz iz Gott!*" "Everything is God!" Not only man in all his glory, but nature in all its splendor too, was ablaze with the divine. The Besht taught that beneath the multiplicity of things and creatures, so utterly different one from the other—stone and insect, animal and flower, cloud and man—there is an unseen, all-pervasive, inner unity which runs as a thread through all creation, joining every form of existence, horizontally, and, even more, binding the beginning to the end of time, vertically. While the Mishnah could have taught that "He who interrupts his studies to remark, 'How lovely is this tree,' is liable to punishment" (Avot 8.7), the Besht saw no necessary contradiction between the book and the tree, spirit and nature. Not only need the one not deny the other, but it might even reflect and continue it. It was at the first breaking of the heavens into the rainbow of dawn which the Ba'al Shem insisted was the proper setting for the morning prayer, a setting more inspiring than any building man could build. The biblical awareness of God's glory in nature—"Let the heavens be glad and the earth rejoice . . . Let all trees of the forest sing before the Lord" (Ps.

96)—which had grown dormant during the medieval period, awoke once again in Hasidism. They found the oneness of God with His world hinted at even by the numerical equivalents of Hebrew words. Thus, "nature," *ha-teva* (5 + 9 + 2 + 70 = 86), and "God," *Elohim* (1 + 30 + 5 + 10 + 40 = 86). The Divine Presence, who dwelt in man and in the Torah, could also be found in nature. For the Besht there was no break in the line that ran from Creator to His creature, His word, and throughout all creation. God was one and His oneness united all, bound all, and gave life to all.[37] "The main thing," taught R. Naḥman of Horodenka, who drank the "sweet medicine" of the Besht, "is to understand that the Lord is everywhere."[38]

One of the Besht's earliest memories as a child, which remained ever fixed in his heart, was his father's last words to him: "Remember one thing, my son, that God is near you and beside you and in you. And because of that you need fear nothing."[39] But if God is so close to man, about him and within him, why, then, the Besht would be asked, does He often seem so far away? Why does man verge on the despair of abandonment and isolation, eclipse and absence? God's remoteness is but an illusion, responded the Besht, offering this parable by way of explanation:

> Once a king built a magnificent palace for himself with many rooms, walls, and corridors. He himself decided to reside in the innermost chamber. When the palace was finished, however, his servants who wanted to pay their respects found they were unable to reach the king because of the labyrinthine maze within which they lost their way. As they pondered the problem, the king's son arrived and went directly to the king. He showed the others that the walls were no walls at all, only human illusions, and that the king was easily accessible to him who could push forward bravely.[40]

The Hasidic teachers insisted that God had not abandoned man to the terrors of solitude. Man's distance from God is self-induced, they argued, only a fiction, a chimera, an illusion. It is man who has distanced himself. The verse "I stand between the Lord and you" (Deut. 5:5) was interpreted to mean that it is the "I", the ego, which stands between God and the self.

Once the grandson of a Hasidic master came weeping to his grandfather. "Why are you crying?" he asked the child. "I was playing hide-and-seek," he answered. "But when I hid no one looked for me." The Zaddik thought to himself, "So it is with the Lord. He hides, but we do not look for Him!"

Just as it is possible to shut out the fiery rays of the sun by holding one slight hand before the eyes, the Besht taught, so man himself can close off the glory of God from his life. He told how once a fiddler began to play in the marketplace and attracted people away from their business through the magic of his melodies. A deaf man, passing by and seeing the stamping and clapping and the empty stores, thought it all mad.

"Where does God dwell?" the Kotzker once asked his disciples. "Wherever man lets Him in!"

Search for Him; remove your hand from before your eyes; ignore the walls of separation; hear the music—let Him in!

That was the startling teaching of Hasidism.

Sometimes the Zaddikim took strange means to enforce this lesson. Rabbi Levi Yizhak called together the Jews of Berditchev on a busy market-day in the central thoroughfare. They expected to be told of some fearful decree by the government. "Jews," he shouted, "you are forgetting that there is a God in the world!"

To them God was not the philosopher's first cause, the unmoved mover, cold, remote, deliberate, oblivious. God cared. That was the point. Emphasis was no longer on His power alone, but on His concern. He cared for each of His creatures, for every Jew, rich or poor, learned or ignorant, Zaddik or disciple. He even cared for the sinner. Typical of their thinking was the way Hasidism rendered the words of the prayer Avinu Malkenu, "Our father, Our king," as "our Father is our King." What greater joy could there be than to know that the father who loves you with an overpowering love and forgives you with an endless compassion is the King Himself, the Creator of heaven and earth!

The Ba'al Shem so succeeded in bringing the reality of the Divine Presence to the people that the love for God which was kindled in their hearts could not abide melancholy. What difference that the stomach was empty and the roof leaked, that life was filled with bitter hardships. The Jews had their Zeese Tatte, their sweet Father in Heaven, before whom they sang and prayed and lived. What else mattered?

It was not that the people had doubts concerning God's existence that they needed to be argued into it or reminded of it. They were neither atheists nor agnostics. They accepted the fact that there was a Heaven above just as there was an earth below. But they ignored it—and Him. What mattered to the Hasidic masters was not His existence but His reality. His power. His presence. God's immanence was not simply to be affirmed but experienced. God is not just "God." He is *Elohim Hayyim*, the *living* God. It is living knowledge that matters. God is not a fact among other facts—there is a table, a house, a man, and God. He is the Fact of all facts. Without Him there could be no other facts, no table, house, or man. Creation is not once and for all; it goes on constantly. Only the divine power enables the world to persist.[41]

The Ba'al Shem taught that the Lord is present *in all things*. God is everywhere. The Hasidic teachers never tired of quoting to their followers the passage from the *Zohar*, "there is no place void of Him" *(let atar panui minei)*. Rabbi Shneur Zalman of Ladi, in his classic volume, the *Tanya*, explains the verse "For the Lord He is God in the heavens above and on the earth beneath; there is none else" (Deut. 4.39) in this manner: "Do not read the words, *'there is none else' ('ein 'od)* to mean, 'there are no other gods but the Lord.' Read it to mean, *'there is nothing else ('ein 'od) but the Lord!'* "[42] This, however, no more means that the Besht or Shneur Zalman were pantheists than that Isaiah was because he proclaimed that "the whole earth is full of His glory." Pantheism is the belief that God *is* the universe and nothing more. Hasidism affirmed that God is not only immanent in the world but transcendent beyond it, as Creator and Revealer. But it taught something else as well, that while God is more than the universe, the universe *is* God. This doctrine may best be called panentheism ("all is *in* God"). "To love the world in God" is how Buber once summed up the Hasidic enterprise.[43]

The opponents of Hasidism, the Mitnagdim, locked horns with them on this very issue. They found this doctrine heretical and made it a source of controversy. The bitterness of the dispute as well as the significance of this doctrine is revealed in a letter by a disciple of Rabbi Shneur Zalman of Ladi and his son, Rabbi Dov Ber. Accused of heresy for teaching that *altz iz Gott*, he defends his masters against this charge.

> I am writing this letter after having calmed down from the anger I felt and the pain I endured because of the accusation against us and our master [Dov Ber]. . . . Listen, my beloved friend! *Nit zog has veshalom az dos is apikorsus* . . . [Do not say this (belief that everything is God) is, Heaven forbid, heresy . . .] *Rak zog dos is emuna shelemah*. [Rather say that it is true belief], through which slumbering souls can be awakened, and dry bones *zollen margish zein Elohim hayyim* [might experience the living God]. *Alle Hasidim . . . hobn die emunah* [All Hasidim have this belief] . . . As for the Mitnagdim . . . *hobn zey kayn ort nit le-emunah zu az altz is Gott* [They have no room for the belief that all is God.] *Ober Hasidim hobn dos le-olam.* [But Hasidim always have this belief.]
>
> . . . I agonized over this belief . . . It began to flower and grow within me . . . but I still was unable to perceive it properly and I wanted to hear it explained verbally . . . [When, at last, his teacher, Dov Ber, finished expounding it to him, he writes,] I remained in a state of trembling, not knowing whether it was day or night . . . the light and the power of the belief that *altz iz Gott*, all is God, shot through me like an arrow, so I wanted to shout it aloud in the streets . . .
>
> As God lives, I have not exaggerated one single word in this letter.[44]

Like parched earth drinks in the new rain, so the startling message that *altz iz Gott*—everything is God—was welcomed by the common and the erudite alike. For the ordinary Jew, crushed by poverty, pursued by hatred, and excluded by his own intellectual aristocracy, the knowledge that God was close to him made life worth living; for the learned it lit a fire, shattering sterotypes and kindling joy in a thousand flames. Something of the wonder with which this new teaching was received is reflected in the following reports:

R. Simḥa Bunim taught: The Hebrew word *makom*, "place," is one of the names of God. Why? Because we should sense Him the way we sense the place upon which we stand, without which we could not exist.

According to another follower of the Besht, what God said to Moses—"Put off thy shoes from thy feet for the ground thou standest on is holy ground"—God says to every man: Put off the stale dullness that encloses you, and you will know that the place on which you are now standing is holy ground. For there is no rung of human life on which we cannot find the holiness of God.

Once Rabbi Shneur Zalman interrupted his prayers and said: "I do not want Your paradise. I do not want Your coming world. I want You, and You only."

The son of the great Maggid Dov Ber, Rabbi Abraham, taught: "Lord of the world, if it were possible to imagine a fraction of a second without your influence and providence, of what avail to us were this world, and what avail to us were that other world? Of what avail to us were the coming of the Messiah, and of what avail to us the resurrection of the dead? What would there be to delight in, in all of this, and what would it be therefore?"

A song attributed to Rabbi Levi Yiẓhak is sung to this day:

Master of the Universe	Ribono shel olom, Ribono shel
I will sing a song to Thee.	olom,
Where will I find Thee?	A ye emtzo-e-kho? Ve-a-ye lo
And where will I not find Thee?	emtzo-e-kho?
Where I go, there art Thou,	Vo ken man dikh yo gefinnen?
Where I stay, there art Thou.	Un vo ken man dikh nit gefinnen?
Only Thou, Thou alone,	Vo ikh geh iz dokh du,
Thou again, and only Thou.	Un vo ikh shteh iz dokh du.
	Rak du, nor du,
	Vieder du, ober du.
When things go well—Thou	Iz emitzen gut, iz dokh du,
And, alas, when things go ill—	V'kholiloh shlekht, oy du.
Thou.	Atoh du,
Thou art,	Ho-yo du,
Thou wast,	Ho-ve du,
Thou wilt be.	Yihye du.
Thou reignest,	Molokh du,

Thou didst reign,	Melekh du,
Thou wilt reign	Yimlokh du.
In heaven art Thou,	Shomayim du,
On earth art Thou,	Eretz du.
Above art Thou,	Maloh du,
Below art Thou,	Matoh du.
Where I turn	Vo ikh kehr mich,
And where I stir	Vo ikh wend mich,
Thou,	Du!
Thou,	Du!
Thou.	Du![45]

How can one describe what transpires within the man who is aware that God is before him? In being overwhelmed by His glory, one can identify at least two characteristics: awe, then contrition. "Holy, holy, holy is the Lord of hosts. The whole earth is full of His glory . . ." said Isaiah. And then: "Woe is me! for I am undone; because I am a man of unclean lips . . . For mine eyes have see seen the King . . ." (Isa. 6:3–4). First *yir'ah*, awe and reverence; afterwards *'anavah*, humility and contrition.

'Anavah, humility, marks the man who truly stands in God's presence. For when God becomes the central reality, the ego is no longer the hub of life's wheel, but a spoke. One who is filled only with himself has no room for God. The Lord cannot abide pride. Man's task, according to the mystics, is to turn his *ani* into *a-yin* (the same Hebrew letters which form the word "I," *ani* form the word "naught," *a-yin*). Concerning the verse in the Scriptures: "I stood between the Lord and you," Rabbi Mikhal of Zlotchov said: "The 'I' stands between God and us. When a man says 'I' and encroaches upon the word of his Maker, he puts a wall between himself and God. But he who offers his 'I'—there is nothing between himself and his Maker. For it is to him that the words refer: 'I am my beloved's and his desire is toward me.' When my 'I' has become my beloved's, then it is toward me that his desire turns."[46]

Rabbi Aaron of Karlin taught:

If a man constantly examines his deeds to determine whether he is a Hasid, it is pride. . . . For what is the essence of melancholy? Melancholy comes about when we worry: do *I* have, do *I* lack— whether it be of material or spiritual matters. Everything is important as it benefits me. But let us consider the matter. What difference does it make if *I* need? What is important is: does Heaven need? If our father Abraham wanted to change places with me, I would refuse. Abraham was a *Zaddik*, a saint, while I am *proste yid*, a nobody. If Abraham became Aaron and Aaron became Abraham, I would profit. But what difference would it make to Heaven? There would still be one saint and one nobody? So why should I wish it?[47]

The humble man achieves inner serenity, a feeling of equanimity. The verse "I have set the Lord before me at all times" was one of the key biblical passages for the early Hasidic teachers, who not only taught it but developed a pattern of exercises to bring it about. The Besht gave this verse an ingenious turn. Taking the Hebrew verb *shiviti*, "I have set," from *hishtavut*, "equanimonous," he read it thus: " 'Because the Lord is before me at all times, I am equanimonous.' I am neither flattered by praise nor offended by scorn."[48] To experience the presence of God is to shift the focus of one's life from the ego to the Divine, from one's own needs to those of heaven. The humble man serves God, not his own pride, because his eyes are on the Lord. Revering God, he fears no man, for what can man do to him who makes his life a dwelling place for the Lord? Freed from fretting over his own needs and hurts, the humble man finds a peace and power, centered in the Divine, which passes understanding.

Humility is a prelude to *devekut*—"the central point," according to Gershom Scholem, "on which Hasidism is focused."[49] To stand in awe before the Divine Presence is to know the selflessness of humility. To step forward into God's embrace is to experience *devekut*. "What is *devekut*, or cleaving to God?" an early Hasidic writer asks. "It comes to one who fulfills God's commandments with devotion. He makes his body a throne for his mind, his mind a throne for the spirit, and his spirit a throne for the light of the Divine Presence that rests upon him. The light spreads forth from him, and he, at the center of that light, trembles in his joy." Or again: "When a man so prays that his words become a throne for

God, an awesome fire seizes him. He no longer can see or hear or know where he is. All this transpires in the flash of an instant—as he rises beyond the world of time."[50]

Devekut, as being utterly lost in God, is reflected in the following two teachings.

Rabbi Yiẓhak of Neskhizh said: "Once my father said to one of his friends in the month before Rosh Ha-Shanah: 'Do you know what day this is? It is one of the days when the fish tremble in the ocean.' " One of the men standing near Rabbi Yiẓhak observed: "People usually say, 'When the fish tremble in the waters.' " "The was my father said it—in a vast endless ocean," Rabbi Yiẓhak replied, "that is the only way it expresses the secret of what occurs between God and the soul of man!"

The rabbi of Kotzk asked: "What did Rabbi Akiba mean when he said that the Lord was *mikveh Yisrael*, 'the waters of immersion of Israel'? He meant that just as the waters of immersion only purify one if he is wholly immersed, so that not even a hair is showing, that is how we should be immersed in God."

Three features were stressed in this Hasidic teaching. (1) *Devekut* is *non-Messianic*. "It is clearly a contemplative value without Messianic implications and can be realized everywhere and at every time. . . . When the Baal Shem and his pupils made it the very center of Hasidic life, the emphasis was shifted from Luria's stress on Messianic action in the process of *tikkun*—i.e., the restoration of the broken state of man and the whole universe to its former harmony and unity—toward a strictly personal relation of man to God. The experience of *devekut* destroyed the exile from within."[51] (2) *Devekut* is *this-worldly*. It is not achieved through the abandonment of this life for the next, a looking to a time *after* this world, so to speak, or a yearning for heavenly bliss or the state of nirvana *away from* this world. It is achieved rather *within* and *through* this world. *Devekut* means communion—only rarely union—with God. Man does not lose his personhood; he remains in the world to do his work. A distinction may be made here between mysticism, as it generally appears in the history of religion, and Hasidism. While mysticism sees the world as an illusion, man's duty, to love God by transcending the world in *unio mystica*, and is customarily antinomian in character, Hasidism sees the world as a reality, a man's task, to love God in the world, and affirms the normative character of society. Hasidism is an "active" or "realistic" mysticism. This is clearly exemplified in the Hasidic doctrine of *devekut*, which could be practiced within and through society as well as by withdrawal from it, or, better, perhaps, by doing both at the same time.[52] (3) *Devekut* was urged upon *all men*. Nahmanides had already read the verse "To love the Lord your God, to walk in all His ways and to cleave unto Him" (Deut. 11:22) as one of the 613 commandments. But for him it was the final stage of the spiritual ascent. For the Besht certain men could even begin there.

Records are available about how some of the circle of the Besht sought to carry out this teaching. For example, Rabbi Naḥman of Kosov employed a servant to do nothing but remind him of the verse "I have set the Lord before me at all times," especially when he was among people, that he might ever be aware of His presence. When he was asked how he could urge others to do this even while earning one's living, he replied: "If you can think of business while you pray, why can't you think of God when you do business?!" Rabbi Yiẓhak of Drobitch had a tray inscribed with this verse set before him when he ate, so that even the most mundane act was accompanied by *devekut*.[53]

IV. God Can Be Served Through Everything

The Besht was able to "banish melancholy and uncover the ineffable delight in being a Jew "because he taught that not only was God *in all things* but that He could be served *through all things*.

Boundaries had been erected that compartmentalized life into the holy and profane, the domain of God and that of man, the realm of ritual and the realm of living, the Sabbath and the week, the "holy"-day and the "every"-day, the synagogue and the marketplace, prayer and ordinary conversation, this world and the world-to-come. God should be served—but within boundaries. Outside lay danger: Approach with extreme care!

A defensive tactic was used by the rabbinic leaders. Better to build ramparts high and thick against the profane world within man—that evil impulse which yearned for pleasure, passion, and power and was so easily deceived by the demon of temptation—and the profane world without man—those mundane, everyday concerns which corrupt and impair—and concentrate on the secure confines of Torah-study, prayer, and ritual. Boundaries are important, and the drawing of distinctions is a fundamental teaching of the Torah. But are the boundaries stationary? Never to be expanded? Yes, was the answer of the time. Yes, they are never to be expanded. And, indeed, it did seem the more realistic way to handle the precarious nature of human life. Especially was such a defensive tactic understandable in a period of unusual social unrest, with the memories of the excesses of the Frankist heresy still so fresh in one's mind that any diversion from the established pattern—a new emphasis in worship, a new pattern of dress, a new expression of enthusiasm—was suspect and condemned. However, to establish fixed boundaries between the holy and the profane, to retreat before God's creation, meant repudiating the goodness *He* said it possessed and the responsibility *He* gave man "to rule over it." It was a distortion of the biblical command, "Serve Him in *all* thy ways" (Prov. 3:6), which the Talmud selects as "that short verse upon which all the Torah rests."[54]

The Besht argued that there are no permanent boundaries and that man possesses the power to conquer all the world; that just as those palace walls which served to prevent people from approaching the king are illusions, for God can be found in every place if only man truly searches for Him with all his heart and all his soul, so can God be served through all things, if only he serves with true devotion. Man need not retreat before God's Creation. It is the Lord's handiwork, and if He said, "It is good," then it *is* good: part actually, part potentially, part obviously, part not so obviously, part easily, part only with great difficulty and even dangerously. But for man to fully become man, he must face all of Creation and seek to transform it. Nature is not some forbidding wall before which man must halt and withdraw, an enemy to be shunned as one would a leper for fear of contamination. Nature is a welcome gate which invites he who understands how, to push it open, enter, and search for signs of the divine which lie within.

One of the "basic motifs" in Hasidism, writes Scholem, is "the sanctification of the profane sphere in the life of the perfect Hasid, its transformation into one single sphere of holy action which leaves no room for the concept of a separate state of 'profane' action."[55]

"Serve Him in all thy ways"—in *all* thy ways—was also the verse upon which the Besht's Torah rested. Hasidism came to complete and extend this teaching. To complete it, for example, by understanding that the injunction "Be holy, for I the Lord thy God am holy" (Lev. 19:2) does not mean *"the hallowing of man away from things"* but *"the hallowing of things through man."* This is why Rabbi Mendel of Kotzk translated the verse "Be holy men, for I the Lord thy God am holy" (Exod. 22:30) in this way: "Be holy *men*," that is to say, "be *humanly* holy"; strive to sanctify all your humanity. Man is to hallow the everyday. In so doing, he extends the realm of the miẓvah, as it was meant to be extended, beyond the sacramental or the ritual, to all of life. Thus

the setting apart a portion of nature removed from hallowing is overcome. All that is allotted to a human person for his use, from cow to tree to field to tool, conceals sparks that wait to be uplifted through man's holy use. . . . But it is not merely in the world that there is no longer a basic division: also in the soul of man. As the things and beings which one has to work with have been entrusted to him, so also the apparently strange conceptions, thoughts, wishes that fall into the soul. In all of them vibrate sparks that want to be redeemed by man. Nothing, in fact, is unholy in itself, nothing is in itself evil. What we call evil is only the directionless plunging and storming of the sparks in need of redemption. It is "passion"—the very same power which, when it has been endowed with direction, the one direction, brings forth the good in truth, the true service, the hallowing. Thus there no longer exist side by side in the soul of man the worldly and the spiritual, qualitatively sundered; there is now only power and direction. He who divides his life between God and the world, through giving the world "what is its" to save for God "what is His," denies God the service He demands, the giving of direction to all power, the hallowing of the everyday in the world and the soul.[56]

One should hallow all that one does in one's natural life. No renunciation is commanded. One eats in holiness, tastes the taste of food in holiness, and the table becomes an altar. One works in holiness, and he raises up the divine sparks which hide themselves in all tools. One walks in holiness across the fields, and the silent songs of nature, which are sung to God, enter the song of one's own soul. One drinks in holiness to one's companions, each to the other, and it is as if one studied together with them in the Torah. One dances the roundelay in holiness, and a splendor shines over the gathering. A man is united with his wife in holiness, and the Shekinah rests over them.[57]

The story of Enoch the cobbler, who while he stitched the upper leather to the sole joined God and His *Shekhinah*, was often quoted by the disciples of the Besht. Their master applied to this ancient tale the verse, "Whatever thy hand finds to do, do with all thy strength" (Eccles. 9:10), explaining that man must unite all his forces, both spiritual and physical, in his effort. And, further, that one's daily work, performed with human wholeness, can help to restore the wholeness of the Divine. "It is the nature of the Ẓaddik," writes the foremost disciple of the Besht, "to join to-together the two worlds . . . the material world with the higher world, the transient to the eternal."[58]

Central to Hasidism, in the life of the individual as well as in the life of the community, is

to overcome the fundamental separation between the sacred and the profane. This separation has formed a part of the foundation of every religion. Everywhere the holy is removed and set apart from the fulness of things, properties and actions which belong to the universal, so that the holy becomes a self-contained holiness outside of which the profane must pitch its tent. The consequences of this separation in the history of man is a two-fold one. Religion is thereby assured a firm province whose untouchableness is always guaranteed . . . but the holy is not given a corresponding power in the rest of life. . . .

In Judaism . . . one needs only note how many everyday actions are introduced by a blessing to recognize how deep the hallowing reaches into what is in itself unhallowed. One not only blesses God every morning on awakening because He has allowed one to awaken, but also when one begins to use a new house or piece of clothing or tool because one has been preserved in life to this hour. Thus the simple fact of continued earthly existence is sanctified at each occasion that offers itself and therefore this occasion itself also. . . . The separation between the realms is only a provisional one. . . . In the Messianic world all shall be holy. In Hasidism this tendency reaches a highly realistic consumation. The profane is now regarded as a preliminary stage of the holy; it is the not-yet-hallowed. Human life is destined to be hallowed in its natural form. "God dwells where man lets Him in!" The hallowing of man means this "letting in." Basically the holy in our world is what is open to God, as the profane is what is closed off from Him, and hallowing is the event of opening out. . . .[59]

When R. Naḥman of Horodenka spoke of the sweet medicine of the Besht, it was his understanding, and that of R. Ya'akov Yosef, that it was composed of two teachings: the belief that God is in all things and can be served through all things. The following lengthy passage, in the typical form of an exposition of a biblical text, Genesis 28:10–17, picks up the central threads of the argument: the reference to R. Shim'on bar Yoḥai's emergence from the cave, R. Nahman's dream about sweet medicine, the former state of intolerance, the new one of compassion, and the understanding that God can be served through all things because He is in all things.

Text

And Jacob went out from Beersheva, and went toward Haran. And he came upon a place . . . and he took of the stones of the place, and put them for his pillows, and lay himself down to sleep in that place. And he dreamed, and behold a ladder fixed into the earth, whose head reached into the heavens; and behold the angels of God were ascending and descending. And, behold, the Lord stood above it, and said, I am the Lord God of Abraham thy father, and the God of Isaac; the land whereon thou liest, to thee will I give it, and to thy seed. And thy seed shall be as the dust of the earth. . . . And in thee and in thy seed shall all the families of the earth be blessed. For behold, I am with thee and will watch over thee every place whithersoever thou goest, and I will bring thee again unto this land; for I will not leave thee, until I have done that which I have spoken to thee of. And Jacob awakened out of his sleep, and said, Surely, the Lord is in this place; and I knew it not. And he was afraid, and said, how full of awe is this place! . . .

Exposition

"And Jacob went out from Beer Sheva," where [according to the Midrash] he had secluded himself within the walls of the school of Shem and Ever, learning Torah. When he "went out" and saw people who were not studying Torah, [but going about their daily affairs,] he condemned them [like R. Shim'on bar Yoḥai]: "Lo, these people are neglecting eternal matters and are busying themselves with matters of the moment." So that he brought down wrath upon the world, as it says, "and he went toward Haran" (Hebrew *ḥaron* = "wrath"). [When R. Shim'on ben Yoḥai and his son emerged from the cave where they were secluded for years in prayer and study and condemned the farmers tilling their fields instead of devoting themselves to prayer and Torah, a Heavenly voice proclaimed: "Do you want to destroy My world? Return to your cave!"] Jacob too was about to escape back into the quarantine of his school, but when he perceived that the world could not endure such persistent wrath, his intent to return departed. For it says, "And he came upon a place," and "Place" is one of the divine Names which stands for the Lord's compassion; which is to say, what had at first evoked rigor was transformed into compassion.

"And he took of the stones of the place," that is, he took the letters of the Divine Name to contemplate them and to contemplate the Torah, [which is composed of the divine letters] that he might be protected from the wild beasts. So he "lay himself down to sleep" in security, "and he dreamed, and behold a ladder fixed in the earth and whose head reached the heavens." That is to say, *from the heavens there was revealed to him a medicine which was sweet and not bitter*, (as I have written of elsewhere in my book) *namely, that one can serve the Lord not alone through Torah and prayer*, for one who thinks this may grow intolerant of others who do not act likewise. It is man who is called the "ladder which is fixed into the earth," that is, into the earthy matter of this world, but . . . "whose head reaches into the heavens," that is, he may serve the Lord with this [earthiness] as well, for man has the freedom to do so.

Therefore, [it is written] "And behold the angels of God were ascending and descending." For it is man who is a *mal'akh* [Hebrew = both "angel" and "messenger"] of the Lord; some ascending with good thoughts and others descending with evil thoughts. Nevertheless, among both the evil and the good I the Lord "stand by." That is, in every place the Lord is present . . . Thus it is written, "And Jacob awakened out of his sleep and said, Surely, the Lord is in this place . . ." That is, even in a place of wild animals and robbers and evil there are the *Shekhinah*'s sparks of holiness, which have fallen there because of the "breaking of the vessels of creation." "And he was afraid and said, how full of awe is this place." That is, trembling, he feared and felt anguish for the anguish of the *Shekhinah*, who dwelt amidst evil; and it was because of this that a *yihud* took place and the *kelipot* (evil) were dispersed . . .

"For behold I am with thee and will watch over thee every place whithersoever thou goest." . . . That is, if all my thoughts cleave truly to the Lord . . . so that God is with me in all the mundane matters of this world, then even when I am not studying Torah and prayer, He will surely watch over me . . . and all assurances will be fulfilled. . . . "For I will watch over you whithersoever thou goest, and I will bring thee again unto this land. For I will not leave thee until I have done that of which I have spoken to thee."[60]

In the above exposition we find the main elements of our study. The sweet medicine of R. Naḥman's dream is analyzed as being composed of serving God through all things because He is in all things. The argument runs as follows. At first the service of God was understood to be limited to Torah-study, prayer, fasting, tears, and the like. This emphasis produced a narrowness of vision which was condemnatory of those who were not scholars, engendering a mood of wrath, the prevailing mood of the period before the Besht. Such an atmosphere was unbearable. The heavenly voice which told R. Shim'on to return to his cave, and would have told Jacob, that is, the leader of the people, to do the same, was understood to mean that a new way was required, one of mercy rather than harshness, compassion in the place of condemnation. In Jacob's dream he is told of the "sweet medicine," a clear allusion to the night vision of R. Naḥman, where heaven itself intrudes. And what is the nature of this sweet medicine? Its marvelous curative powers derive from an understanding of man as the ladder fixed in the earth whose head reaches the heaven, that is, whose earthy existence can be lifted to heaven, who can serve God with his daily needs as well as through exalted moments of Torah and prayer. For man is a "messenger," who is sent into this world freely to serve God. He can serve freely if he understands what Jacob learned, namely, that "God is in this place," that is, in *every* place, which means that since "sparks of holiness" reside in all things, all things can be a means of serving God. Ever holding God's image before him, man pursues his destiny.

'*Avodah be-gashmiut*, a technical term in Hasidic literature, means serving God through the corporeal world. Hasidism appropriated and expanded the teaching that one can worship God by means of his bodily acts, with both the "good" and "evil impulse," through eating, business, and sex, by turning one's natural desires into a vehicle for the worship of God. It is man, says the ancient Midrash, who makes the impulse *(yeẓer)* evil *(ra)*.

A parable is told in the name of the Besht which explicates this notion.

A king's son was taken captive. He possessed a secret letter from his father which was the key to his redemption. His captors removed him to a tavern and then began to drink. The captors drank for the sake of drinking. The prince drank, too, but for a different reason. In the mood of joy which prevailed because of the liquor, he was able to rejoice in his father's letter.[61]

The argument behind this parable, central to the understanding of the way of the Besht, seems to be something like this: If man was created to serve God, and man is made of body as well as soul, then it must be wrong to believe that the soul alone can achieve creation's purpose without concern for the body. Or, to

put it differently and more to the point: since man is both body
and soul (*nefesh* or "person" in the biblical sense), then man qua man
cannot properly serve God unless the body too serves Him.

"In other words there is no way to be liberated from the
captivity of corporeality except by ostensibly cooperating with
it."[62] One does not reach the spiritual by turning away from the
material but by using it. Indeed, there are times when the
spiritual can be reached only through the material. After the death
of his wife, the Besht would not let himself be comforted and said:
"I had hoped to journey to Heaven in a thunderstorm like Elijah,
but now it has been taken from me, for I am now only half a
body."[63] Nor is this tension between the spiritual and the material
limited to the individual. Quite the contrary, it is also representative of the unique society which emerged out of the relation
between the Ẓaddik and his disciples. Indeed, it is precisely in the
full life of the Hasidic community that the spiritual process finds a
major expression. From his understanding of the Hasidic society,
Buber extrapolated much for his earlier teachings regarding
socialism and his later design for the Zionist kibbutz.[64]

> Hasidism has meant to Buber the most impressive effort made at
> the realization of true community from the days of the prophets to
> the time of the beginnings of halutziut in Palestine in recent years.
> "Hasidism was the one great attempt in the history of the Diaspora
> to make a reality of their original chosenness and to found a true and
> just community based on religious principles. . . . This structure
> found its perfection about two centuries ago in Hasidism, which was
> built on little communities bound together by brotherly love. . . .
> [It] failed for a number of reasons, among others because it did not
> aim for the independence, for the self-determination of the
> people . . ."[65] [Buber's] Zionism is essentially a call to take up the
> task which Hasidism attempted and at which it failed, under condi-
> tions appropriate to the task. This task is the "unperformed task"
> that has hung over Jewry from the days of the prophets, the task of
> building true community. "At that time [in the days of the
> prophets], we did not carry out that which was imposed upon us; we
> went into exile with our task unperformed; but the command re-
> mained with us, and it has become more urgent than ever. We need
> our own soil in order to fulfill it; we need the freedom to order our

own life; no attempt can be made on foreign soul and under foreign statute. . . . Our one desire is that at last we may be able to obey."[66] [67]

We have observed that Hasidism teaches that man need not reject the material world around him nor the emotional world within him, but rather should meet and transform them by raising them up in the service of God. Sometimes human passion, even sexual passion, can become not only a means but a model for serving God. This theme, developed by Heschel in his Yiddish book *Kotzk*, I shall attempt to summarize here.

Over the generations, under the influence of the *Zohar* and the later Kabbalah, the tendency developed among some Jews to despise the body and to see physical pleasure as sinful. In the eighteenth century the *Musar*, or ethical literature, frowned upon intimate relations between husband and wife even to fulfill the command "Be fruitful and multiply," understanding sexual intercourse as a kind of hardship, as if one were acting under compulsion. Had not Maimonides in his *Guide* observed more than once that "the sense of touch is repulsive," and did not Nahmanides (to Lev. 18:6) observe that "sexual intimacy is loathsome and rejected by the Torah, except to propagate mankind"?

The Besht spoke otherwise. Do not be ashamed of pleasure, afraid of passion, or frightened by desire, even sexual desire. "Hide not yourself from your own flesh" (Isa. 58:7), he wrote to his beloved disciple, Rabbi Ya'akov Yosef, who was given over to self-mortification.[68] Consider, the Besht might have argued, could man have been created by God with endless desires and passions, only that they be uprooted or trampled upon? Must He not have meant them for something more? It had been assumed that holiness had to do "with fulfilling the law in all its strictness" (*ḥumrot*), and not at all with the corporeal world. But, observed the Besht, perhaps the material world is intertwined with the spiritual world? Perhaps the dimension of human experience can reflect, or even enhance, the divine dimension? Could it be that the reason human passion had to be given to man was that through it he might learn the passion for God? Even when man sins with a

woman—to take an extreme example—what drives him to do it
except love, and is love not a divine quality; no less divine in
origin because man desecrates it? "Erotic love is like an unripe
fruit which falls from the tree. When human love ripens, then it is
love for God."

But even erotic love itself has a higher purpose. The body can
become an avenue of the spirit. The verse in the Song of Songs
7:7, "How beautiful and how sweet among pleasures, is love," is
interpreted by the Besht to mean: How beautiful and how sweet it
is that through his coarse delights, man can come to the love of
God! Each pleasure one experiences might be understood as a
divine hint on how to take pleasure in God. Human passion, then,
would seem to function on two levels: the first, a purely creaturely
one; the second, a lesson in how to serve the Creator. The
prophets, and the talmudic rabbis after them, had long before
used the model of human love to enable us to comprehend Divine
love, while still later, in the Kabbalah, sexual symbolism takes on
major proportions. It is not, however, so much the complex sexual
symbolism so central to the Kabbalah as erotic desire which the
Besht uses for an example of service to God. Indeed, can man
truly come to the love of God without experiencing human love?
Against the teaching of those who condemned sexual pleasure, the
Besht argued that "intimate relations should be performed with
fire, desire, and joy." And just this was to be a model for the
spiritual life of Torah study and prayer: "the same fire, the same
desire, and the same joy."[69]

At the heart of the Besht's teaching of hallowing the everyday
lies the mystical formula of the "doctrine of sparks." What was
this doctrine?

In the process of creation, according to the teaching of Rabbi
Yizhak Luria, the great sixteenth-century Kabbalistic master of
Safed, the vessels containing the divine light were shattered,
leaving traces throughout all creation. The Lurianic teaching of
restoring these holy sparks to their source, through special mystical thoughts and deeds performed by the initiated in order to

hasten the Messiah, was transformed by the Ba'al Shem into a task incumbent upon every man to perfect himself through the hallowing of all things. Consequently it is the duty of man to serve God with everything he encounters through *devekut*, cleaving to God, and with *kavanah* performing one's deeds with utter sincerity. Whether it be in work or eating or talking to one's neighbor, man may succeed in redeeming the sparks. Hasidism drew upon a profound teaching of Lurianic mysticism and turned it from an apocalyptic-Messianic purpose into a humanistic one. In a word, "Kabbalah had become ethos."

An example of this teaching, as expressed by one of the classic Hasidic writers, can be seen in the book *Kedushat Levi* by Rabbi Levi Yiẓhak of Berditchev.

Everything that the Holy One, blessed-be-He, created in this world was created only for His glory—even material things. For example, when a man sits down to eat and drink, let his mind dwell upon the thought that he nourishes his body in order that it might better serve his Creator in strength and health; or when he performs his marital duties, let him understand that he is fulfilling the commandment of the Lord. And so it is with all matters of the flesh. For in this way he is able to raise up the hidden holy sparks to their divine source. When you desire to eat and drink or to perform other worldly desires, and you keep in mind the thought that it is for the love of God that you do this, then you elevate physical desire into spiritual desire, and, consequently, you are able to draw out the holy spark that dwells within it.

. . . And this is the mystery of the blessing over the washing of the hands, *netillat yadayyim*, for *netillah* means "raising up." And this too is the secret of the blessing over the bread, ". . . Who brings forth bread from the earth," for "bread" is a mystical symbol of holiness, and "earth" refers to earthy, material qualities, thus implying that one "brings forth" the hidden sparks [bread] from the material world [the earth]. When a man walks in this path, he gives evidence of the deep and abiding love that dwells within him for the Holy One, blessed-be-He, and there is no path greater than this. For in every place that a man walks and in everything that a man does—even seemingly unimportant things of this world—he is able to serve the Creator, blessed-be-He.[70]

Hasidism succeeded in making the esoteric Lurianic doctrine of sparks into a powerful program of daily living by seizing upon and developing that aspect of it which was most humanistic and personal. Scholem describes how this was achieved. The Kabbalah speaks of two kinds of sparks, those of the *Shekhinah* and those of Adam, for as the vessels containing the divine light were shattered, so was the soul of Adam when he sinned and failed to restore the original harmony by lifting up those sparks. The task of restoring the sparks of the *Shekhinah* is ontological, Messianic, and the task of every informed man. The task of restoring the sparks of Adam is anthropological and limited to the sparks which relate to each particular person. In Hasidism the doctrine of the sparks of the *Shekhinah* is subsumed under and merged with that relating to the individual man. In other words, it is *non-Messianic, humanistic, and directed to the individual,* for no one can raise up a spark not of his own root. The metaphysical becomes personal.

> All that belongs to a man [the early Hasidic sources tell us] be it his servants and animals, be it even his household effects—they are all of his sparks which belong to the root of his soul, which he must raise to their upper root. . . . A man's food, his clothing, his home, and his business—all these belong to the sparks of his own soul which he is called upon to lift up. . . . This is the hidden meaning of the verse, "Know Him in all thy ways" (Prov. 3:6), because *whatever man experiences is to enable him to lift up the sparks of his own soul, which are, at the same time, the sparks of the Shekhinah.* . . . Everyone must go to those places which contain sparks from the root of his own soul in order that he might free them.[71]

Through this interpretation, the role of the individual achieves preeminence. Each soul is related to holy sparks which only he can redeem. And each person is commanded to redeem those sparks. Each man is in effect given a task which no other man can perform in his place. "There is a specific sphere in man's environment that mystically belongs to him, and to him alone, and can be touched by nobody else."[72] Such a teaching raises the esteem of each man in that it provides for his own individual circumstances and leads him to serve God through the mundane affairs of his own particular world. Consequently, there is no one way to serve God. "What is the most important task for a man? A Zaddik asked his Hasid. "The Sabbath, Torah study, or prayer," the latter suggested. "No," he was told, "the most important task a man can undertake is whatever he happens to be doing at the moment!" Thus, to the uniqueness of the person must be added the uniqueness of the situation.

The sense of man's individuality is paradoxically expressed by Rabbi Mendel of Kotzk: "If I am I because you are you and you are you because I am I, then I am not I and you are not you. But if I am I because I am I and you are you because you are you, than I am I and you are you!" In other words, man's worth depends not so much on whether he reaches the level of others, or excels in imitation, as on whether he fulfills his own particular destiny by standing his own ground, being what he, and only he, can be, what he was created to be. Rabbi Sussya of Hanipol said this to his disciples on his deathbed: "When Sussya dies and appears before the heavenly court, they will not ask, 'Sussya, why were you not a Maimonides or an Akiba or a Moses?' For I could reply that I had neither their mind nor spirit. But they will ask me something far more difficult. 'Sussya,' they will ask, 'why were you not Sussya?' And then what shall I say?"

The fashioning of man in God's likeness is repeated twice in the verse—"And God created man in His own image; in the image of God created He him" (Gen. 1:27). Why? A Hasidic master offered this answer.

In Hebrew there is no distinction between capitals and small letters. Therefore the word "His" in the first part of the sentence could just as well be read "his," referring not to God at all but to man. Thus: "And God created each man in *his own image;* in the *image of God* created He him." If that were the case the verse would teach that man was made in two images: his own and God's. Why two images? Because this is indeed the nature of man. Each man possesses *his own image,* that is to say, what is uniquely his own and none other's. For each man is different from every other man, and none can do the work of another, because each one occupies a special rung upon the ladder of life upon which no one else stands. But man is also made in the *divine image;* and it is this which provides the deepest meaning of his existence. Man's task, then, is twofold: to discover that peculiar image in which he was made, who he in fact is; and, then, having found his own image, to labor to make of that image the image of God.

The life of man is not only a part of the life of nature but also a part of the life of God. That man partakes in the dimension of nature is obvious: made of matter, he is born, ages, dies, eats, procreates, is pained, diseased, and driven by animal-like impulses. That man also partakes in the "holy dimension" and is part of the life of God *(ḥelek Eloha mi-ma'al)* is, however, a startling notion. It means that irrespective of his learning, man qua man owns, so to speak, a piece of God! It is self-understood, of course, that one must strive to learn how to think and feel and act so that the divine within becomes manifest. But that is another matter. It is the fact itself which is—and was understood then to be— momentous. One consequence of this concept, for example, can be observed in how the Hasid understood prayer. He saw it not simply as a dialogue between God and man, but rather communion between "the divine within" and "the divine above." Or, as Rabbi Pinḥas of Koretz put it: "People think they pray *to* God, they are wrong. Prayer itself *is* God."

III. Conclusion

Let us sum up our argument.

Intellectualism had been overestimated among the Jews of eighteenth-century Poland. Torah study was transformed into a search for subtle dialectics. Books became little more than anthologies of *pilpul,* intriguing for those who were engaged in scholarly fireworks, but without a message of piety, a lesson in how to live, an answer to the people's questions. The scholars were immersed in the problems of the law. The Talmud said thus and so, but Maimonides in his code said so and thus: apparently there was a contradiction. But no, the opinions could be reconciled through sharp reasoning, and all would be put right! For the problems of the scholar this may have been a delight, but what about the problems of life—sickness, death, envy, pride, earning a livelihood, and marital discord? They seem to have been all but ignored. To the rabbi of the time came people who had problems with the law; but to whom were people who had problems with life to come? Was external obedience to the law the only answer?

Furthermore, this was no way to contend with that portion of the population which had been caught up in the fantasy of Messianic redemption, which at one fell swoop promised to free them from the exile, return them to their own land, and hail the coming of the Awaited One. That dream, as we know, failed: Shabbeti Zevi converted to Islam in Istanbul. Hearts that had been broken when the vision of redemption turned into a nightmare would not be mended by *pilpul* and dialectics.

The bitter medicine of the rabbis did not heal the hurt, serving only to stir up the malady of melancholy which threatened the life of the people. It was the sweet medicine of the Ba'al Shem which restored the health of eighteenth-century Jewry.

Hasidism was able "to banish melancholy and uncover the ineffable delight in being a Jew" because it taught that God was in every place and could be served through everything. The command to serve God in "all one's ways" was forged into a vital program for daily living, so that it encompassed not only special days or times or places but every day and every moment. All was to be hallowed. Beneath the program was the teaching, the doctrine of sparks, which the Besht related to each man's private world: to which he and only he was obligated, and which only he was able to redeem. "The cosmos is potentially holy; the encounter with man makes it actually holy," Buber wrote. "Hasidism teaches this through its doctrine of worship of God through the corporeal and worldly dimension of God's being."

Judaism can be summed up in a single sentence: *God can be beheld in each thing and reached through each pure deed.* In the Hasidic teaching, the whole world is only a word out of the mouth of God. Nonetheless, the least thing in the world is worthy that through it God should reveal Himself to the man who truly seeks Him; for no thing can exist without a divine spark, and each person can uncover and redeem this spark at each time and through each action, even the most ordinary, if only he performs it in purity, wholly directed to God and concentrated in Him. Therefore, it will not do to serve God only in isolated hours and with set words and gestures. One must serve God with one's whole life, with the whole of the everyday, with the whole of reality. The salvation of man does not lie in his holding himself far removed from the worldly, but in consecrating it to holy, to divine meaning; his work and his food, his rest and his wandering, the structure of the family and the structure of society. It lies in his preserving the great love of God for all creatures, yes, for all things. Hasidism took the social form of a great popular community—not an order of the secluded, not a brotherhood of the select, but a popular community in all its medley, in all its spiritual and social multiplicity. Never yet in Europe has such a community thus established the whole of life as a unity on the basis of the inwardly known. Here is no separation between faith and work, between truth and verification, or, in the language of today, between morality and politics; here all is one kingdom, one spirit, one reality.[73]

The peoples of the earth also believe that there are two worlds, taught a Hasidic master. They too say: "in the next world." The difference is this: they think that the two worlds are separate and cut off from each other. But Israel knows that the two worlds are one in their essence and that one day they shall become one in their reality.

NOTES

1. A comprehensive review of the conflict brought about by the rise of Hasidism has not yet been published. The English reader is referred to articles in the *Encyclopaedia Judaica*, as well as the following: B. Weinryb, *The Jews of Poland* (Philadelphia, 1972), pt. III; "Hasidism and Its Opponents: The Hostile Phase," by M. Wilensky, and "The Phase of Dialogue and Reconciliation," by N. Lamm, in *Tolerance and Movements of Religious Dissent in Eastern Europe*, ed. Kiraly (Columbia University Press, 1976), pp. 89–129; Dubnow, *History of the Jews in Russia and Poland* (Philadelphia, 1916), vol. 1, pp. 229–242, 370–390; S. Dresner, *The Zaddik* (New York: Schocken, 1974). Hebrew studies included: M. Wilensky, *Hasidim U-Mitnagdim* (Jerusalem: Mosad Bialik, 1970), 2 vols.; R. Mahler, *Ha-Hasidut Ve-ha-Haskalah* (Merhavya: Sifriat Poalim, 1961); A. Wertheim, *Halakhot Ve-Halikot Ba-Hasidut* (Jerusalem: Mosad Ha-Rav Kook, 1960); Dubnow, *Toldot ha-Hasidut* (Tel Aviv: Dvir, 1960); E. Zweifel, *Shalom al Yisrael* (Zhitomir, 1868–69); M. Teitelbaum, *Ha-Rav mi-Ladi* (Warsaw: Tushiah, 1914).

2. Cf. J. Abelson, *The Immance of God in Rabbinic Literature* (London, 1912).
3. Cf. Dubnow, *Toldot ha-Hasidut*, pp. 380–381; N. Lamm, *Torah Lishmah* (Jerusalem: Mosad ha-Rav Kook, 1972), pp. 208–218.
4. *Toledot Ya'akov Yosef*, R. Ya'akov Yosef of Polnoy (Koretz, 1780), f. 202a; cf. *In Praise of the Baal Shem Tov*, ed. Ben-Amos and Mintz (Bloomington, Ind., 1970), p. 156, #133; Abraham Heschel, "Unknown Documents for the History of Hasidism," *YIVO Bletter*, vol. 36 (1952), p. 117.
5. Dubnow, *History of the Jews in Russia and Poland*, vol. 1, p. 203–204.
6. Ibid., pp. 113–131.
7. Ibid., p. 202.
8. *Ben Porat Yosef*, R. Yaakov Yosef (Koretz, 1781), f. 64a.
The significance of this passage has not yet been noted by scholars. A central doctrine of the Besht was the transformation of evil by locating the spark of holiness which inhered in it and thereby raising it up in the service of God (see Piekanz, *Bi-Yemei Zemihat Ha-Hasidut* [Jerusalem, 1978], pp. 204–280). Thus, in the case of "evil thoughts" *(mahshavot zarot)* which may occur while engaged in prayer or Torah-study—for example, the thought of a woman—one is encouraged not to cease one's prayer or study, but to penetrate to the core of the thought—beauty in this case—find its source in divine beauty, and use the power of that quality in more fervent prayer or study. So the Besht taught in regard to other undesirable human traits. Not so with '*azvut*. "*Azvut*" itself "is a *kelipah*," R. Ya'akov Yosef, the author of the passage quoted, goes on to say, and thus it is a quality unredeemable through the normal process of sublimation. There is no redeeming potential, it would seem, no spark of holiness to be searched out. Melancholy itself must be removed, if only for a moment, in order for *yihud* or *devekut* to be possible. That the Besht found it necessary to make so special a place in his thinking for '*azvut* suggests how oppressive must have been the mood of the time and thereby contributes to our understanding of the social and spiritual conditions. (The author intends to deal with this subject in a separate article.)
It should be added that R. Ya'akov Yosef goes on to say that "just as it is not possible [for the Zaddik] to join to God one who is in a state of '*azvut* because it is a *kelipah*, so is this the case with the arrogant, for he is removed from holiness" (ibid.). R. Ya'akov Yosef is referring to the contemporary scholars, an indictment of whom is a central theme of his works. (Cf. Dresner, *The Zaddik*, chap. 4.)
9. Ben Amos and Mintz, *In Praise of the Baal Shem Tov*, loc. cit.
10. Shabbat 33b.
11. *Toledot Ya'akov Yosef*, f. 202a. Italics mine.
12. Ibid.
13. See Dresner, *The Zaddik*, pp. 34–35.
14. R. Barukh of Mezebosh, *Butzina di-Nehora*, f. 18d. Italics mine.
15. A. J. Heschel, *The Earth Is the Lord's* (New York, 1950), pp. 75–76.
16. *Zava'at ha-Rivash* (Brooklyn: Kehot, 1975), pp. 14–16, #44–46. Much of the material in this work is found in books by R. Dov Ber, the Maggid of Mezritch. For a parallel to this passage see *Likutim Yekarim* (Jerusalem, 1974), #23; *Or ha-Emet* (Brooklyn, 1960), f. 103b.
17. *Or Yesharim*, M. Kleinman (Pietrokov), p. 221, n. 112. For a study of joy in Hasidism, see E. Shohet, "*Al Ha-Simhah ba-Hasidut*," *Zion*, 1951, pp. 30–43. Cf. *Toledot Ya'akov Yosef*, f. 124c.

18. G. Scholem, *Major Trends in Jewish Mysticism* (New York: Schocken, 1941), pp. 230–231.

19. *Toledot Ya'akov Yosef*, f. 18d.

20. *Likutim Yekarim*, R. Dov Ber (Jerusalem, 1974), p. 1, #4.

21. *Divrei David*, R. David of Czortkof (Husiatin, 1904), pp. 65–66.

22. Shohet, op. cit., p. 43. "Without *simḥah* there can be no service of God [*avodah*]" (*Toledot Ya'akov Yosef*, f. 63a).

23. Taanit 22a. See *Toldot Yaakov Yosef*, f. 120d.

24. Shabbat 30b.

25. R. Moshe of Mogelenitza, *Or Yesharim*, p. 221, n. 112.

26. *Toledot Ya'akov Yosef*, f. 72b; *Zohar*, par. Teẓaveh, f. 184b.

27. A. J. Heschel, *A Passion for Truth* (New York, 1973), pp. 47–48.

28. *Keneset Yisrael* (Warsaw, 1906), p. 145. See Heschel, *Passion for Truth*, p. 76.

29. *Zekher Ẓaddik*, R. Aaron of Kaidenov (Vilna, 1905), p. 19.

30. R. Naḥman of Bratslav, *Ha-Midot* (Warsaw, 1914), pp. 116–117, 149–150.

31. Heschel, *Passion for Truth*. For the place of humor in the Besht's thinking, see *Ben Porat Yosef*, 38b.

32. *Toledot Ya'akov Yosef*, f. 18d.

33. Ibid., f. 201a.

34. *Divrei Shalom*, Shalom of Kaidenov (Vilna, 1882), *derush* for Ḥanukah, f. 29d.

35. *Divrei Ẓadikim*, quoted by S. Vendik, *Sefer Ba'al Shem Tov*, vol. 1, p. 25.

36. A. J. Heschel, "Hasidism As a New Approach to Torah," *Jewish Heritage*, Fall–Winter 1972, p. 15.

37. See M. Orion, *The Exalted* (Jerusalem: Masada, 1975), chaps. 21, 23 (Hebrew).

38. *Toldot Ya'akov Yosef*, f. 201b.

39. Ben Amos and Mintz, *In Praise of the Baal Shem Tov*, p. 11, #3.

40. See G. Scholem, *The Messianic Idea in Judaism* (New York, 1971), p. 224.

41. "It is written: 'Forever, O God, Your word stands firm in the heavens' (Ps. 119:89). The Ba'al Shem Tov, of blessed memory, explained 'Your word' [to mean the words of creation]: 'Let there be a firmament in the midst of the waters' (Gen. 1:6). That is to say these very words and letters [that is, the Divine force which brings creation into existence out of nothing] stand firmly forever as the firmament of heaven and are hidden within all the heavens in order to give them life, as it is written, 'The word of our God shall stand forever' (Isa. 48), and 'His words live and stand forever' (Morning Service). For if the letters were to depart for even an instant and return to their source, all the heavens would crumble away as before creation. And similarly with all creation in the lower world as well as the upper world, even this physical earth . . . If the letters of the Ten utterances (Avot 5.1), by which the earth was created during the six days of creation, were to depart from it but for an instant, heaven forbid, the earth itself would be turned to naught as it was before the six days of creation.

"This same thought was expressed by the ARI (*'Eẓ Ḥayyim*, 'shaar man u-mad,' sec. 3), of blessed memory, when he said that even in completely inanimate matter, such as stones or earth or water, there is a soul and spiritual life force . . . which give life and existence to inanimate matter." (Shneur Zalman of Ladi, *Likutei Amarim*, "shaar ha-yiḥud," chap. 1).

42. Ibid. chap. 6.

43. L. Jacobs, *Seeker of Unity* (London, 1966), p. 11. "In the Hasidic message the separation between 'life of God' and 'life in the world,' the primal evil of all 'religion,' is overcome in genuine, concrete unity. But a rejoinder is also given here to the false overcoming of the separation through the abstract dissolution of the difference between God and the world. Hasidism preserves undiminished God's distance from and superiority to the world in which He nonetheless dwells. In this distance Hasidism sets the undivided wholeness of human life in its full meaning: that it should receive the world from God and act on the world for the sake of God. Bound to the world, receiving and acting, man stands directly before God—not 'man', but this particular man, you, I" (Buber, *Origin*, p. 99).

44. Jacobs, *op. cit.*, Appendix. For a fuller version of this letter see Heschel, *Man's Quest for God* (New York: Scribners, 1954), pp. 73–76. "When a Jew dwells upon the fact that the Holy One, blessed-be-He, is literally all-present in the higher and lower worlds, that He literally fills the heavens and earth, that the whole world is literally full with His glory, and that He searches out each mind and heart and word and counts his every step—then will humankind be filled with awe for the Lord, and turn away from evil to do good" (*Likutei Amarim*, chap. 42).

45. *Levi Yitzḥak*, pp. 106–107.

46. M. Buber, *Tales of the Hasidim* (New York, 1948), vol. 1, p. 149.

47. *Keneset Yisrael, loc. cit.*

48. *Zava'at ha-Rivash*, p. 1, #2.

49. Scholem, *Messianic Idea*, p. 209.

50. Green and Holtz. *Your Word Is Fire*, pp. 82–84.

51. Scholem, *Messianic Idea*, pp. 185–186.

52. The difficulty in achieving this state is reflected in the statement of Rabbi Ya'akov Yosef of Polnoy, the main source of the teaching of the Besht, about his master. "Because of his fervent *devekut*, the Ba'al Shem could not talk to people, but would mutter to himself. Then his teacher, the prophet Ahiyah, taught him which psalms to recite each day, so that he might be able to talk to people while cleaving to God" (*In Praise of the Baal Shem Tov*, p. 129, #104).

53. *Toledot Ya'akov Yosef*, f. 183c; see A. J. Heschel, "R. Nahman of Kosof," *Jubilee Volume for H. Wolfson* (Jerusalem, 1965), p. 5, n. 4 (Hebrew).

54. Berakhot 63a.

55. Scholem, *Messianic Idea*, p. 206.

56. M. Buber, *The Origin and Meaning of Hasidism* (New York, 1960), pp. 98–99.

57. Ibid., p. 55.

58. *Ben Porat Yosef*, f. 64a.

59. M. Buber, *Hasidism and Modern Man* (New York, 1958), pp. 28–29. Gershom Scholem in *The Messianic Idea* (Schocken, N.Y., 1971, pp. 227–251), and Rivkah Shatz-Uffenheimer in *The Philosophy of Martin Buber* (Open Court, 1967, pp. 403–435), have questioned the validity of Buber's interpretation of Hasidism. They argued against Buber's understanding of "the service of God in corporeality" and "hallowing the everyday" which Buber found central to Hasidism. Scholem and Shatz-Uffenheimer pose the doctrine of *devekut* against this, the problem becoming, "to be in *devekut* with God all day long and still to

fulfill the obligations of flesh and blood on earth" (*Philosophy of Martin Buber*, p. 406). Buber, she argues, distorts the doctrine of "sparks," reducing it to an ethical theory, while the task of the Zaddikim was essentially gnostic; not "how to hallow the everyday" but how to return the world to its original state of "primordial creation," how "to turn 'being' into 'nothing' . . . which is true being. . . ." (ibid. p. 408) "Man's contact with creation which is an inescapable necessity, did, it is true in Hasidism, turn into an added ideal and a mission, a mission that demanded of man the nullification of creation and of the concrete as such. In this more than anything else, Hasidism demolished the locus of the 'dialogical' encounter which in Buber's eyes is the central concern of Hasidism, whereas in the sources its role is only that of the mystic point of transformation to 'nothing' " (op. cit., pp. 408, 409).

In the same volume Buber responds, arguing that there are several strands of thought in Hasidism, one Kabbalistic-gnostic represented by the Maggid, the other, in line with his own exposition, represented by the Besht (op. cit. 731–741 and *Commentary*, 1963, pp. 218–225.) "The way of spiritualization comes into Hasidism with its great thinker, the Maggid of Mezritch; the second way, the hallowing of all life, was introduced by his teacher, the Baal Shem Tov" (*Commentary*, p. 222).

The following passage, by R. Yosef Yizhak Shneirson, a successor to the throne of R. Shneur Zalman of Ladi, the founder of the Lubavitch dynasty, is presented as a tradition from the Besht, and would seem to lend support to Buber's view:

> "When you observe a donkey (*hamor*) belonging to your enemy prostrate under the weight of its burden and would refrain from helping him, you must nevertheless help him" (Exodus 23:5).
>
> *Exposition*
>   When you observe a *hamor*. That is, when you truly observe your body (*hamor* = "donkey" is related to *homer* = "matter" or here "body"), you will notice two things: first, that your body is "your enemy," that is, the enemy of your soul; for the soul yearns for spirituality while the body is attracted to earthiness. Second, you will notice that the body "is prostrate under the weight of its burden," that is, the burden which God has given the body to become purified through the study of Torah and the fulfillment of the mizvot. And since the body is too lazy to fulfill its responsibilities and is prostrate under the weight of its burden, it might occur to a God-fearing man to "refrain from helping him," that is, to refrain from helping the body fulfill the mission that God has laid upon it. Instead, you may prefer to heap affliction and deprivation, such as fasting, etc. upon the body, in order to break its crassness. Know that this is not the way to enable the light of Torah to dwell in the body; but only by understanding that "you must nevertheless help him," that is, to elevate and refine the body, but not to break it with self-imposed afflictions. (*Ha-Tamim*, vol. 8, 1938, p. 49; cf. *Keter Shem Tov*, Kehot, Brooklyn, 1972, *hosafa* p. 18; *Likuttei Sihos*, vol. 1, p. 32, vol. 7, p. 254.)

60. *Toledot Ya'akov Yosef*, f. 23a, b, c.

Two other passages from the *Toledot Ya'akov Yosef* should be noted:

> At first it was thought that serving the Lord meant only Torah-study, prayer, fasting, weeping, and the like. Consequently, anyone who did not conduct himself in

this manner provoked anger; [as with R. Shim'on bar Yohai who, departing from his cave and seeing people tilling the field instead of engaged in prayer or Torah-study, cried out:] "Lo, these people are forsaking eternal matters for things of the moment!" And anger brought such a spirit of wrath upon the world, that the heavenly voice proclaimed: "Return to your cave!" Then they understood that the purpose of this [heavenly voice] was to teach them a better way, the way of compassion, by which is meant, that one may serve the Lord through all one's deeds, if one understands that the Lord is there too . . . as I heard from my teacher [the Besht]. . . . To remove melancholy one should understand that anything can be a means for *yihud*. Even when one encounters something unpleasant in another or is deterred from Torah-study, he should know that this is for his benefit, as I have written, "Serve the Lord in all your ways" (Prov. 3:6). And it is as I have written, "I have set the Lord before me [*kenegdi*] at all times" (Ps. 16:18), that is, even when He seems "*against* me" [*kenegdi*]. It is then that "my heart rejoices" (Ps. 16:9), stirring up compassion and happiness in the world, for "even my flesh will find peace." (*Toledot Ya'akov Yosef*, f. 23b.)

It appears to me that I learned from my teachers and my friends that one should act compassionately with every man. Even when one observes something unpleasant in another, he should consider that there too is the Name of God; for there is no place void of God, and it may be for man's welfare that he experiences something unpleasant so that he himself might repent, as I have mentioned in the last section of my book, in the name of R. Nahman of Horodenka. For example, when one is interrupted from Torah or prayer by conversation or the like, he should consider that perhaps this is for his welfare; or if he does not pray or study with the proper spirit or does not have the proper *kavanah*, etc., he should understand that this may truly be for his own improvement, as it is written, "And I shall set the Lord before me at all times" (Ps. 16:18). For just as wheat grows out of ugly earth, so can good emerge. . . . And through this, compassion is stirred up in our world, and the Lord blesses it, as in the case of R. Shim'on bar Yohai and his son when they came forth from the cave the second time. For it is written, "And I shall set the Lord *against* me [*kenegdi*] (ibid.), "that is, even when there are those things which are "against me," preventing me from Torah and prayer, I should understand that this is ordained for my welfare. . . . Thus must one understand the verse of the Psalm (16:9), "And my heart rejoices," . . . for all . . . one's thoughts will be good if they flow from heartfelt joy. Thus is compassion stirred up in the world for the common man and for one's material needs, which are called "my flesh," as it is written, "even my flesh will dwell in peace . . ." (*Toledot Ya'akov Yosef*, f. 19b.)

61. *Toledot Ya'akov Yosef*, f. 203c.

R. Ya'akov Yosef brings an explanation of the Besht to the following passage from the Talmud: "One is obligated to drink on Purim until he can no longer distinguish between [the words] 'blessed is Mordecai' and [the words] 'cursed is Haman' " (Megilah 7b): "One is obligated to drink on Purim," that is, to rejoice the body, in order that the spirit might cleave to the Lord. Thus one [the body] becomes the throne for the other [the spirit], for through the physical act of eating and drinking man achieves spiritual *devekut*. In like manner did Haman become the throne for Mordecai . . . Until one can no longer distinguish between 'blessed is Mordecai' and 'cursed is Haman,' [that is, until] there is no difference any more between one [the body] and the other [the soul]. . . . as my master [the Besht] explained" (*Toledot Ya'akov Yosef*, f. 63b). Cf. *Toledot Ya'akov Yosef*, f. 63a.

62. R. Shatz, *Encyclopaedia Judaica*, vol. 7, col. 1492.

"Melancholy and physical needs prevent one from fulfilling the *mizvah* with joy. Therefore good counsel is found in the verse [dealing with the Sabbatical year]: 'then shall the earth have a release, and there shall be a Sabbath unto the Lord' (Lev. 25:2). That is, when the earthiness of the body has 'a release' through physical rejoicing, then is the soul able to rejoice. And this is 'a Sabbath unto the Lord'. For both [bodily and spiritual joy] are required to keep the Sabbath. As I have heard from my master [the Besht]" (*Toledot Ya'akov Yosef*, f. 119d).

63. Ben Amos and Mintz, *In Praise of the Baal Shem Tov*, p. 169, #146.

64. See Dresner, *The Zaddik*, p. 136.

An interesting sidelight is given by the veteran Zionist writer Yehuda Yaari, who observed that the extreme left-wing Hashomer Hatzair first acquired the name "kibbutz" from a Hasidic source.

> Our camp was called the corps (*gedud*) of *Hashomer Hatzair*. And the name "corps," even though we were used to it from the days of our youth in the movement, (where there were *kvutzot, gedudim*, and *plugot*), didn't work for us any more. During a discussion one of the members, who had just then returned from a trip to Jerusalem, got up and started to speak, not of the future, but of the past. He said that while in Jerusalem he had fallen in with a group of Bratzlaver Chassidim, and for him, their encounter had been a deep experience. He spoke enthusiastically because they were a kind of revelation for him. In Galicia, from which he came, nothing was known of this group. Only those of us who had read Martin Buber's book, *Seven Tales of Rabbi Nachman of Bratzlav*, knew about them, and he had not read Buber.
>
> He spent several days in their company. He related to us a story of honest and righteous people, who live on the modest earnings they derive from manual labor, about their conversations with him and with each other, and about the Rebbe's tales. At the end he said: The Bratzlaver Chassidim assemble regularly once a year at *Rosh Hashana* (New Year) for prayer, and for study of the books of their teacher, Rabbi Nachman of Bratzlav. Before the (First) World War, they used to assemble in the town Uman, which is in the Ukraine, where Rabbi Nachman is buried, and now they get together in Jerusalem, and in other places around the world. That gathering on New Year's Day, the Bratzlaver Chassidim call by the name "Kibbutz."
>
> "Why shouldn't we also call our camp *kibbutz?*" he asked.
>
> Our people decided to accept the suggestion of that *chaver*, and since then our camp was called, *Kibbutz Hashomer Hatzair*.
>
> And behold, wonder of wonders: before long all of the *chavurot, gedudim, plugot* and the big *kvutzot* changed their name to *kibbutz*.
>
> I have told this story both in order to publicize the origin of the name, and to demonstrate that there is a continuity in Jewish life, which doesn't always operate in the open. We would never have assumed that the name of the most magnificent creation of our generation in this century—the kibbutz—is derived from the treasure-store of the Bratzlaver Chassidim. (*Shdemot*, no. 9 [1978], p. 49–50.)

65. M. Buber, *Israel and the World*, "On National Education," p. 159; *At the Turning*, "The Silent Question," p. 43. *Israel and the World*, "On National Education," p. 159.

66. *Israel and the World*, "The Land and Its Possessors," pp. 229–30.

67. W. Herberg, *Buber* (New York: Meridian Books, 1956), pp. 35–36.

68. *In Praise of the Baal Shem Tov*, p. 65.

69. See Heschel, *Kotzk* (Tel Aviv, 1973), vol. 1, pp. 235–243. Two striking examples, brought by Heschel, illustrate this teaching: "Just as in sexual converse one can only beget if the male member is vital with joy and pleasure . . . so in

spiritual converse, the word of Torah and prayer must be vital with joy and pleasure in order to beget" (*Keter Shem Tov* [Zholkava, 1894], p. 4). "Prayer is converse with the *Shekhinah*. Just as at the beginning one moves and then halts, so when one begins to pray, he first sways and later stands quiet, cleaving to the *Shekhinah* in a deep embrace" (*Zeva'at ha-Rivash*, p. 20, #68).

Heschel points out, however, that Hasidism was by no means all of a piece in its approach to sexuality. In such figures as Rabbi Yaakov Yizhak of Psyshkha, Rabbi Nahman of Braslav, and Rabbi Mendel of Kotzk a different opinion prevailed. It was the custom among other Zaddikim for Hasidim to come for a Sabbath or holiday, remain a few days, and return home. In Kotzk, however, one stayed away from his home and wife for an entire year or longer. Especially did Rabbi Mendel urge young men to come just after marriage, so that by taking on sexual desire at its height, he could crush it once and for all and turn man's love to God alone. "Deprived of biological release, the body might weep, but the imagination would remain fresh and pure . . ." The Kotzker "demanded a discipline of continence . . . since the conquest of sexual drive alone can assure total commitment to spiritual pursuits. . . . Sensuality was the only powerful alternative to absolute religion" (Heschel, *Passion for Truth*, p. 220). Love for women, even one's own wife, he saw as removing something from love of God. The Kotzker prided himself on being able "to take a young man drowning in fleshly passion and so disgust him with it, that he would no longer hear of it, and if he did, would vomit up what he had already devoured." Another Hasidic figure argued that one should engage in sexual relations but not feel pleasure, otherwise a blessing would have been prescribed before this act just as it is before enjoying certain other pleasures of nature (*Kotzk*, pp. 243–248).

70. S. Dresner, *Rabbi Levi Yitzhak of Berditchev* (New York, 1974), pp. 148–149.

71. *Degel Mahaneh Efrayim* (Koretz 1810), f. 38a; *Toledot Ya'akov Yosef*, f. 84b; *Ketonet Passim* (Lvov, 1866), ff. 35a–b; quoted by Scholem, op. cit., pp. 186–189.

72. Scholem, *ibid.*

73. Buber, *Hasidism and Modern Man*, pp. 49–50.

SELECTED BIBLIOGRAPHY

In addition to the works cited in note 1, page 168:
Buber, Martin. *Hasidism and Modern Man*. New York: Harper and Row, 1966.
———. *Origin and Meaning of Hasidism*. New York: Horizon Press, 1972.
Dresner, Samuel. *The Zaddik*. Bridgeport: Hartmore House, 1974.
Jacobs, Louis. *Hasidic Prayer*. New York: Schocken, 1973.
Rabinowicz, Harry M. *The World of Hasidism*. Bridgeport: Hartmore House, 1970.

Conflicting Jewish Responses to Modernity

STEVEN BAYME

Yeshiva University

ALTHOUGH HISTORIANS past and present have differed as to the exact origins of Jewish modernity, the consensus is that the onset of modernity posed definite challenges to the existence and self-identity of the Jew. Modernity connoted the acceptance of Western categories as criteria by which Judaism could be evaluated. In this sense Benedict Spinoza weighed Judaism by the category of universal reason and found it wanting. Haskalah, as will be demonstrated, attempted to interpret Judaism by the standards of Western cultural norms. In other words the medieval Jew perceived himself as superior to the external culture. In contrast the modern Jewish temper demanded acceptance by the standards of the external culture and began to acknowledge the greatness of Gentile society.

Unquestionably certain medieval Jews, notably Maimonides, appreciated the value of secular learning. Yet modernity meant the collapse of the traditional medieval synthesis of faith and reason. Where Maimonides had supremacized faith over reason, modern culture demanded that reason evaluate items of faith. In this sense the European Enlightenment markedly differed from medieval rationalism much as the Jewish Haskalah deviated from the paths of medieval Jewish philosophy.[1]

For Ashkenazic Jews, modernity also meant a departure from the medieval educational curriculum. As will be seen, efforts were made to transform the medieval *heder* into an institution that emphasized both Judaic and secular instruction.

Finally, modernity brought the collapse of the traditional Jewish communal structure. Autonomy and corporate status disintegrated as emancipation came in stages to the various Jewish communities of Western Europe. The rise of modern nation-states meant that members of separate, private autonomous corporations such as the medieval Jewish community had to be either integrated into the nation-state body politic, i.e. as citizens, or expelled from the body politic altogether. In this sense the emancipation of the Jew became a necessity for the modern nation-state.[2]

These changes did not occur overnight. Their origins may be traced to the first stirrings of discussion regarding Jewish emancipation in the seventeenth century. For Sephardic Jewry many of these trends can be traced even earlier.[3] Yet the thrust of these changes challenged the very self-identity of the modern Jew. His dilemma became one of rationalizing his own continued separate existence in a world in which medieval religious differentiations had been blurred.

These challenges to Jewish identity spawned a variety of ideologies propounding change and adjustment in Jewish life. Perhaps the first such ideology was that of the Haskalah, or Jewish enlightenment. Haskalah, a word derived from the He-brew *hiph'il*, or causative form, aimed at both the introduction of secular culture into Jewish life and an effort to enlighten the Jews themselves. In other words, the Haskalah, as will be seen, con-stituted an effort to transform the Jews socially, culturally, and economically.

For example Naftali Herz Wessely (1725–1803), a Haskalah poet and biblical exegete, published in 1782 his *Divrei Shalom Ve'emet* in response to Joseph II's Edict of Toleration, which granted the Jews limited freedoms of occupation and residence.[4] Wessely's pamphlet advocated educational reform in the Jewish schools. The author perceived the dispersion as an opportunity rather than a punishment and urged the Jews to abandon national redemptive hopes and instead to participate fully in the modern culture. Such participation necessitated fundamental changes in Jewish education. A graded curriculum and greater emphasis upon secular and extratalmudic content would mark a significant departure from the traditional *heder* program. For Wessely, secular education, or *Torat Ha-Adam*, chronologically preceded the Torah of God and assumed the stature of a religious command.[5]

Wessely's pamphlet by no means comprised the entire thrust of the Haskalah. The movement contained different intellectual currents and varied according to both geography and chronology. In Western Europe the Haskalah of Moses Mendelssohn and the *Meassefim*, the group of Mendelssohn's disciples who published the educational and literary journal of the Haskalah, was generally quite conservative. In Eastern Europe, where Enlightenment was to arrive a half-century later, the Haskalah became less religiously oriented and more overtly polemical against the established Orthodoxy.

These differences in both tone and content can be explained in terms of varying social contexts. In Western Europe Jewry received emancipation on the condition that the Jews become men of enlightenment. The Haskalah originated as an ideology for change within the Jewish world and for Jewry's acceptance within the Gentile environment. The conditional grant of emancipation to the "enlightened" Jew created new options of Jewish identity for acculturated Jewish intellectuals. Such individuals now sought to encounter the Gentile upon territory in which religion constituted a negligible difference between them. In such a context Moses Mendelssohn, the "exception Jew" par excellence, attempted to interpret Judaism for enlightenment circles.[6]

This grant of emancipation followed a general secularization of society. The modern capitalist economy, with its stress on individual wealth and worldliness, permitted the Jew to be evaluated as an individual rather than as a member of a group. Even more importantly, the modern nation-state simply could not allow private corporations, e.g. the Jewish *kehillah*, to remain as a "state within a state" and thereby attenuate the centralized nation-state. Finally, the emerging secular culture, with its emphasis upon universal reason, theoretically held little room for religious bigotry and intolerance.

Yet this very grant of emancipation posed new problems of Jewish identity and continued existence. Jewish identity as defined by membership in the community was now placed upon a voluntaristic basis. The very continuation of communal group life was questioned by the proponents of emancipation. Similarly the challenge of modern secularism and its attacks upon religious culture extended to modern Judaism and questioned the necessity for continued religious differentiation between Jew and Christian.[7]

Internal changes paralleled the threats to Jewish identity from without. Rabbinic authority, the traditional power center of Jewry, began to wane. Accusations of closet Sabbetianism, reciprocal bans of excommunication, and widespread envy of rabbinical positions, culminating in the infamous Emden-Eybeschuetz controversy of the 1750s, all contributed to a general decline of prestige for the organized rabbinate. In such a context, advocates of changes within Jewish life that necessitated diminished rabbinic authority found a ready audience.[8]

The world-view of Moses Mendelssohn, most renowned of the Western *Maskilim*, may be understood as a response to these challenges to Jewish identity. In general Mendelssohn's theories epitomized the ideology of the Haskalah in the West. For Mendelssohn Judaism equaled the religion of pure reason. Whereas Christianity demanded belief in irrational doctrines, e.g. Incarnation, Virgin Birth, and Resurrection, Judaism allegedly knew of no dogmas. The truths of Judaism consisted of purely rational propositions discoverable by anyone who reflected upon religious matters. Revelation for the Jew consisted of a corpus of legislation binding upon every Jew as a member of God's Chosen People. Philosophically Judaism stood united with rational religion. The two differed solely in the realm of religious ritual.

The validity of Mendelssohn's position depends upon the definition of dogma. Obviously belief in the revelation of law constituted belief in a truth accessible only through faith. Moreover, the very concept of a Chosen People defied rational analysis. Similarly Mendelssohn's explanation of miracles as a realm of physical fact, i.e. events which historically occurred, yet upon which the truths of religion do not depend, failed to satisfy the test of reason.

Yet Mendelssohn did not regard these areas as "dogmas" in the salvational sense. He argued, following Joseph Albo, the fifteenth-century Spanish-Jewish philosopher and communal leader, that Judaism contains many truths, which the individual ought to accept, yet one's personal salvation does not depend upon belief in such doctrines. In that sense Mendelssohn portrayed Judaism as less "dogmatic" than Christianity. This reading of Judaism certainly approximated the standard of rational religion first adumbrated by Tillotson and Locke.[9]

Mendelssohn's somewhat questionable formulation of Judaism did not comprise the core of his significance. Rather he contributed primarily toward the formulation of a defensive Jewish ideology. The presuppositions of a modern culture questioned the necessity for continued Jewish separateness. Challenged by the question of the compatibility of Judaism and its legalistic system with a modern system of democracy, Mendelssohn responded in *Jerusalem* that the two were indeed compatible.

The problem of compatibility had been first raised in the seventeenth century by Benedict Spinoza. In his *Theological-Political Treatise*, the Dutch-Jewish philosopher portrayed Judaism as a system of law applicable solely to a political nation-state. The implication for Spinoza was clear. Judaism and modernity could not coexist, and therefore Jewry constituted an anachronism in the modern world.[10]

Ironically the ultra-Orthodox Moses Sofer, better known as the Hatam Sofer, adopted a similar line of reasoning in the nineteenth century. Sofer agreed that Judaism and modernity were in mutual contradiction. In consequence he and his community waged bitter war against modernism on the slogan "*Hadash 'asur min ha-Torah*" ("Innovations are prohibited scripturally").[11]

Mendelssohn attempted to refute these assumptions. The very title of *Jerusalem* signified that the holiest Jewish city continued to symbolize the eternality of Judaism and traditional observance even though the city itself had lost its earthly splendor and political power.

The analysis of Jerusalem as a spiritual force rather than a political power lay at the base of Mendelssohn's philosophical originality. For reasons totally alien to the thought of Montesquieu and Jefferson, Mendelssohn advocated separation of church and state. The political Jerusalem had been historically unique; the spiritual Jerusalem continued as a religious model more rational and inspiring than that of Christianity. In other words, whereas Christianity possessed dogmas and potentially idolatrous symbols, Judaism knew of no dogmas and possessed only *mizvot*, i.e. commands to action.

This social theory rested upon a somewhat odd reading of history. For Mendelssohn, as for Hobbes and Locke, the State of Nature had evolved into a social contract. The terms of that social contract, however, dictated that men had duties to the state but none to the church. The church could advise and teach but possessed no compulsive power. Similarly the Jewish institution of the *herem*, or ban of excommunication, constituted at best an anachronism and at worst a fundamental infringement upon the political rights of freedom of expression. Moreover, by denying the individual religious instruction to remedy his disbelief, excommunication would be religiously incorrect.

Mendelssohn's desire to abolish the *herem* must be understood within an historical context. Generally his political theory was quietist. He believed, following Leibniz, that whatever unfolded represented the divine will and should therefore be accepted. Men ought to attempt little by themselves although certain modest steps might be taken. Mendelssohn here took such a modest step. He pleaded for full equality and emancipation for the Jews. Whereas earlier *shtadlanim*, or court Jews, e.g. Menasseh ben Israel, had requested tolerance for the Jews, Mendelssohn demanded full emancipation.

Yet Mendelssohn realized that emancipation carried a heavy price. Wilhelm Döhm, who had earlier argued for improvement in Jewish civil status at Mendelssohn's bequest, had urged temporary retention of the *herem* until the Jews fully entered general culture. Mendelssohn wished immediate entry. The secular authorities clearly did not desire the retention of corporate powers or a "state within a state." Therefore although Mendelssohn did advocate the retention of certain Jewish courts, the *herem* had to be rejected.

In most other respects Mendelssohn remained remarkably conservative in his call for change within the Jewish community. Medieval Jewish philosophy had already portrayed Judaism as essentially rationalist, and the aforementioned Joseph Albo had reduced the number of dogmas within Judaism to three. Although disagreeing on the presence of any dogmas within Judaism, Mendelssohn perceived himself as the heir of Maimonides, one who straddled both the world of Judaism and that of secular culture, wishing to introduce general trends into Jewish life.[12]

In sharp contrast with Mendelssohn's Western version of Haskalah stood the later East European wing of the Jewish enlightenment, epitomized by men such as Abraham Mapu, Isaac Erter, and Joseph Perl.[13] Where Mendelssohn had defended traditional Judaism, these Eastern *maskilim* bitterly attacked the rabbinical establishment for its conservatism and obscurantism. For example, Mapu, the father of the modern Hebrew novel, utilized the medium of historical fiction to mock the bosses of the contemporary Russian *kahal*. By romanticizing biblical heroes as *maskilim*, Mapu characterized the younger intellectuals of his own day as giants towering above the contemporary rabbis of Eastern Europe. Allied authors singled out Hasidism for abuse. *Maskilim* such as Erter and Perl utilized the short story for satirizing the alleged primitivism and backwardness of Hasidim in Eastern Europe.

Yehuda Leib Gordon, pioneer of modern Hebrew poetry, epitomized the polemical thrust of the East Europeah Haskalah. Moreover, Gordon represented the shift in the mood of Haskalah from one of optimism to one of despair. Gordon had hoped to implement Haskalah education through government-sponsored schools. Yet as the dean of such an institution, he quickly encountered opposition and even persecution. As a means of counterattack, Gordon turned to poetry. In one of his most famous poems, Gordon ridiculed rabbinical divorce procedures by illustrating how an incomplete *yod* in a bill of divorce could result in the tragedy of an *agunah*, a woman forbidden from remarrying because her former husband could not be found.[14] Like Mapu, Gordon turned to history as a medium for expressing contemporary social criticism. In discussing the rebellion against Rome, Gordon mocked the rabbis for failing to fulfill the injunction of "teach the sons of Judah the martial arts." On the contrary the rabbis of Roman times had been too preoccupied with the minutiae of halakhic discourse to confront pragmatic questions of self-defense. Prophetic political theory suffered the same abuse. Gordon's Jeremiah personified a defeatist who consistently counseled quietistic surrender rather than self-defense.[15]

The historical portraits may not be taken uncritically. Modern research points to the full participation in the Great Revolt against Rome on the part of most Pharisaic teachers. Rabbi Yoḥanan ben Zakkai at most represented a minority view among the rabbis. Moreover Gordon obscured the political wisdom inherent in the approaches of Jeremiah and Yoḥanan ben Zakkai. To suggest that the Jews make peace with ancient empires rather than continue to fight on to the last man may well have been prudence rather than defeatism. In the final analysis the political theory of Yavneh triumphed over that of Jerusalem.[16]

Distortion of historical fact results, for Gordon, in distortion of contemporary reality. Behind the poems lay a critique of the rabbis for failure to organize Jewish self-defense units against the Russian *pogromchiks*. Gordon rightly despaired of the failure to resist, a despair that permeated the entire Russian-Jewish community and led to organized self-defense, primarily by the Bund, during the next round of pogroms in 1904–1905, seven years following Gordon's death. Yet one must question whether the rabbis were solely to blame for this failure.

Jewish revolutionaries, eager to minimize the divergence between themselves and their colleagues in the revolutionary movement, some of whom greeted the outbreaks as healthy albeit unfortunate indications that the Russian peasants had begun to concentrate upon their real social and economic difficulties, similarly muted their responses to the pogroms or minimized their anti-Jewish aspects. One could hardly expect a stranger rendition of the phrase "Anti-semitism is the socialism of fools."[17]

To replace traditional rabbinism Gordon advocated numerous reforms within Jewish life. He urged that the Jew learn Russian and love the Gentile in the hope that Jew and Russian would socialize one with another. In the economic sphere Gordon urged that the Jews abandon mercantile occupations for "productive" labor. In particular farming appealed to him. Much as Tolstoy had idealized man's attachments to the soil, so Gordon extolled farming as that occupation which would root the Jew in soil and nature as well as solidify the Jewish presence in Russia. Politically the Jew ought to demonstrate his civic virtue through service in the army and prompt payment of taxes. Finally the Jew ought to relegate religious distinctiveness to his home life and become indistinguishable from the Gentile in public.[18]

Certain common themes permeated the writings of Mendelssohn and Gordon. In particular they both stressed the virtues of good citizenship. However, the differences in terms of Gordon's satirical and anti-Orthodox style and rhetoric outweighed these similarities. Such variations must be understood as consequences of the differing social context in which East European Haskalah flourished. Although the questions of emancipation in Eastern Europe resembled those of Western Europe, the order of prospective change was reversed. In other words, emancipation in Eastern Europe meant that the Jews would first have to transform themselves, and only then would they receive their civic rights. Consequently East European *maskilim*, as proponents of change, bitterly attacked the Orthodox, who resisted such change on the grounds that it would ultimately mean the disappearance of the Jew. Haskalah polemics and sharp-edged satire only reflected the bitterness of the underlying struggle for control of the dynamics of the Jewish community.

These differing ideologies varied greatly in the degree of their successes. In Western Europe the Haskalah generally recorded success. Jewry attained complete emancipation by the mid-nineteenth century, and virtually every country established a non-sectarian school system in which Jews participated. The Western Jew, whether Orthodox or assimilationist, reflected the impact of modern culture.

As a consequence the traditional communal or *kehillah* structure of medieval Jewry disintegrated. Although the processes of decline of the *kehillah* had antedated the development of Haskalah, e.g. through the rise of Hasidic communities,[19] Haskalah itself functioned as an ideology for change in Jewish communal organization. The *maskilim* attacked rabbinical authority in general and the institution of the *herem* in particular. At least one historian has noted their class orientation as spokesmen of the rising Jewish middle classes and thus in opposition to the aristocratic leaders of the *kehillah*.[20] Through their emphasis on the Bible, e.g. in the curriculum of the Haskalah *Freischule* at Berlin, Hinukh Nearim, the *maskilim* implicitly attacked the Talmud, whose values formed the crux of rabbinic Judaism.[21] The postemancipation Jew no longer viewed his life-style as sharply restricted by synagogal legislation.

In contrast, Haskalah in Eastern Europe failed on most counts. Acts of apparent enlightenment and liberalism, e.g. the Crown School system, which promised Jewry secular education but in actuality furthered conversionist purposes, only masked far more reactionary policies.[22] So long as the Czar remained in power, Russian Jewry never attained the grant of political emancipation. On the contrary, the false dawn of enlightenment quickly gave way to the onset of terrible pogroms. By the close of the nineteenth century, Haskalah in Russia had virtually expired. The Russian-Jewish youth and intelligentsia had generally drifted into alternative movements, such as Zionism and the revolutionary Left, or had abandoned Russia for the more liberal shores of America. These alternatives signified an exasperation with remaking Russian Jewry internally. Only fundamental changes in Russian society could make Haskalah viable. Rooted in the assumption that Russia could evolve peacefully into a modern constitutional and democratic state, Haskalah waned as the revolutionary movement strengthened. Even Y. L. Gordon himself questioned to whom he might address his poems if the best of the youth had already chosen the path of revolution over that of reform.[23]

Yet Haskalah—both in Western and in Eastern Europe— created certain changes in Jewish life. Certainly a new attitude toward the value of secular learning developed. Even the traditonalist camp of the Gaon of Vilna to some extent incorporated the new intellectual currents.[24] Similarly the rabbinic *ḥeder* gave way to the new broadly-based curriculum envisioned by the *maskilim*.

These changes did not come easily. Tensions between the *maskilim* and the defenders of the status quo often erupted into full-scale warfare. Similarly the Hasidim, right-wing critics of the established Orthodoxy, soon joined forces with their erstwhile opponents to combat the new currents of Enlightenment. As Kabbalists the Hasidim defended the irrational and the mythic against the strictures of rationalism. Moreover, they criticized the Mendelssohnian conception of a purely transcendental deity. Such a Deity could never satisfy the religious needs of the common people, who needed to sense God in the here and now. Clearly the Hasidic emphasis upon an immanent deity who permeates this world directly contradicted the deity Mendelssohn portrayed.

The *mitnagdim* also opposed the new currents of enlightenment and secularization. In their eyes the *maskilim* were at best naive and at worst destructive. Although the *maskilim* had hoped for an alliance with the *mitnagdim* against the Hasidim, the rise of Haskalah and its arrival in Eastern Europe signaled the close of the Hasidic-mitnagdic rivalry and the forging of new bonds between Hasidim and *mitnagdim*. Thus, Haskalah, through its attacks against Orthodoxy, ironically helped repair a major rift within the Orthodox camp.

In particular the *mitnagdim* opposed emancipation and defended rabbinic education. Perhaps their greatest victory lay in their opposition to the Crown Schools, theoretically institutions of Enlightenment and therefore enthusiastically supported by the maskilim, but in reality conversionist agencies. The naivete of the *maskilim* in their unqualified enthusiasm for the Czarist-backed project confirmed the *mitnagdim's* suspicions of the new currents.

These conflicts between the *maskilim* and their opponents frequently assumed ugly forms. Bans were issued against the reading of Haskalah literature and occasional book-burnings occurred. At times the secular government received requests for intervention and responded by censoring a number of works of the Haskalah.[25]

In Western Europe the mitnagdic rabbis were more restrained in their opposition to Haskalah, and some even agreed on the desirability of emancipation. Yet Haskalah and its ideals struck a sensitive chord. Mendelssohn's expressed wish for an end to the use of the *ḥerem* implied the surrender of traditional rabbinic authority. Wessely's educational reforms aroused a storm of controversy although the proposals for secular education and a graded curriculum were not terribly far removed from the desires of the renowned Gaon of Vilna. Yet whereas Wessely's earlier works had received wide-ranging *haskamot*,[26] or approvals, his pamphlet on education seemed so widely at variance with contemporary practice that his erstwhile friends among the rabbis were the quickest to attack his theories.

Fortunately such conflicts eventually subsided. Even Wessely ultimately regained the approval of the rabbinic world. In this sense West European Haskalah could succeed as even the rabbis became enamored of emancipation. Secular education became a desirable endeavor for most Western Jews.

In a wider scope Haskalah signified another in a series of periods in Jewish intellectual history in which Jewish thought and culture partially integrated with general culture. Obviously the political condition of Jewry had to stabilize as a prerequisite for such integration to take place. Yet given a period of tranquility in Jewish-Gentile relations, Haskalah could and did interact with the European Enlightenment. Haskalah shared the Enlightenment's desire to create a religion devoid of superstition and solidly rooted in principles accessible through reason alone. Little differentiated Mendelssohn's religion of reason from that of Tillotson or Locke. Similarly the *maskilim* shared the general veneration of the Bible common to Herder and Lessing.

Yet the Haskalah never endorsed the openly anti-religious polemic of Voltaire and Bayle. For the *philosophes*, organized religion remained the stronghold of superstition and even immorality. Mendelssohn and the early *maskilim* argued that Judaism as it existed equaled the religion of reason. Thus Solomon Maimon defended even the Talmud against those who argued that it consisted of the Jewish equivalent to *l'infâme*. In this respect the Haskalah approximated the German Enlightenment in contrast to the openly anti-religious French Enlightenment.[27]

In other words the *maskilim* were also apologists for Judaism to the world of Enlightenment. Yet their apologetics frequently had deleterious effects. The *maskilim* created an image of Judaism as a compilation of rational and universal truths coupled with a corpus of legislation mysteriously commanded to the Jews alone. Liberal Protestant circles, particularly Kant, Hegel, Schleiermacher, and Harnack, quickly caricatured contemporary Judaism in the original language of the Gospels. Borrowing the Mendelssohnian image of Judaism, these men understood Judaism as strictly legalistic and devoid of mysticism. Jesus for them represented the reformer who wished to restore ethical autonomy into a religion badly encumbered by a list of do's and don'ts.[28]

In assessing the impact of Haskalah on modern Jewish history, both a positive and a negative legacy emerge. Certainly the Haskalah signified the revival of the Hebrew language and the renaissance of Hebrew literature.[29] Moreover the new relationship to secular culture captured the hearts of all but the most extreme elements within Jewish life. Finally the spirit of rebellion against rabbinic and *kehillah* authority did produce positive changes in the social, communal, and economic structures of nineteenth-century European Jewry.[30]

Yet these accomplishments must be weighed in conjunction with the negative side-effects of the Haskalah's legacy. Undoubtedly many quickly leaped from Haskalah to total assimilation. David Friedlander in Germany, a disciple of Mendelssohn, contemplated total conversion to Christianity upon deistic principles until rebuffed by a more devout Lutheran pastor.[31] Similarly Y. L. Gordon bewailed the nearly complete assimilation of Russian-Jewish youth so that few still bothered to read his Hebrew poems.[32] In other words, the assimilatory motif in the sense of a desire to join the modern world, common to both West European and East European Haskalah, succeeded in weaning many completely away from any semblance of Jewish identity or wish for Jewish survival. Occasionally this process could even evolve into Jewish self-hatred.[33]

Moreover Haskalah polemics shattered the cohesiveness of European Jewry. The critiques of the Talmud, the Polish *melamdim*, the *kehillah* leadership, and Hasidism all signified the creation of rigid barriers between the enlightened West Europeans and the seemingly backward *Ostjuden*. German Jewry's rediscovery of the *Ostjuden* during World War I indicated how a century of polemical battles had in reality created two separate Jewries with few bridges between them.[34]

Finally, the religion of reason preached by the *maskilim* could not ensure the survival of Judaism. Ultimately rationalist theology failed to convey much meaning to men in need of faith. The religion of reason suited an age of optimism and hope in a better world. The resurgence of modern anti-Semitism and the rise of global warfare shattered this optimistic reading of history and evoked "theologies of crisis" with much more personal and demanding forms.

In this respect, perhaps the greatest failure of the Haskalah was that it quickly became outdated. One might go further and suggest that other modern Jewish ideologies similarly fell "behind the times." Much as Jewish Enlightenment arose in the final stages of the general European Enlightenment, so the Jewish Kantianism of Hermann Cohen and Leo Baeck arose only during the final stages of Kant's sway over European philosophy. More tellingly the modern political Zionism of Pinsker and Herzl postdated the heyday of European nationalism.

In effect Haskalah represented an early effort by the Jews to join modernity. Subsequent ideologies, e.g. religious movements, *Wissenschaft des Judentums*, and political Zionism, similarly represented attempts by the Jews to integrate themselves into the idiom of the modern world. In the case of the latter, the Haskalah's program for the economic regeneration of Jewry was co-opted and transformed in locale from Eastern Europe to Palestine. In this sense the Haskalah did not influence these ideologies directly but rather initiated such an effort and set the groundwork for subsequent attempts to define the identity of the Jew in the modern world.

In particular the Haskalah failed to exert a direct influence upon *Wissenschaft des Judentums*, a movement to initiate the academic study of Jews and Judaism. The *maskilim* wrote biographies of great personalities in Jewish history whom they envisioned as role-models and proto-*maskilim*. For them, history served to edify and inspire its student. The men of *Wissenschaft* attempted something far different. They wished to integrate the study of Jewish

history into general history and to legitimize Jewish scholarship
as respectable academic work. For them the act of scholarship
itself became the medium of expressing Jewish identity and translating Jewish culture to the outside world rather than a search for
historical role-models and edification.[35]

The connection between Haskalah and modern Zionism was
perhaps more direct. Certainly the Zionists co-opted many of the
themes of the Haskalah, e.g. the use of Hebrew, the need for
productive labor, particularly farming, and the development of a
Jewish identity built upon the acceptance of secular norms and
criteria of evaluation.[36] More important, Zionism arose only after
emancipation had failed to solve the problem of anti-Semitism. As
a result Pinsker entitled his work *Auto-Emancipation*, namely that
the Jews must now emancipate themselves through normalizing
themselves as a people.[37] In other words the ideology of the
Haskalah pointed to the need for changes in Jewish life. If those
changes could not be secured in the Gentile world, i.e. through
emancipation, then they had to be secured elsewhere, e.g. Palestine. In this sense Y. L. Gordon, as noted earlier, symbolized the
shift in the mood of Haskalah from one of optimism that the
necessary changes might be secured in the Gentile world to one of
despair and disappointment in Gentile society. Political Zionism
arose on the base of such despair and disappointment.

More generally, study of the Haskalah suggests certain thoughts
concerning the general significance of ideological conflicts in
modern Jewish history. Ideological conflicts, whether between
maskilim and Hasidim, reformers and Orthodox, or Zionists and
anti-Zionists, shared a universal preoccupation with the problem
of modern Jewish identity. Ideological content often became the
central component of Jewish identity. For example, the commitment to *Jewish* scholarship at times became the medium for expressing Jewish identity for the practitioners of *Wissenschaft des Judentums*. Similarly the conflicts of the *maskilim* centred around the
question of the Jew's relationship to the culture of the Enlightenment. For Mendelssohn and Wessely, Jewish identity necessitated
immersion into the general culture. Their opponents, particularly
in Eastern Europe, feared that the general culture negated Jewish

identity. Yet both sides shared a commitment to continued Jewish presence and identity.

In this sense one can appreciate the reasons for the vigor with which the conflict was waged. The ideological protagonists and antagonists were not merely splitting hairs over fine points of theory. Their real question was the forms which Jewish identity would assume after undergoing (or in some cases without undergoing) the experience of modernity. The very future of Jewish civilization seemingly rested upon the outcome of the ideological polemic.

The immediate outcome, of course, did not have such far-reaching effects. Modern Jewish history has witnessed the emergence of pluralistic forms of Jewish identity. In that sense modern Jewish ideologies and the conflicts between them helped create the pluralism that is the hallmark of Jewish identity today.

The legacy of ideological conflict in modern Jewish history does not point to the victory of any particular ideology. Rather the various ideologies themselves suggest variant formulations of modern Jewish identity. Haskalah and the conflict it engendered constituted ideological expressions of those differing and pluralistic formulations.

NOTES

1. Carl Becker has attempted to demonstrate continuity between thirteenth-century medieval rationalism and the eighteenth-century Enlightenment. See his *The Heavenly City of the Eighteenth-Century Philosophers* (New Haven: Yale University Press, 1932), passim. This view has been refuted conclusively by Peter Gay, *The Party of Humanity* (New York: North Books, 1971), pp. 188–210. See also idem, *The Enlightenment: An Interpretation*, vol. 1, *The Rise of Modern Paganism* (New York: Vintage Books, 1967), passim. Gay argues that the Enlightenment was an age of criticism, a spirit of critical reasoning rather than rational thought developed on the basis of authoritative scripture, which had characterized medieval rationalism. A similar distinction can be drawn between the rationalism of Saadia and the critical analysis of Spinoza. The *maskilim* generally rejected the critical spirit in terms of the Bible, but they certainly subjected Jewish life, thought, and institutions to critical analysis.

2. Salo W. Baron, *A Social and Religious History of the Jews*, (New York: Columbia University Press, 1937), vol. II, pp. 224–229.

3. Frances Malino, *The Sephardic Jews of Bordeaux* (University, Ala.: University of Alabama Press, 1978), p. 25. Yosef Yerushalmi detected similar trends among

the Marrano population during its reentry into the Jewish world. See his *From Spanish Court to Italian Ghetto* (New York: Columbia University Press, 1971), pp. 44–50, and more generally throughout the biography.

4. For the terms of the edict, see Rapheal Mahler, *A History of Modern Jewry, 1780–1815* (New York: Schocken Books, 1971), pp. 253–255. Although the edict did grant the Jews entry into a variety of professions heretofore restricted, special taxation on Jews remained, and numerous clauses restricted their actual entry into many of these professions. Moreover, the Jews, as will be seen, were now required to either enter the general school system or build such schools for themselves.

5. Naftali Herz Wessely, "Words of Peace and Truth," *Various Letters* (Hebrew), (Vienna: Anton Edlin Schmid, 1827), chap. 1. The term *Torat Ha-adam* has been variously interpreted as secular education, natural religion, and natural law. By all accounts, however, it is clear that Wessely placed the learning of *Torat Ha-adam* as prior to the learning of the Torah of God in terms of educational sequence. See Moshe Pelli, "The Impact of Deism on the Hebrew Literature of the Enlightenment in Germany," *Eighteenth-Century Studies*, VI (1972), pp. 51–52.

6. Jacob Katz first developed this them in a number of studies. See his *Exclusiveness and Tolerance* (New York: Schocken Books, 1962), chap. 24; idem, *Tradition and Crisis* (New York: Schocken Books, 1971), p. 255, and most recently idem, *Out of the Ghetto* (Cambridge: Harvard University Press, 1973), chap. 4, wherein he modified the term to "semineutral society."

7. Salo W. Baron, "Modern Capitalism and Jewish Fate," reprinted in Baron, *History and Jewish Historians* (Philadelphia: Jewish Publication Society, 1964), pp. 52–56.

8. See in general the final chapters of Katz, *Tradition and Crisis*. In 1751 Jacob Emden accused Jonathan Eybeschuetz of closet Sabbetianism, an accusation which shook the entire communal establishment of Central European Jewry as it initiated a bitter controversy between the partisans of both sides. See Gershom Scholem, *Kabbalah* (New York: Quadrangle Books, 1974), pp. 405–408, and bibliography cited therein.

9. Moshe Pelli correctly drew the distinctions between Mendelssohn's theology and that of the Deists, which rejected historical revelation. See Pelli, pp. 45–51. For the distinctions between Deism and rational religion, e.g. the theologies of Locke and Tillotson, see Peter Gay, ed., *Deism: An Anthology* (Princeton: D. Van Nostrand Co., 1968), pp. 25–26, 52–53.

10. See *Works of Spinoza*, trans. R. A. Elwes (New York: Dover Publications, 1951), p. 195. Julius Guttmann suggested that Mendelssohn, in *Jerusalem*, was replying virtually directly to Spinoza's political theory and its challenge to Judaism. See Guttmann, "Yerushalayim le-Mendelsohnn veha-masekhet ha-teologit ha-medinit le-Spinoza," *Dat U-Mada'* (Jerusalem: Magnes Press, 1965), pp. 192–195.

11. The Hatam Sofer opposed Mendelssohn specifically on the grounds that reason could not be utilized to evaluate Judaism. See Jacob Katz, "Kavim La-Biographia shel Hatam Sofer," in E. E. Urbach, ed., *Studies in Mysticism and Religion Presented to Gershom Scholem* (Jerusalem: Magnes Press, 1967), Hebrew sec., pp. 140–142.

12. The best study of Mendelssohn is the recent comprehensive biography by Alexander Altmann, *Moses Mendelssohn: A Biographical Study* (Philadelphia: Jewish Publication Society, 1973), which brilliantly places Mendelssohn within the context of the German Enlightenment. On the imagery of Mendelssohn as a second Maimonides, see James Lehmann, "Maimonides, Mendelssohn and the Me'asfim: Philosophy and the Biographical Imagination of the Early Haskalah," *LBIYB*, 1976, pp. 87–94.

13. Abraham Mapu (1808–1867) was best known for his historical novels, especially *'Ahavat Ziyyon* and *'Ayit Zavu'a*. See David Patterson, *Abraham Mapu* (London: East and West Library, 1964). Isaac Erter (1791–1851) was known especially *'Ahavat Ziyyon* and *'Ayit Zavu'a*. See David Patterson, *Abraham Mapu* (London: East and West Library, 1964). Isaac Erter (1791–1851) was known primarily as a satirist, especially in his book *Ha-Zofeh Le-Veit Yisrael*. He also participated in the founding of *He-Haluz*, a Hebrew periodical dedicated to religious reform. Joseph Perl (1773–1839), a Galician *maskil*, was most famous for his satires against Hasidism, especially in his *Megaleh Temirin*.

14. See Y. L. Gordon, "Kozo shel Yud," *Writings* (Tel-Aviv: Dvir, 1959), pp. 129–140.

15. "Zedkiyahu Be-veit Ha-Pequdot," ibid., pp. 98–101, on Jeremiah. See also "Bein Shetei Ariot," ibid., pp. 103–107, for the critique of the rabbis for failure to teach self-defense against the Roman Empire.

16. On the victory of the political theory of Yohanan ben Zakkai over that of Masada, see the stimulating essay by Ismar Schorsch, "On the Political Judgement of the Jew," *Leo Baeck Memorial Lecture*, 1977, pp. 9–10.

17. Robert Wistrich, *Revolutionary Jews from Marx to Trotsky* (New York: Harper & Row, 1976), pp. 12–13. See also ibid., pp. 85–86, for a comparison with the very similar reaction of Rosa Luxemburg to later pogroms. See also Lucy Dawidowicz, ed., *The Golden Tradition* (Boston: Beacon Press, 1967), pp. 405–411, and Salo W. Baron, *The Russian Jew under Tsars and Soviets*, 2d ed. (New York: Macmillan Co., 1976), pp. 138–139.

18. Gordon, "Ha-Qizah Ami," *Writings*, p. 17.

19. See the final chapter of Katz, *Tradition and Crisis*.

20. Mahler, p. 228, and more generally chap. 13.

21. Ibid., pp. 224–225.

22. In 1844 the Russian government offered the Jews the right to set up their own schools in which both religious and secular subjects would be taught with Jewish teachers responsible for instruction in religion. Dr. Max Lilienthal, a young German Jew, was imported to direct the project. Although the *maskilim* eagerly supported the project, it failed because the Orthodox remained suspicious. In reality Lilienthal soon recognized that the project was indeed conversionist in intent and abandoned Russia for America. See Louis Greenberg, *The Jews in Russia* (New York: Schocken Books, 1976), I, pp. 33–37.

23. Gordon, "Le-Mi Ani 'Amel," *Writings*, p. 27.

24. Mahler, pp. 540–543.

25. See Moshe Carmilly-Weinberger, *Censorship in Jewish History* (New York: Hermon Press, 1977), pp. 111, 117–122. See also Greenberg, I, pp. 28, 67.

26. See Altmann, pp. 356–357, on the *haskamot* given Wessely.

27. Altmann in particular, as noted above, placed Mendelssohn within the context of the German Enlightenment. See especially pp. 25–50 and more

generally throughout the work. See also ibid., pp. 477–487, for the controversy over Wessely. On the anti-Judaism and anti-Semitism of the French Enlightenment, see Arthur Hertzberg, *The French Enlightenment and the Jews* (New York: Schocken Books, 1970), especially chap. 9.

28. On Kant and Hegel's image of Judaism, see Nathan Rotenstreich, *The Recurring Pattern* (New York: Horizon Books, 1964), and more recently Emil Fackenheim, *Encounters Between Judaism and Modern Philosophy* (Philadelphia: Jewish Publication Society, 1973). On Harnack, see his *What Is Christianity?* (New York: Harper & Row, 1957), pp. 47–48, 91–92, 103. On Schleiermacher, see Michael Meyer, *Origins of the Modern Jew* (Detroit: Wayne State University Press, 1967), pp. 104–105.

29. Shalom Spiegel, *Hebrew Reborn* (Philadelphia: Jewish Publication Society, 1962), pp. 20–24. Spiegel suggests that the Haskalah's role in the revival of Hebrew was an unintentional one.

30. Obviously here the Haskalah may not be taken out of context. It is closely interconnected with a wide variety of political, social, economic, and cultural factors, which taken together transformed the modern Jewish community. Certainly one might ascribe to the Haskalah the role of ideological social protest.

31. See Mahler, pp. 207–209, Altmann, pp. 350–352, and the full chapter on Friedlander in Meyer, *Origins of the Modern Jew.*

32. Gordon, "Le-Mi Ani 'Amel," *Writings,* p. 27.

33. Perhaps the most telling example is that of Karl Marx, especially in his "On the Jewish Question," reprinted in Ellis Rivkin, ed., *Readings in Modern Jewish History* (Cincinnati, Hebrew Union College, 1957), a work which has attracted great attention. See in particular Solomon Bloom, "Karl Marx and the Jews," *JSS*, 1942, pp. 3–16, Edmund Silberner, "Was Marx an Anti-Semite?" *Historia Judaica,* XI (April 1949), pp. 3–52, and Nathan Rotenstreich, "For and Against Emancipation: The Bruno Bauer Controversy," *LBIYB,* IV (1959), pp. 23–27. Interestingly, Rotenstreich suggests that Marx's conception of Judaism as egoism derived from Mendelssohn's definition of Judaism and in turn was developed by Kant and Feurbach, ibid., pp. 25–26. See also more generally the biography by Sir Isaiah Berlin, *Karl Marx* (New York: Oxford University Press, 1963), pp. 25–27. Berlin suggests that Marx's hostility toward religion generally and Judaism in particular flowed from the unnatural position of German-Jewish converts to Christianity in the early nineteenth century. This conversion movement, as noted earlier, was to some the logical culmination point of Haskalah ideology.

34. Franz Rosenzweig brilliantly portrayed this rediscovery of East European Jewry as an encounter with "authentic" Jews. See Nahum Glatzer, ed., *Franz Rosenzweig: His Life and Thought* (New York: Schocken Books, 1958), pp. 74–78.

35. On the aims of *Wissenschaft,* see Ismar Schorsch, "Ideology and History in an Age of Emancipation," in Heinrich Graetz, *The Structure of Jewish History and Other Essays* (New York: Jewish Theological Seminary, 1975), pp. 4–9. A good example of the difference between Haskalah historical writing and that of the men of *Wissenschaft* is the treatment of Rashi. Leopold Zunz, an archetype of *Wissenschaft,* insisted on placing Rashi with a medieval context and ridiculed those who wished to portray him as a modern man. See Michael Meyer, *Ideas of Jewish History* (New York: Behrman House, 1974), pp. 23–25. On the search for role-models in Haskalah biographies, see Lehman, pp. 94–108.

36. See the introduction to Arthur Hertzberg, *The Zionist Idea* (New York: Atheneum, 1969), pp. 15–100, especially the section on Ahad Ha-'Am, pp. 63–72.
37. Ibid., pp. 43–45. See also my M.A. essay, "Conceptions of History in Zionist Thought" (Columbia University, 1973), pp. 3–9.

SELECTED BIBLIOGRAPHY

Altmann, Alexander. *Moses Mendelssohn: A Biographical Study.* Philadelphia Jewish Publication Society, 1973.

Baron, Salo W. *The Russian Jew under Tsars and Soviets.* 2d ed., rev. New York: Macmillan Co., 1976.

Barzillay, Isaac. "The Ideology of the Berlin Haskalah." *PAAJR.* XXV (1956), 1–37.

———. "The Italian and Berlin Haskalah." *PAAJR.* XXIX (1960–61), 17–54.

———. "National and Anti-National Trends in the Berlin Haskalah." *JSS* XXI (1959), 165–192.

Dubnow, Simon. *History of the Jews in Russia and Poland.* 3 vols. Trans. by I. Friedlander. Philadelphia: Jewish Publication Society, 1916.

Ettinger, Shmuel. "The Beginnings of the Change in the Attitude of European Society towards the Jews." *Scripta Hierosolymitana,* VII (1961), 193–219.

Fackenheim, Emil. *Encounters Between Judaism and Modern Philosophy.* Philadelphia: Jewish Publication Society, 1973.

Gay, Peter. *The Enlightenment.* 2 vols. New York: Norton Books, 1977.

Greenberg, Louis. *The Jews in Russia.* 2 vols. New Haven: Yale University Press, 1944, 1951. Reprinted New York: Schocken Books, 1976.

Hertzberg, Arthur. *The French Enlightenment and the Jews.* New York: Schocken Books, 1970.

———. *The Zionist Idea.* 1959. Reprinted New York: Atheneum Books, 1969.

Halkin, Simon. *Modern Hebrew Literature.* New York: Schocken Books, 1971.

Katz, Jacob. *Exclusiveness and Tolerance.* New York: Schocken Books, 1962.

———. *Out of the Ghetto.* Cambridge: Harvard University Press, 1973.

———. *Tradition and Crisis.* New York: Schocken Books, 1971.

Krieger, Leonard. *Kings and Philosophers.* New York: Norton Books, 1970.

Levitats, Isaac. *The Jewish Community in Russia.* New York: Columbia University Press, 1943.

Mahler, Raphael. *A History of Modern Jewry: 1780–1815.* New York: Schocken Books, 1971.

Mendelssohn, Moses. *Jerusalem and Other Jewish Writings.* Edited and translated by Alfred Jospe. New York: Schocken Books, 1969.

———. *Moses Mendelssohn: Selections from His Writings.* Edited and translated by Eva Jospe. New York: Viking Books, 1975.

Meyer, Michael. *The Origins of the Modern Jew.* Detroit: Wayne State University Press, 1967.

Patterson, David. *Abraham Mapu.* London: Horowitz Publishing Co., 1954.

Rotenstreich, Nathan. "For and Against Emancipation: The Bruno Bauer Controversy." *LBIYB.* IV (1959), 3–36.

————. "Mendelssohn's Political Philosophy." *LBIYB*. XI (1966), 28–41.
————. *The Recurring Pattern*. New York: Horizon Books, 1964.
Schorsch, Ismar. "Ideology and History in an Age of Emancipation." In Heinrich Graetz, *The Structure of Jewish History and Other Essays*. New York: Jewish Theological Seminary, 1975.
Spiegel, Shalom. *Hebrew Reborn*. Philadelphia: Jewish Publication Society, 1962.

The Clash of Modern Ideologies of Judaism

GILBERT S. ROSENTHAL

I

EMANCIPATION AND ENLIGHTENMENT were the two great upheavals that affected Jews and Judaism profoundly in the eighteenth and nineteenth centuries. Their impact on Jewish religion and culture was enormous; the shock waves are still felt today.

What were the goals of Enlightenment and Emancipation? And how did this new approach to life affect Jews and Judaism? Enlightenment sought to awaken within the Jewish community a sense of human values and human dignity so as to appreciate secular values and a secular society. It set out to cut the Gordian knot between religion and state and to create what Professor Jacob Katz calls the "neutral society."[1] The esthetics of European humanism were extolled; the beauty of language, art, music, poetry, drama, and dance was idealized; nature was deified and God was identified with nature; other-worldly salvation was replaced by this-worldly human fulfillment; and reason and rationality were enthroned at the cost of faith and piety. In a word, the human mind and reason became the new gods of the pantheon of Western Europe.

Actually, Baruch Spinoza (1632–1677) had prepared the mood for this revolution in European life. He was really the first "secular" man in Europe—neither Christian nor Jew. He denounced dogma and revelation; he argued for freedom of religion; he espoused biblical criticism; he denied that Jews are the chosen people; he placed conscience above revelation. He laid the foundation upon which the English Deists and French *philosophes* built their systems.[2]

The French *philosophes*, such as Voltaire, D'Holbach, and Diderot, favored Emancipation for Jews with several caveats. They were to forsake their orientalism and separatism; they were expected to renounce their rabbinical authorities and autonomous communities; they were to become rational, reasonable, unprejudiced, enlightened *hommes* and *philosophes*. [3]

If Enlightenment was concerned with freeing the *spirits* of the Jews, Emancipation dealt with the freeing of their *bodies*. Emancipation was the process by which the Jews of Europe left the ghettos, entered the mainstream of the political and economic life of Europe, and began the tortuous climb to civic equality with their Christian neighbors. As Professor Salo W. Baron points out, however, not all Jews wanted Emancipation, and Emancipation was not offered without a heavy price. [4] The price was clear: Jews were required to relinquish their autonomous community and surrender rabbinic authority to control and discipline their people. Malesherbes made this clear already in 1787 in supporting the Act of Toleration in France, and Clermont-Tonnere stated it bluntly in the debates over the liberation of French Jews in 1790–91 when he proclaimed: "To the Jews as men, everything; as a nation, nothing." And he added ominously: "If they accept this, well and good; if not, let them be banished!" Some French Jews understood this and were prepared to pay the price by surrendering autonomy and communal controls and even going so far as to agree to religious reforms to hasten the process. [5] In like fashion, Felix Libertaté in Holland developed liberal religious patterns in order to win civic emancipation for Dutch Jews. [6]

When Napoleon summoned an assembly of rabbis and Jewish merchants to Paris in 1806, he spelled out the price of freedom for all European Jews. He asked bluntly whether Jews considered themselves Frenchmen or Jews; whether the rabbis were autonomous or not; whether intermarriage was valid or not. When the delegates shouted that they were loyal to France *jusqu'à la mort* and renounced rabbinic police powers, *herem* (excommunication), and Jewish autonomy, they indicated that henceforth and forevermore the laws of the prince would be supreme. [7]

How did Jews react to the new winds that were blowing over

Europe? Some were overjoyed and leaped into new cultural and religious streams with reckless abandon. Many, such as Heinrich Heine and Daniel Chwolson, converted to Christianity. Others, such as Abraham Geiger, Yom Tov (Leopold) Zunz, Nachman Krochmal, Solomon Judah Rapoport, and Moritz Steinschneider, created *Wissenschaft des Judentums*, the scientific and critical study of Judaism, in an attempt to make Judaism a modern academic discipline. Zunz and Geiger utilized this new discipline for reforms of Jewish religious life; Steinschneider studied Judaism in a totally detached, objective fashion in order to give Judaism a "decent burial."[8] Still others developed Jewish nationalism and ultimately Zionism. And large numbers of Jews reevaluated Jewish religious norms and ideals in developing new interpretations of classical religious positions.

II

Reform Judaism was the first significant religious reaction to the new trends in European life and thought. Some critics accuse Reform of being merely a way station to assimilation and conversion, of surrendering to the *Zeitgeist* and capitulating to every changing whim. Its partisans are equally insistent that Reform suceeded in stemming the tide of Jewish defection because it was prepared to adapt to the changing mores and new climate of the times. In reality, both are right: Reform did succumb to the *Zeitgeist* in a frequently servile fashion while holding on to Jews who might well have gone the way of baptism. Let us recall two criticisms of the Enlightenment: first, the leaders of Enlightenment posited an invidious dichotomy between a human being or *philosophe* and a Jew; second, they argued that Judaism was a separatist oriental entity that refused to become integrated in Western culture. The Reform movement labored tenaciously to blunt both criticisms. It endorsed the philosophy of Enlightenment, "Be a Jew at home and a human being outside" (as if the two were inimical!); it also struggled to strip itself of any "orientalisms" so as to be accepted in Western society. Reform also blunted the accusation of separatism by accepting the decisions of the Napoleonic Sanhedrin that Jews were no longer a nation but loyal citizens of their adoptive country and Jews by religious persuasion only. Finally, Reform set out to abolish distinctions between Jew and gentile and break down religious barriers by lopping off ritual practices with abandon. Professor Gershom Scholem suggests that Reform grew out of the ruins of the old Sabbatean heresy, which was antinomian and free-wheeling. Perhaps so. But it has not been clearly established that Reform was a direct derivative of Sabbatean or Frankist heresies.[9] In any event, Israel Jacobson set up the first Reform temple in Seesen in 1810 in an attempt to purge Judaism of "ritual offensive to reason as well as our Christian friends."[10] Subsequent Reform temples introduced the organ, mixed choir, German sermon and prayers, and stripped the prayers of references to the Messiah or the hope to return to Erez Yisrael. The new Reform *Vereine* spread quickly to Hamburg, Frankfort, Vienna, Metz, London, Berlin, Pesth, and other places. The Frankfort group was most radical and bowed to the anti-talmudic canards of the *philosophes* by rejecting the authority of the Talmud, belief in a personal Messiah, and a return to Zion since "Germany is our fatherland." The Orthodox were appalled; fights became bitter as partisans ran to civil court. When the brilliant Reformer Abraham Geiger was elected associate rabbi to Rabbi Solomon Tiktin of Breslau, the aged Orthodox sage reacted ferociously, and the case dragged on for years.[11]

Reform Judaism held a series of rabbinical conferences in Brunswick (1844), Frankfort (1845), Leipzig (1869), and Augsburg (1871). The message of these synods was clear: Judaism must be modernized in the light of the dictates of reason; it must delete outmoded "oriental" practices and add new rites; it must be studied scientifically and critically and keep pace with the spirit of the times. Needless to say, as Reform proclaimed itself a religious sect rather than a nation, and as it deleted rituals such as *kashrut*, Sabbath observance, the use of Hebrew, and other ancient practices, the clash between it and the Orthodox became more clamorous and sharp. Eminent Orthodox rabbis denounced the Reformers as heretics and sectarians. A conference of Orthodox rabbis met in 1860 and proclaimed a ban against rabbis who preached sermons in the vernacular, wore a gown, or placed the *bimah* (reader's stand) in front of the synagogue. But the day of excommunication had passed, and although Reform Judaism exceeded the sectarianism of Karaism, which merely denied the sacredness of the Talmud, the Reform movement was never treated by the Orthodox as another sect beyond the pale of Judaism. Reform had its greatest successes in Protestant countries rather than in Catholic lands; but it was in the New World that Reform would win its greatest victories.[12]

Why was Reform so successful in America? This was a pioneer land with a free-wheeling, frontier mentality, where great latitude was afforded in political, social, and religious life. America had no formal, established church; rather, a conglomeration of sects and faiths. Here the *Zeitgeist* was liberal, and progressive theologians, such as Theodore Parker and Henry W. Beecher, were widely respected. Here there existed no formal Jewish community, no *Cultusgemeinde*, to strangle budding reforms, and no chief rabbis to excommunicate or ban "heretics." Americans preferred the congregational rather than the hierarchical or diocesan system, so that each synagogue was free to choose its own path. And here there existed a drive to be Americanized quickly, even if it meant dropping rituals.[13]

The earliest attempt at Reform came in Charleston, South Carolina, in 1824 at the historic old Beth Elohim Congregation. Isaac Harby and David N. Carvalho led a group of petitioners in requesting a shorter, more intelligible service with a weekly English sermon, English prayers, and Torah commentary. While disclaiming any move to abolish "such ceremonies as are considered land-marks to distinguish the Jew from the Gentile," Harby's group evidently wanted to duplicate the moderate reforms of the Germans. But the leaders of the congregation rebuffed the group, forcing a secession. The new group issued a new prayer book, introduced an organ and liturgical reforms, and charted a course to adapt Judaism to the "situation of an enlightened world." The Reformed Society of Israelites issued "The Charleston Creed," which eliminated belief in a personal Messiah and bodily resurrection, and by 1836 Beth Elohim went Reform. Its German-trained minister, Gustave Poznanski, proceeded to abolish various rituals as he proclaimed: "This is our *temple*, this city our Jerusalem, this happy land our *Palestine*." That slogan was to become the theme and philosophy of Reform for an entire century.[14]

With the arrival of German and Bohemian Reform rabbis, such as Isaac M. Wise, David Einhorn, Kaufmann Kohler, Max Lilienthal, and Samuel Hirsch, Reform Judaism began to take shape and formulate its ideology. It created the three major institutions: the Union of American Hebrew Congregations (1873), the Hebrew Union College (1875), and the Central Conference of American Rabbis (1889). Ideologically, Reform propagated its program to free Judaism of its superstitions, orientalisms, and mystical excrescences, and it enthroned reason and Western rationality. New York's *Cultus Verein* (forerunner of Temple Emanu-El) was of the opinion that by its reforms it would "win for Jews a position of greater respect among fellow citizens, enable Jews to worship together with greater dignity, and attract the rising generation."[15]

The mood of the new Reformers was radical and iconoclastic. It was the conviction of men such as Wise and Kohler that Judaism had been encumbered with rabbinic excrescences; that talmudic legalism and medieval mysticism had obscured the beauty and truth of pure monotheism and prophetic social justice. Reason was the god of the day; rationalism was in the saddle; social Darwinism was the mood of the time. In the rush to attract the new generation and the Western mind, orientalisms were to be purged and the *Shulḥan Arukh*, the code of Jewish law, became the villain of Jewish life, for it had obscured the pure flame of Jewish ethical monotheism. Moreover, true to the *Wissenschaft* school of Jewish critical studies, Reform laid heavy stress on the fact that Judaism, in Kohler's words, had always been "a religion of historical growth" that had evolved and changed, and that its main goal was to spread a message concerning one God to an undivided humanity. Traditional Judaism glorifies the past and idealizes the merits of forefathers, wrote Kohler. "Reform Judaism, on the contrary, looks forward with hope for a far brighter future, beholding in the Messiah the ideal of mankind to be realized by the Jewish people through all the factors and agencies of civilization and progress . . ."[16] Kohler rebuffed the traditionalists who accused Reform of breaking with past traditions by arguing that Reform was really a continuation of past progress and reforms but that in an age of historical research and reason these reforms must be conscious and deliberate.[17] In bowing to the mood of universalism, the Reformers denounced narrow, parochial interests and Jewish nationalism, insisting that the only national loyalties owed were to the country of residence. Yet the Reformers were still chauvinistic enough to argue that Israel, by virtue of some "racial genius," had a mission to bring ethical monotheism to mankind. The heady optimism of the day can be detected in the almost ludicrous view of Isaac M. Wise that in twenty-five years the religion of *all* America—perhaps even of *all* the world—would be Reform Judaism![18]

These ideas crystallized in the historic Pittsburgh Platform of 1885, "the utterance most expressive of the teachings of Reform Judaism," in the words of David Philipson, historian of the movement. The Platform's eight points were revolutionary and radical and hewed closer to the line of David Einhorn and Kaufmann Kohler than to that of the more moderate Isaac M. Wise. The Platform declared that Judaism "presents the highest conception of the God-idea" and preserved and defended it amid continual struggles and trials "as the central religious truth for the human race." The framers recognized the Bible as "the record of the consecration of the Jewish people to its mission as priest of the One God," and as the most potent instrument of instruction. But they declared that the doctrines of modern science and historical research were not antagonistic to the doctrines of Judaism, since the Bible reflects "the primitive ideas of its own age" and clothes divine providence in "miraculous narratives." The Platform accepted as binding "only the moral laws" and ceremonies that "elevate and sanctify our lives" while rejecting those not adapted to "the views and habits of modern civilization." The Platform repudiated Mosaic and biblical rules of diet, priestly purity, and dress as being of pagan and foreign origin, as out of step with modern times, and as apt to "obstruct rather than further modern spiritual elevation." The fifth point described the modern era of culture and intellect as the realization of the Messianic hope. In blunt terms it affirmed:

> We consider ourselves no longer a nation but a religious community, and therefore expect neither a return to Palestine, nor a sacrificial worship under the administration of the sons of Aaron, nor the restoration of any of the laws concerning the Jewish state.

The Platform proceeded to articulate its conviction that Judaism was a religion of reason that would work closely with Christianity and Islam in establishing truth and righteousness among men. The seventh point emphatically denied bodily resurrection and Heaven and Hell; instead it affirmed a notion of spiritual immortality. Finally, the Platform called on every Jew "to participate in the great task of modern times, to solve on the basis of justice and righteousness the problems presented by the contrasts and evils of the present organization of society."[19]

The Pittsburgh Platform became the charter of Reform until well into the twentieth century. It reflected the views of "classical" or "radical" Reform Judaism; it was symptomatic of the *Zeitgeist* of German Reform; it appealed to the New World Jew as did no other movement. And it precipitated counter-reforms in Conservative and neo-Orthodox circles, as we shall presently see. But these eight guiding principles were concretized in fifty years of the work of Reform. The Reformers developed a liberal, naturalistic theology. Their *Union Prayer Book* and liturgical works reflected their anti-mystical, non-supernatural theology as well as their denationalization of Judaism. Reform's deep antagonism to Zionism also reflected their opposition to Jewish nationalism and their worldly, humanistic views. In their approach to ritual, the Reformers wielded a sharp scalpel: they dropped *kashrut* rules, relaxed Sabbath and Festival regulations, moved Sabbath services to Sunday, added an organ and mixed choir to worship, deleted most of the Hebrew prayers, and revised personal status by sanctioning mixed marriage without valid conversion and by dropping the requirements for a *ketubah* (Jewish marriage contract) and *get* (Jewish divorce). The Reform movement became deeply involved in social action and interfaith activities, much to the outrage of the more traditional elements in the Jewish community.

Ironically, while the Reform movement viewed the Orthodox as medieval fanatics who were hopelessly chained to the letter of the law, and the Conservatives as merely timid Reformers, they were profoundly influenced by them, and the newer version of Reform owes much to the interraction with the traditionalist groups. To be sure, the *Zeitgeist* changes; and since Reform is the most sensitive of all Jewish groups to changing winds, it reflects societal developments. Rationalism, social Darwinism, the naive belief in unbounded human progress which marked nineteenth-century thought, declined by the 1930s and 1940s. The rise of Nazism and Communism, the Second World War, the Holocaust, the birth of the State of Israel—all did their part in revising Reform thinking. Then, too, the influx into Reform temples of East European Jews, who demanded "warmer" services with more rituals, affected the movement, as did the growing number of Reform rabbis of East European rather than German origin. The growing Conservative movement, the new Reconstructionist philosophy of Mordecai M. Kaplan, the resurgent Modern Orthodoxy, all helped change the face of Reform. Never isolated or inert in the past, Reform interracted and was changed by its environment and sister movements in dramatic fashion, culminating in the Columbus Platform of 1937.

The Columbus Platform began by recognizing the changes in modern life that had necessitated the restating of Reform principles. It defined Judaism as "the historical religious experience of the Jewish people" whose history shows progressive development in teaching the universal message of one God, with whom man is a partner in shaping the world. The Platform then talks of Torah as the progressive revelation of God. Both the written and oral Torah enshrine "Israel's ever-growing consciousness of God and of the moral law." While certain specific laws have lost their "binding force," Torah remains "the dynamic source of the life of

Israel," and each age must adapt the teachings of Torah to its basic needs. Point five uses the long-taboo phrase "the Jewish people" and in a sharp about-face proclaims: "In the rehabilitation of Palestine, the land hallowed by memories and hopes, we behold the promise of all Jewry to aid in its upbuilding as a Jewish homeland by endeavoring to make it not only a haven of refuge for oppressed but also a center of Jewish culture and spiritual life." The Platform reiterates Israel's mission to strive with other nations and religions for the ideals of universal brotherhood, justice, truth, and peace. It carries on the Reform theme of social justice and urges an end to all forms of slavery, tyranny, and poverty while demanding universal disarmament. The final section is almost as radical as are the sections dealing with Palestine, for it urges synagogue and home rituals and prayer, reminding its partisans that Judaism is a way of life requiring concrete symbols such as the Sabbath and Festivals, customs and ceremonies, as well as the Hebrew language.[20]

Reform Judaism responded to the new program almost immediately. More Hebrew was introduced into the new *Union Prayer Book*, and the Sunday School program was beefed up. Long-discarded rituals, such as Bar Mitzvah, crept back into temples. Reform rabbis and laymen moved into the forefront of the Zionist movement, and men such as Rabbis Stephen S. Wise and Abba Hillel Silver became spokesmen for world Jewry in arguing the case of the State of Israel. Guides to Jewish practices were issued by several Reform scholars, and while Reform was not about to become a new Orthodoxy or adopt a modern *Shulḥan Arukh*, its swing back to tradition has been unmistakable. Professor Solomon Freehof, premier legal scholar of the movement, has welcomed the new interest in ritual and *Halakhah* and has described it as a return to the "mind" of Judaism. He notes that as chairman of the Committee on Responsa of Reform Jewry for forty years, he had received but a handful of ritual queries. But currently, he handles over two hundred annually.[21] The "new" Reform movement is not going to accept Orthodoxy's view of a divinely mandated *Halakhah;* it is committed to individual choice of *miẓvot* on a subjectively selective basis. The current mood can be best summed up in Freehof's phrase that *Halakhah* should be our guide rather than our governance. Clearly, Reform has been reforming itself. If constancy is the hallmark of Orthodoxy, flux is the symbol of Reform.

At the centennial of the founding of the Hebrew Union College, a statement of principles was issued by the Reform movement. It goes beyond the Columbus Platform in projecting the newest views of Reform. It affirms that "most modern Jews within their various religious movements, are embracing Reform Jewish perspectives." The Centenary Perspective agrees that the Holocaust has "shattered our easy optimism about humanity and its inevitable progress." It reaffirms its acceptance of the universalist mission of the Jewish people in working towards messianic fulfillment at the same time as it gives the survival of the Jewish people "highest priority." The Perspective urges the restoration of Torah study as "a religious imperative and whose practice is our chief means to holiness." Whereas Judaism emphasizes action rather than creed as the primary expression of a religious life, the religious life encompasses both the ethical and the ritual, including family devotion, private and public worship, daily religious observance, keeping the Sabbath and the holy days, celebrating the major events of life, and so on. To be sure, when approaching observance, Reform Jews are called upon "to exercise their individual autonomy, choosing and creating on the basis of commitment and knowledge."

The statement on Israel is extraordinarily positive:

> We are bound to that land and the newly reborn State of Israel by innumerable religious and ethnic ties. . . . We have both a stake and a responsibility in building the State of Israel, assuring its security, and defining its Jewish character. We encourage *aliyah* for those who wish to find maximum fulfillment in the cause of Zion. We demand that Reform Judaism be unconditionally legitimitized in the State of Israel.

At the same time, the Perspective reaffirms the mandate to create strong Jewish communities wherever we live, centered around the synagogue. It also reminds Reform Jews of their duty to be concerned with both universalistic and particular causes; to develop a passion for our people as well as mankind. Finally, it reiterates its basic optimistic faith that "the existence of the Jew is an argument against despair; Jewish survival is warrant for human hopes," for "we remain God's witness that history is not meaningless" and people "are not powerless to affect their destiny."[22]

Obviously Reform has been highly receptive to changing times. But even as it has interacted with and influenced the other movements in Jewish life, so has it been the recipient of their impact. In the earlier days, Reform was vilified by the Orthodox and responded in kind, viewing them as hopeless fanatics. Similarly, Reform leaders such as Philipson and Eisendrath considered it but a matter of time before the Conservatives and Reconstructionists would go Reform. Times have changed, however. The Reform's swing to an interest in *Halakhah* is doubtlessly due to the impact of a surging neo-Orthodoxy with thousands of day school graduates, some of whom belong to Reform temples and serve as Reform rabbis and have changed the face of contemporary Reform. Likewise, Orthodox and neo-Orthodox, neo-Hasidic and existentialist thinkers, such as Rabbi Joseph B. Soloveitchik, Franz Rosenzweig, Abraham Joshua Heschel—just to mention three—have profoundly shaped the theology of newer Reform thinkers such as Jacob J. Petuchowski and Eugene Borowitz, even as religious humanist Mordecai M. Kaplan had a seminal influence on an older generation of Reform ideologues, such as Charles Shulman and Roland Gittelsohn.[23] That newer Reform leaders, such as W. Gunther Plaut, attack the classical stress on Bible and ethical monotheism and call for guides to Jewish law and *Halikhah* if not outright *Halakhah*, is striking corroboration of the impact of traditionalism on the new Reform, as is the creation of several all-day Reform parochial schools.[24]

Conservative Judaism and Reconstructionism have had their impact on Reform as well. Reform's new passion for the Jewish People, for communal involvement, for Erez Yisrael, for the needs of world Jewry, can be directly traced to Solomon Schechter's stress on "Catholic" or world Israel, as well as Mordecai M.

Kaplan's lesson of Jewish peoplehood. Today it would be terribly difficult to find a Reform rabbi or layman who would refuse to cooperate with fellow Jews of other stripes or who would spurn efforts in behalf of Soviet Jewry or the State of Israel. In every Federation, in every UJA drive, in every Soviet Jewry organization, Reform Jews are at the helm. The old Germanic contempt for *Ostjuden*, the "Our Crowd" condescension toward East European Jews, has been long buried. Reform has learned the lesson of peoplehood—and learned it well.[25]

There are several dramatic pieces of evidence indicating the influence of other movements in Jewry on Reform. The new version of the *Union Prayer Book, Gates of Prayer* (1975), is 800 pages long; it is replete with Hebrew; it has restored references to Zion and prayers for Jerusalem; and it has reintroduced long-discarded prayers for the *tallit, tefillin,* Purim, Tish'a Be-Av—just to mention several. The Reform movement has formed its own Zionist organization, called ARZA (1977), and it is now officially linked to the World Zionist Organization. Its views on mixed marriages have undergone change. At the 1909 meeting of the Central Conference of American Rabbis, the body declared that "mixed marriages are contrary to the tradition of the Jewish religion and should therefore be discouraged." But at the 1973 convention, a resolution was adopted declaring the Conference's "opposition to participation by its members in any ceremony which solemnizes a mixed marriage."

Clearly, Reform's process of reformation owes much to interaction with Orthodoxy, Conservatism, Reconstructionism, and Zionism. It no longer views them as hostile, outmoded, or dangerous threats to progress. On the contrary: it is closer to them, perhaps, than ever before.

III

The second religious response to Emancipation was the Conservative movement. It represented, at least at the outset, a counteraction to the Reform movement, whose views it considered too radical a surrender to the *Zeitgeist*. Conservative Judaism was born in Germany and was the creation of Rabbi Zachariah Frankel, historian Heinrich Graetz, and the premier scholar of *Jüdische Wissenschaft*, Yom Tov (Leopold) Zunz. Frankel attended the early Reform rabbinical conferences in the 1840s and was considered a "moderate Reformer." But when the rabbis voted at the Frankfort conference of 1845 that the Hebrew language was no longer objectively a *sine qua non* for Jewish life and learning, Frankel broke irrevocably with the Reformers. He did not form a new movement; rather, he created a school of thought called the "positive-historical trend in Judaism." It was "positive" in that it was positively oriented toward traditional practices and laws. It was "historical" because Frankel and his colleagues accepted the findings of *Jüdische Wissenschaft* that Judaism and its institutions had evolved historically, that it is fallacious to assume that today's Judaism is identical with medieval or ancient Judaism, and that Jewish law and institutions must be studied historically and critically. Frankel developed his theories in his writings and at his new Jewish Theological Seminary of Breslau. He battled both Geiger and the Reformers as well as Samson Raphael Hirsch and the neo-Orthodox group. He acknowledged the need for change that comes about via *evolutionary* rather than *revolutionary* means; he insisted that the will of the community must ultimately decide the fate of law and lore. Frankel's views had limited effect in Europe. The growth of Conservative Judaism would come in America.[26]

There was an unofficial group of rabbis and laymen in America who gave impetus to the ideas of the positive-historical school in Judaism. Reverends Isaac Leeser and Sabato Morais and Rabbis Benjamin Szold, Marcus Jastrow, and Alexander Kohut battled against what they considered to be the excesses of the Reform movement, which was chipping away at *Halakhah*, changing the traditional liturgy, and destroying basic rules of the Sabbath, Festivals, dietary laws, and family status. On the other hand, these men were not Orthodox, and they were prepared to introduce new practices in synagogue worship and to alleviate some of the anachronisms of Jewish law. At first, these proto-Conservative leaders sought to join forces with Isaac M. Wise and his colleagues. But gradually the rift widened between the two camps.

The issuance of the new Reform prayerbooks, such as Wise's *Minhag America*, upset Morais and his colleagues. When the Board of Delegates of American Israelites was absorbed into the Union of American Hebrew Congregations in 1878, the traditionalists believed that they had lost their voice. The first commencement dinner of the Hebrew Union College in 1883 was, incredibly, a non-kosher dinner, much to the outrage of Morais, who walked out incensed. The final blow came with the Pittsburgh Platform of 1885. Morais, Szold, Jastrow, and Kohut were shocked; Szold and Jastrow pulled their congregations out of the Union of American Hebrew Congregations; they determined to chart their own course and establish their own seminary.[27]

And so was born the Jewish Theological Seminary of America, founded in 1886 in New York. The preamble indicated immediately why the new school could not accept the Hebrew Union College:

> The necessity has been made manifest for associated and organized effort on the part of Jews of America, faithful to Mosaic Law and ancestral tradition; for the purpose of keeping alive the true Jewish spirit; in particular by the establishment of a Seminary where the Bible shall be impartially taught and rabbinic literature faithfully expounded, and more especially where youth, desirous of entering the ministry, may be thoroughly grounded in Jewish knowledge and inspired by precept and the example of their instructors with the love of the Hebrew language, and a spirit of fidelity and devotion to Jewish law.[28]

The institution would preserve the knowledge and practice of "Historical Judaism"; it would safeguard "Judaism in America" rather than "American Judaism" (an obvious thrust at Isaac M. Wise). Unofficially, Kohut and others began referring to the new school of thought as the "Conservative" trend. The term had two connotations: (1) it implied a conservative rather than a radical philosophy; (2) it suggested the desire to *conserve* or *preserve* Jewish values and traditions, unlike Reform.[29]

The new Seminary languished and nearly died until a group of laymen revived it and brought over Solomon Schechter as its new president. Schechter had made a great name for himself as discoverer of the Cairo *Geniza* and as professor of Jewish studies at Cambridge and at the University of London. He was a rare combination of Rumanian Hasidism, Viennese *Wissenschaft des Judentums*, and British crispness of style. He declared that his newly organized Seminary would be a "theological centre which should be all things to all men, reconciling all parties, and appealing to all sections of the community." Moreover, he expected that the faculty would include raving mystics, advanced critics, and the strictly orthodox, so that academic freedom and critical scholarship for all schools of thought would be preserved. From 1902 to 1915, Schechter maintained that goal.[30]

Schechter helped develop the organization of Conservative rabbis, the Rabbinical Assembly, founded in 1901. He was the driving force behind the United Synagogue, the congregational arm, established in 1913. The preamble to its Charter states its purposes:

> The advancement of the cause of Judaism in America and the maintenance of Jewish tradition in its historic continuity.
> To assert and establish loyalty to the Torah and its historical exposition;
> To further the observance of the Sabbath and the dietary law,
> To preserve in the service the reference to Israel's past and the hopes for Israel's restoration,
> To maintain the traditional character of the liturgy with Hebrew as the language of prayer,
> To foster Jewish religious life in the home, as expressed in traditional observances,
> To encourage the establishment of Jewish religious schools, in the curricula of which the study of the Hebrew language and literature shall be given a prominent place . . .[31]

The Conservative movement has been a protean coalition movement of the near-Orthodox, the virtually Reform, and the vast center. Unlike Reform Judaism, the movement has issued no formal "platforms" or creedal declarations. It is more of a pragmatic movement; life has been a greater determining factor than ideology. It has drawn heavily on the traditional norms and commitment to *Halakhah* and *mizvot* of the Orthodox wing at the same time that it accepts the critical scholarship of *Wissenschaft* and the need to update and change Jewish laws as espoused by Reform. The key words "tradition and change" have become the philosophy of the movement. Conservative Judaism has criticized Orthodoxy's extraordinary stress on ritual and has taken Reform to task for overly emphasizing the ethical at the expense of the ritual. Thus, it has attempted to strike a delicate balance between the two; it has sought to walk a fine line between *Halakhah*, "the science of deeds," and *Aggadah*, "the art of being," to quote Abraham Joshua Heschel.[32] Moreover, Conservative Judaism differs from its sister movements in its focal point: Orthodoxy starts with *Halakhah*; Reform begins with God; Conservatism takes off from the Jewish People. In other words, in its view, Jewish life, law, and lore exist to enhance and insure the creative survival of *Kelal Yisrael*, world Jewry.

Conservative thinkers berated Reformers such as Geiger and Kohler for having reduced Judaism to a mere religious sect, stripped of national content. Likewise, Conservative leaders have criticized the Orthodox, such as Rabbi Joseph B. Soloveitchik, for having reduced Judaism to *Halakhah* and laws. Schechter, Israel Friedlander, Abraham Joshua Heschel, and Mordecai M. Kaplan all argued that Judaism is not just a creed: it is a whole complex of laws, ideals, customs, culture, mores, and traditions. As Mordecai M. Kaplan has defined it, "Judaism is an evolving religious civilization."[33] This definition has been accepted by virtually all Conservative thinkers and philosophers.

Conservative ideologists have approached the idea of God in much the same way as the Reformers. They espouse varied theologies, ranging from naturalist-humanism of the school of Mordecai M. Kaplan to the religious existentialism and neo-Hasidism of Abraham Joshua Heschel. Most Conservative thinkers are non-literalists in explaining revelation, and few share the Orthodox notions of miracles or supernaturalism.

The Conservative view of *Halakhah* is inconsistent and hard to define. It certainly disagrees sharply with Reform's view that only the ethical commandments are eternally binding and that each individual is free to pick and choose the ritual *mizvot* that suit him. On the other hand, the movement rejects Orthodoxy's stress on *Halakhah* as preeminently the unchallenged, unchanging will of God. Heschel derided this view of Rabbi Soloveitchik as a reduction of Jewish law to "sacred physics," and he calls such theoreticians "pan-Halakhists":

> It is a distortion to say that Judaism consists exclusively of performing ritual or moral deeds, and to forget that the goal of all performing is in *transforming* the soul. Even before Israel was told in the Ten Commandments what *to do* it was told what *to be: a holy people.*[34]

The Conservative movement has developed the notion that the *people* are the final arbiters of Jewish practice. Solomon Schechter dealt with the subject in several brief passages. He wrote that the center of authority had actually been removed from the Bible "and placed in some *living body* which, by reason of its being in touch with the ideal aspirations and the religious needs of the age, is best able to determine the nature of the Secondary Meaning." This living body Schechter called the "collective conscience of Catholic Israel as embodied in the Universal synagogue." Catholic Israel was composed of the Prophets and Psalmists, the rabbis throughout the ages, and above all, general custom, which "forms the rule of practice."[35] This notion of Catholic Israel as the final authority became popular in Conservative circles. But it created problems: If Catholic Israel no longer observes *kashrut* or the Sabbath, does that imply these laws are dead forever? Professor Robert Gordis has reinterpreted Schechter's view in an attempt to overcome the problem. He writes that "Catholic Israel is the body of men and women within the Jewish people who accept the authority of Jewish law and are concerned with Jewish observance as a genuine issue."[36]

For a long time, the United Synagogue and the Rabbinical Assembly had been reluctant to authorize changes in Jewish law or liturgical practices. In fact, the United Synagogue's original Charter had indicated that while the United Synagogue would not endorse innovations introduced by its constituents, it would embrace "all elements essentially loyal to traditional Judaism" and in sympathy with the stated purposes. At the outset, congregations that worshipped with bare heads or prayed from the *Union Prayer Book* were excluded, while those with organs or mixed seating were not. The Law Committee of the Rabbinical Assembly was kept in check by the Seminary faculty, including Professors Louis Ginzberg and Boaz Cohen and Seminary Chancellor Louis Finkelstein, so that even mildly radical proposals were sidetracked. Then, too, the new movement was still seeking (vainly, as it turned out) some recognition and legitimization from the Orthodox, who were weak, dispirited, disunited, and not overly vituperative at that point. Consequently, whenever a proposal to amend laws such as the *agunah* (abandoned wife) was put forth, it was done so gingerly lest Orthodox sensibilities be offended. When the Orthodox reacted violently, such proposals were invariably withdrawn. As the Orthodox have grown stronger and more assertive and have become less tolerant of Conservative actions, the movement has begun to move off in its own direction, less sensitive to Orthodox reactions.

In 1948 the Law Committee of the Rabbinical Assembly was reorganized, giving a voice to the left as well as the center and the right. A series of sweeping legal decisions was undertaken in defiance of Orthodox protests and in obvious emulation of Reform procedures. For example, in 1950, the Committee permitted riding to synagogue on Sabbath and Festivals, and allowed the use of electricity on those days. In 1954, the Rabbinical Assembly adopted a new *ketubah* (marriage contract) with a clause designed to force a recalcitrant husband to issue a *get* (writ of divorce). This measure provoked a storm of criticism among the Orthodox, who questioned the legitimacy of such marriages. In 1967, the Law Committee went still further by allowing the nullification of marriages in order to free a wife from a recalcitrant husband. In 1969 the Law Committee voted to make the observance of the Second Day of Yom Tov optional in keeping with the Israeli calendar and in emulation of Reform practices. The new status of women in society has affected the Law Committee and the entire movement in convulsive fashion. In 1973, the Rabbinical Assembly agreed to count women for the *minyan* (worship quorum) and give them *'aliyot* (Torah honors) at services, much to the outrage of Orthodox leaders, who described these moves as acts of desperation to bolster sagging attendance at Conservative synagogues. More recently, the movement has been sharply divided over the question of the ordination of women. Following the lead of the Reform and Reconstructionist seminaries, Chancellor Gerson D. Cohen has openly espoused the idea of ordination for women. But the Seminary faculty has been badly split over this issue, and the Rabbinical Assembly and the United Synagogue, while leaving the final decision to the faculty, are also sharply divided. The more traditional elements have decried these legal steps as creeping reforms which will destroy the traditional coloration of Conservative Judaism; the liberal wing accuses the other of being nostalgically Orthodox. At this writing, the issue is unresolved, and the bitterness and vituperations are creating havoc and threatening to break up the century-old coalition of Conservative Jewry. But as Reform veers back to tradition, and as the Conservatives adopt a more liberal legal posture, the gap between the two groups seems to have narrowed considerably.[37]

While Conservative Judaism has provoked clashes with the Orthodox by its legal decisions and evoked some Reform gibes by its hair-splitting indecision, it has been the most concerned with Jewish peoplehood of all groups and has done more to foster intergroup harmony in Jewish life than either the Orthodox or Reform. On the whole, Conservative Judaism has eschewed partisanship and vituperation; its leaders have refused to respond to assaults from the left or right and have refrained from name-calling. Solomon Schechter set the tone long ago in stressing "Catholic Israel." He worked harmoniously with Kaufmann Kohler of the Hebrew Union College and sought to bring the Orthodox elements under the common banner of the United Synagogue and the Seminary. And while he criticized Reform as "Paulinism" for having stripped Judaism of law, he wrote that "life is too short for feuds," and he set an example of intergroup cooperation and community concern followed by his successors.

The Conservative movement has been the most ecumenical and cooperative of all the movements in Jewry.

True to its stress on peoplehood, Conservative Judaism has been loyal to the ideal of Zion reborn and has supported the Zionist movement from the outset. Schechter believed that a return to Zion was essential for Israel to achieve its sacred mission, and in 1905 he publicly announced his affiliation with the Zionist movement. He declared that Zionism was a great bulwark against assimilation and that it "was, and still is, the most cherished dream I was worthy of having." But he cautioned against severing Jewish nationalism from its sacred roots, and he felt drawn to Aḥad Ha-Am's cultural Zionism and to the nascent Mizrachi wing, with its stress on religious Zionism.[38] The Conservative movement has remained in the leadership of the political, financial, and spiritual struggle to create and sustain the Jewish State. In recent years, as its presence has grown in Israel and as it has been treated, in its view, as second-class citizens in the young state, Conservatism has grown more critical of the Orthodox establishment and Chief Rabbis. It has battled for recognition of Conservative rabbis in Israel; it has established its own synagogues; it has followed the Reform lead and created its own Zionist group, MERCAZ, as a constituent member of the World Zionist Organization.

In sum, as the Conservative movement has been rebuffed and even abused by Orthodoxy, it appears that the liberal wing is prevailing and Conservatism is moving more and more away from traditionalism and ever closer to a more liberal posture in a variety of key areas.

IV

Orthodoxy, the oldest of Jewish religious groups, was slow in reacting to the twin challenges of Emancipation and Enlightenment. Oriental Jewry was basically untouched by new trends or liberal winds. Consequently, it never developed a Reform or Conservative movement, and Orthodoxy preserved its monopoly. European Orthodoxy responded in two opposite fashions. The

East European fundamentalists steadfastly rejected both Enlightenment and Emancipation and refused the blandishments and blessings of integration into the modern world, considering those blessings dangers to Torah and Jewish autonomous life. Rabbi Ezekiel Landau of Prague (d. 1793) opposed German culture as corrosive, and he proscribed the *Biur* (Commentary) to the Bible of Mendelssohn and Wessely as well as the writings of the Maskilim. The Vilna Gaon opposed both the Hasidim as well as the Maskilim, and Rabbi Moses Sofer of Pressburg (d. 1839) rejected the reforms of Francis II and any attempt to mingle with gentiles in the new world of Enlightenment. In a pun on an ancient rabbinic ruling, he declared that "the new is taboo." Shneur Zalman of Ladi, confronted by the imminent capture of Moscow by Napoleon Bonaparte, prayed for his defeat, as did Reb Yisrael, the Maggid of Kozienice. Shneur Zalman allegedly proclaimed:

> Should Bonaparte win, the wealth of the Jews will be increased and their position will be raised. At the same time their hearts will be estranged from our heavenly Father. Should, however, our Tzar Alexander win, the Jewish hearts will draw nearer to our heavenly Father, though the poverty of Israel may become greater and his position lower.[39]

The Frankfort Reformers were put in *ḥerem* (excommunication) by Orthodox rabbis. In 1860, a rabbinical conclave issued a ban against sermons in the vernacular, gowns for rabbis, and the placing of the *bimah* (reader's stand) at the front of the synagogue. In some cases, Orthodox zealots even resorted to violence against the Reformers and spread seditious rumors about them to the government in an attempt to gain government support for closing Reform temples.

Fundamentalist Orthodoxy, referred to by Charles Liebman as "the sectarians," established his own *yeshivot* (talmudic academies) in Europe and America, generally rallied to the flag of the Agudat Israel party, staunchly opposed Zionism and even the newly established State of Israel, and shunned cooperation with the non-Orthodox, whom it viewed as heretics. Even the liberal Orthodox and Mizrachi wings have been subjected to attacks by these groups, and some of the great leaders of the more worldly Orthodox, including Rabbi Joseph B. Soloveitchik, have been accused of compromising Jewish principles. The fundamentalists have transported their ideas and institutions to America and Israel. Generally foreign-born and of the lower economic brackets, they cluster in self-imposed ghettos in Brooklyn, Lakewood, Spring Valley, Me'ah She'arim in Jerusalem, and B'nai Berak, near Tel Aviv. Their spiritual leaders are the heads of the various *yeshivot* or Hasidic rebbes. They shun secular education, television, movies, and worldly pursuits, apart from earning a livelihood. For them, the challenges of the post-Emancipation world do not exist.[40]

The fundamentalist trend was not able to strike roots in America for a long time. In the early days, few pious Jews ventured forth to the impure, *trefa* New World. Consequently, the Agudat Israel was very late in starting here. Only after World War II have the fundamentalist groupings of Hasidic and non-Hasidic Jews begun to come to America in large numbers and develop their own *shuls*, *yeshivot*, and institutions. As their numbers and influence have increased, they have been less inhibited about attacking the non-Orthodox. For example, in 1955, eleven eminent *yeshivah* heads, including Rabbi Moshe Feinstein and Rabbi Ahron Kotler, issued a ban against participation in the New York Board of Rabbis, the Synagogue Council of America, and other umbrella groups consisting of non-Orthodox rabbis and laymen:

We have been asked by a number of rabbis in the country and by alumni and *musmochim* of *yeshivos*, if it is permissible to participate with and be a member of the New York Board of Rabbis and similar groups in other communities, which are composed of Reform and Conservative "rabbis."

Having gathered together to clarify this matter, it has been ruled by the undersigned that it is forbidden by the law of our sacred Torah to be a member of and to participate in such an organization.

We have also been asked if it is permissible to participate with and to be a member of the Synagogue Council of America, which is also composed of Reform and Conservative organizations.

We have ruled that it is forbidden by the law of our sacred Torah to participate with them either as an individual or as an organized, communal body.[41]

When the leader of the liberal and more worldly Orthodox wing, Rabbi Joseph B. Soloveitchik, was queried on the same matter, he declined to respond. He did, however, respond to a query in 1955 concerning participation in a non-Orthodox synagogue on Sabbaths and Festivals, replying that the Torah itself prohibits worshipping in such places. Better to stay at home, he wrote, then to worship in a synagogue with mixed seating.[42] The same view has been taken by the Chief Rabbis of Jerusalem, Yaakov Zolti and Shalom Mashash, who issued a legal ruling on the eve of Rosh Hashanah, 1979, that the Torah prohibits praying in or listening to the *shofar* at Conservative congregations.[43] Clearly, the fundamentalist trend in Orthodoxy has been consistent: it refuses to recognize any need for change or updating of ritual; it rejects any compromises within modern Orthodoxy; it views the non-Orthodox as heretics and inauthentic Jews.

But the fundamentalist wing of Orthodoxy was not destined to capture the minds and hearts of American Orthodoxy. Rather, it was the more worldly philosophy of Samson Raphael Hirsch and German Orthodoxy that was to win out in the New World.

Hirsch was born in Hamburg in 1808 and died in Frankfort in 1888. He received a traditional *yeshivah* training and was awarded ordination by Rabbi Jacob Ettlinger. But Hirsch was no parochial Orthodox rabbi: he pursued secular studies and began writing extensively in German rather than Hebrew. In his early days, he was clearly influenced by the young Reform movement. He dressed in a Protestant clergyman's garb and did not sport a beard. Moreover, he was favorably inclined toward Emancipation and wrote: "I bless Emancipation when I see how the excess of oppression drove Israel away from a normal life."[44] This great apostle of modern Orthodoxy, who described himself as a *religiös erleuchtet*, wrote that the Jew's duty to the state is unconditional even if the state is harsh and tyrannical. He borrowed a page from the Reformers when he blessed the Diaspora because it enabled Israel to fulfill its mission to the gentiles. He did not believe that land or soil are Israel's bond of union but only the Torah; he wrote his commentaries on the Bible and prayerbook in German. He scandalized the fundamentalists by dropping the *Kol Nidre* prayer and by establishing a school for girls. His motto was "Torah and *Derekh Erez*"—Jewish life and learning plus secular learning and worldly living.[45]

Later on in his career, he became an ardent foe of Reform and the proto-Conservatives. In Frankfort, where he served from 1851 until his death, he shaped the neo-Orthodoxy that was to make such an impact on Western European Jewry and later on American Jewry. Hirsch demanded, and won, the right of the Orthodox group to secede from a local Jewish community which included the non-Orthodox. In 1876, the Prussian Parliament passed the Law of Secession (*Austritt*) and the Orthodox community went off on its own. By denuding Judaism of nationalism, Hirsch and his followers Breuer and Hildesheimer became Germans of the Mosaic (albeit Orthodox) persuasion very much as the Reformers had become Germans of the Mosaic (albeit Reform) persuasion. Whether he admitted it or not, Hirsch, despite his call for "Torah-true Jews" and rejection of Reform, was more profoundly influenced by Emancipation, Enlightenment, and Reform than he realized.

American Orthodoxy followed Hirsch's example in its development and ideology. Early Sephardic Orthodoxy left few permanent achievements. It was the arrival of German and later the masses of East European Orthodox that changed the face of Orthodox Jewry. Interestingly, although Orthodoxy officially denounced the Reform and Conservative groups, it emulated them organizationally and, to a lesser degree, ideologically as well. First, Orthodoxy organized a *yeshivah* (Etz Chaim in New York in 1886) to teach young boys Bible, Talmud, and Hebrew in accordance with Orthodox Judaism. The *yeshivah* would also teach secular subjects, in keeping with Hirsch's views rather than with those of East European *yeshivah* heads who proscribed secular learning.

In 1897, the Rabbi Isaac Elchanan Theological Seminary was established in New York for advanced talmudic studies and in order to prepare students for the "Hebrew Orthodox Ministry." Secular subjects were taught in the afternoon. In 1915, both schools merged under the leadership of Rabbi Bernard Revel, himself the holder of a Ph.D. Revel shaped the schools into Yeshiva College in 1928 to combine Torah education and secular learning. He was fearful of the secular and even anti-Semitic atmosphere of the colleges, and he hoped that the school would be a blend of "Orthodox Judaism and Americanism" and would produce English-speaking rabbis. The ultra-Orthodox sniped at Revel for adding secular learning, and the Reformers sneered at the parochial East European greenhorns. But the experiment worked, and the little yeshivah grew into Yeshiva University.[46]

In 1898, a group of Orthodox rabbis and laymen (including some non-Orthodox) created their response to the Union of American Hebrew Congregations by establishing the Union of Orthodox Jewish Congregations. They flung the gauntlet at Reform and its Pittsburgh Platform by outlining as their goals the advancement of "positive Biblical, Rabbinical, Traditional, and Historical Judaism." They affirmed their belief in Divine revelation of the Bible and ceremonial laws; they emphasized a commitment to "the authoritative interpretation of our rabbis as contained in Talmud and Codes and the Maimonidean Thirteen Principles of Faith." The delegates clearly rebuffed the Reformers by affirming their belief in a personal Messiah, circumcision, and ritual immersion for converts, and they protested strongly against intermarriage. Finally, they denounced the Pittsburgh Platform's stand on Zion and Jewish nationhood by stressing, "We are a nation, though temporarily without a national home," and they reaffirmed their belief in the return to the Holy Land, rejecting the Reform charge of dual loyalty. In 1903, the new Union endorsed the Isaac Elchanan Theological Seminary as the only legitimate training school for rabbis in America, thus cutting forever its ties with the Conservative group.[47]

In 1902 the Agudat Ha-Rabbanim, or Union of Orthodox Rabbis, was born. Its purpose was "the training of ordained rabbis, teachers and preachers who have mastered the English language and who will be fit to wage combat against the forces of Reform." The Union disavowed graduates of the Conservative Jewish Theological Seminary as lacking proper credentials, and it endorsed the Isaac Elchanan Theological Seminary as the only *bona fide yeshivah* in the land. Thus it declared war on both Reform and Conservative Judaism. With the passage of time, however, the Union of Orthodox Rabbis declined in numbers and prestige, and the Rabbinical Council of America (founded in 1935) replaced it as the leading mouthpiece for modern Orthodoxy in America.[48]

What does Orthodox Jewry stand for? Ideology has never been its *forte*, and Orthodoxy has preferred to stress *Halakhah* and ritual rather than ideas or theology. Yet some of the younger men have acknowledged external pressures and the need to formulate a theology in the light of outside challenges. Reform and Conservatism have forced Orthodoxy, willy-nilly, to rethink and restate its position. Rabbis Shubert Spero and Norman Lamm have urged that Orthodoxy turn to theology in an age of science and doubt and in order to demonstrate "its superiority over rival Jewish theologies." Consequently, we have seen some profound theological studies issue forth from Rabbis Joseph B. Soloveitchik, Emanuel Rackman, Eliezer Berkovits, and others.[49]

Orthodoxy has not been constrained to formulate formal ideological positions. Rather, it has been generally content to restate the classical ideological views of Maimonides or Albo or Hirsch. Judaism, in Orthodoxy's view, is a *religion*, not a civilization, and it is based on Divine revelation of Torah. A Jew is fundamentally expected to adhere to *Halakhah* and divinely revealed *mizvot* as the commands of a supernatural Deity. He is part of a chosen people whose mission it is to disseminate Torah and ethical monotheism to humanity.

Orthodoxy's focal point is *Halakhah*, which is viewed by all Orthodox thinkers as the will of God. Most Orthodox theologians insist that *Halakhah* is the objectification of religion, and that the laws do *not* reflect human caprice or socioeconomic factors. Nor are they the result of any evolution or development, growth, or change. The *Halakhah* we know today is precisely that which God

revealed at Sinai. In short, Orthodoxy rejects the critical scholarship of *Wissenschaft des Judentums* and the findings of scholars such
as Geiger, Zunz, Graetz, and Louis Ginzberg. The more liberal
thinkers, such as Samuel Belkin, Emanuel Rackman, Leo Jung,
and Eliezer Berkovits, do seek the higher purpose of the law and
concede the need for legitimate applications of precedents to new
situations (*ḥiddushin*). Rackman goes so far as to concede that "man
plays a role in the development of *Halakhah*." Eliezer Berkovits is
even more liberal: he berates the Orthodox for becoming advocates of "non-authentic *Halakhah*" and for developing into
"ivory-tower scholars" who ignore past adaptations of *Halakhah*
and who defend archaic and obsolete laws and are oblivious to
pressing problems. Rabbi Mendell Lewittes has issued a call for
frank confrontation with modern dilemmas in order to curb "the
alarming growth of the Reform and Conservative movements and
take the wind out of their sails."[50]

Orthodoxy has been untroubled by liturgical problems. Virtually no Orthodox theologian has suggested revision of the liturgy.
Concepts such as bodily resurrection, the personal Messiah, and
the restoration of animal sacrifices in a rebuilt Temple in
Jerusalem may not be taken too seriously by the Orthodox, but
they have not been deleted from the traditional prayerbook.
Rackman has decried attempts to revise the liturgy as "immodest"
and "arrogant behavior." Yet despite its rejection of any liturgical
reforms, the more modern Orthodox synagogues have been affected by non-Orthodox practices. Many Orthodox synagogues
are really synagogue-centers as envisioned by Mordecai M. Kaplan. The rabbis do preach in English. More significantly, many
Orthodox synagogues, euphemistically referred to as "traditional"
synagogues, have mixed seating of men and women in clear violation of Orthodox practice. Non-Orthodox trends have obviously
made inroads in Orthodox services.[51]

The Orthodox community has been ambivalent over the question of a Jewish state. The extreme groups, such as the Satmar
Hasidim, are implacable foes of the Jewish state, refusing to even
recognize it and denouncing it as a secular creation that violates

God's laws. They insist that only with the coming of the Messiah will the state be reborn and legitimatized. Consequently, these zealots condemn the Mizrachi wing of Zionists who are part and parcel of Israel reborn. In the eyes of the zealots, they are as bad as the secularist-Zionists and are guilty of forcing God's hand in history. The bulk of the fundamentalists, however, are part of the Agudat Israel group. They have made an uneasy peace with the State of Israel; they vote in elections, field their own candidates for Parliament, and participate in the government. Their philosophy is simple: Israel must be run along the lines of Torah and *mizvot* is interpreted by the sages and *yeshivah* heads rather than Israel's Chief Rabbis.

The mainstream of Orthodoxy, however, is in the camp of the Mizrachi, in this country called the "Religious Zionists of America." They are passionately devoted to the State of Israel; they want to see it run according to the rules of *Halakhah* so that it might fulfill a higher purpose than mere national rebirth; they regard the Chief Rabbis of Israel as their ultimate authorities. As Rabbi Soloveitchik has written, the Jewish state is a means to a higher end—the way of fulfilling the destiny of "the community of the committed." The slogan of the religious Zionists has been, "The Land of Israel for the people of Israel according to the Torah of Israel." This has led to sharp clashes with the secular Zionists as well as the non-Orthodox Zionists. Since Orthodoxy perceives Reform and, especially, Conservative Judaism as serious threats, it has adamantly opposed legitimatizing non-Orthodox rabbis in Israel or extending state help to non-Orthodox congregations. The same Orthodox leaders who call for pluralism and equal rights for non-Christian groups in America would deny those rights to the non-Orthodox Jews in Israel. Their argument is that the non-Orthodox groups are heretics who inject divisiveness into the State of Israel and whose views will corrupt the citizens of the Holy Land.[52]

As to interreligious cooperation, Orthodoxy has roundly chided the Reform and Conservative leaders for joining with Christians either in worship or community projects, accusing them of sycophancy and compromising Jewish principles. Virtually no Orthodox rabbis participate in interfaith activities, and few will ever set foot in a church.[53]

When it comes to cooperation with other Jewish groups, Orthodoxy seems willing to work with others if it serves Orthodox Judaism's purposes. Since 1962, the Orthodox community has broken ranks over the question of public aid to parochial schools. Likewise, the Orthodox groups have been at loggerheads with the non-Orthodox over liberal abortion laws, insisting that abortion on demand is immoral and that feticide is contrary to *Halakhah*. More and more it appears that the Orthodox community, now greatly Americanized and psychologically secure, is going off on its own, less willing or anxious to cooperate with the non-Orthodox segment than in the past.[54]

Of late, the Orthodox community has taken a sharp swing to the right in an obvious fundamentalistic resurgence. The right-wing groups have grown enormously by virtue of population explosion. They have become more outspoken in criticizing liberal Orthodox groups as well as the non-Orthodox. They have not been reluctant to express their contempt for "heretics." Rabbi Moshe Feinstein, for example, premier legal expert of the fundamentalist wing, has ruled that Conservative and Reform Jews are invalid as witnesses; hence, marriage ceremonies utilizing such witnesses and performed by non-Orthodox clergy are invalid and null. The various Hasidic groups have resorted to violence against one another and against the non-Orthodox as well. Even the formerly liberal element within Orthodoxy has taken a fundamentalist turn. Many refuse to refer to non-Orthodox clergy by the title of "rabbi" so as to deny them any sense of legitimacy. As Rabbi Ralph Pelcovitz wrote: "By submerging ourselves we lose our identity, we sacrifice our unique voice, we forfeit our opportunity to project our viewpoint in a clear, decisive, unequivocal manner."[55] The Conservative movement has been more sharply vilified than the Reform because, being closer to Orthodoxy, it represents a greater threat.

For the present, it appears that Orthodoxy will continue to cooperate with the non-Orthodox in matters of Jewish communal welfare, notwithstanding theological qualms. But for the future, it seems that the clash of ideologies will be disruptive, and Orthodox Jewry will go its own way oblivious to the other groups.

V

Reconstructionism is the fourth religious response to the modern era and its challenges. It is unlike the other movements in a number of striking respects. First, it is the creation of one man, Rabbi Mordecai M. Kaplan, so that in order to understand its position one must read Kaplan's works. Second, it is essentially an American phenomenon, and although several Reconstructionist synagogues and ḥavurot (fellowships) have sprung up in Canada, Israel, Curaçao, and elsewhere, it is basically an American movement whose ideology is typically American even though European thinkers, such as Durkheim, Spencer, Mills, Darwin, and Aḥad Ha-Am, have had an obvious impact on Kaplan's views.[56] Finally, Reconstructionism originally resisted the temptation to become a separate movement in Jewish life, perferring to remain a "quality of Jewish life" and influence the other movements. Only in the last decade has Reconstructionism formally set off on its own course.[57]

Mordecai M. Kaplan, the creator of Reconstructionism, was born in Lithuania in 1881 into a eminent family of Orthodox rabbis. Brought to this country at an early age, he was educated in New York at the City College and Columbia University and was ordained by the Jewish Theological Seminary. Although quite Orthodox in practice, Kaplan held radical views at an early age. He had studied biblical criticism with Arnold B. Ehrlich and his belief in the Divine origin of the Torah was undermined. His readings in philosophy and anthropology also changed his fundamentalist views. For a time he served in two eminent Orthodox pulpits, but his doubts grew. When Dr. Solomon Schechter invited him to teach at and run the new Teachers Institute of the Jewish Theological Seminary, he eagerly accepted.

At the Seminary, Kaplan was free to expound his views that Judaism is more than a religion: in fact, that it is an "evolving religious civilization."[58] He rejected the idea of a supernatural deity, preferring a naturalist-humanist notion of God as "the power or process that makes for human salvation."[59] He also denied that the Torah is the literal revelation of God.[60] These views caused friction with the Seminary leadership, and Kaplan almost resigned from the faculty on several occasions and very nearly accepted Stephen S. Wise's invitation to become president of the recently organized Jewish Institute of Religion. But Kaplan's loyalties to his *alma mater* transcended his personal ego. He steadfastly refused to create a new movement, for he believed that Judaism was already overly fractionalized. His loyal coterie of followers, including Rabbis Eugene Kohn, Milton Steinberg, Ira Eisenstein, and others, as well as a group of Reform rabbis, communal leaders, and men and women of eminence in Jewish life, begged him to chart his own course, free of the restraints of the Seminary; but Kaplan rebuffed them. It was not until the 1960s that he despaired of capturing the hearts of the Conservative movement and officially seceded.

For this reason, Reconstructionism was the last of the religious trends to crystallize into a formally organized movement. In 1940, the Reconstructionist Foundation was established, consisting of Reform and Conservative rabbis and lay leaders as well as secularists and Zionists who supported Kaplan's views. The Foundation published the *Reconstructionist* magazine and issued the Reconstructionist Haggadah, Sabbath prayerbook, Festival *Mahzor*, and daily prayerbook as well as books and pamphlets by Kaplan and his followers. In 1950, the Reconstructionist Rabbinical Fellowship was organized. In 1959 a formal Fellowship of Reconstructionist Congregations was established, and finally, in 1968, the Reconstructionist Rabbinical College was opened in Philadelphia to train men and women for the rabbinate under the presidency of Kaplan's long-time protégé and son-in-law, Rabbi Ira Eisenstein. Obviously, Reconstructionism has become, albeit reluctantly, the fourth religious movement in Jewry.

The essence of Reconstructionist philosophy can be gleaned from Kaplan's writings. The contributions of his disciples are really variations on Kaplanian themes. Kaplan had surveyed all of the contemporary movements in a searching critique and had found each one wanting.[61] He wrote that Reform was wise in accepting the need to adapt Judaism, but that it denationalized Jewish civilization and neglected its ritualistic aspect. Neo-Orthodoxy did elicit greater sacrifice than the other groups and insisted on maximum education and living; but it desiccated nationhood by treating it as a theological concept, and it was obsessed with supernaturalism. Conservative Judaism stressed the primacy of the Jewish People and its historical quest to live. But it was overly afflicted with romantic nostalgia and lacked the courage to revise or update Jewish law. Zionism is based on the ineradicable nature of anti-Semitism and rightly appeals to the will of the Jewish People to live and create in its own land. But it has failed to reckon with the Jewish People as a whole in the Diaspora. Consequently, nothing short of the reconstruction of Jewish life can save Judaism. Since the era of Emancipation, Jews have been thrust into an open society as members of a free world with no vestiges of Jewish self-rule. Therefore, we must teach our people to live in two civilizations simultaneously, borrowing the best in the American civilization and enriching Judaism in the process.

Kaplan views Judaism as more than merely a religion. It includes various elements: religion, culture, language, mores, folkways, dress, peoplehood, land, and so on. In short, it is a civilization that has evolved and changed. Since religion has been so vital a part of that civilization, it is a *religious* civilization. Kaplan's concept of God is naturalist-humanist, and he firmly rejects supernaturalism and miracles. For him, God is a power or process in man and nature that makes for human fulfillment or salvation. This theological position has scandalized the Orthodox, who accuse him of being a pantheist or a heretic.[62] But he has scandalized the Orthodox even more in his approach to revelation: Kaplan denies that revelation of Torah ever took place. The Reform movement accepts the notion of revelation of the ethical commandments of Judaism; Orthodoxy believes that the entire Torah is God's word; Conservatism affirms the notion of progressive revelation of Torah. Only Reconstructionism denies revelation entirely. Reconstructionism accepts the findings of biblical criticism and *Jüdische Wissenschaft;* it views the Torah as the creation of men over the centuries as they searched for God. In Kaplan's words, "The Torah reveals God to man."[63]

In view of Reconstructionism's concept of God and revelation, it is understandable why it rejects the notion of *Halakhah* and *mizvot.* Kaplan argues that each religion creates its heroes, sacred days and holy deeds—in a word, its *sancta.* He refers to *mizvot* as "folkways and customs," whose function is to bind the Jewish People together in religious fellowship, foster their group survival, and spiritualize their lives. The decision as to what rules to uphold or reject is left to the people, and Reconstructionists argue that since we live in a democratic era, we must decide by popular vote what is to be deleted and what is to be retained:

> Our position is that those *mitzvot* which, in tradition, are described as applying "between man and God" should be observed, insofar as they help to maintain the historic continuity of the Jewish People and to express, or symbolize, spiritual values or ideals which can enhance the inner life of Jews. Their observance, however, should be reckoned with, not in the spirit of juridical law which is coercive, but in the spirit of a voluntary consensus based on a general recognition of their value. We shall therefore refer to our approach to Jewish ritual observance as the *voluntaristic approach.*[64]

Mordecai M. Kaplan and the Reconstructionists have followed the Conservative movement in laying heavy emphasis on the central importance of the Jewish People in Jewish civilization. In a sense, Kaplan's views represent a revolution in Jewish life because instead of placing God at the center of Judaism, as does Reform, or *Halakhah* at the center, as does Orthodoxy, Kaplan sets the Jewish People as the focal point. Consequently, he argues that Torah and all facets of Jewish civilization exist to guarantee the survival of the Jewish People.[65] At the same time that he stresses peoplehood, he breaks with all other religious groups in rejecting the notion of chosen people, which he labels chauvinism, racism, and undemocratic.[66] Still, Kaplan does not totally shed the concept, for he borrows the idea of mission or vocation from the

Reform movement and writes that we have heard a "divine calling in which all peoples can have a share," and we must show the way to human salvation by teaching mankind the moral and spiritual uses of power over nature and by impelling men to create a social order based on justice, freedom, peace, and love. In a word, we Jews must become "a People in the image of God."[67]

Kaplan has been a Zionist from his youth, but his Zionism is of the cultural-spiritual brand. Heavily indebted to the views of Aḥad Ha-Am, he has placed the Land of Israel at the center of the Jewish world, hoping that it will fulfill Aḥad Ha-Am's dream of becoming a "spiritual center," united to the Diaspora by religion, ethics, and culture. He has written that only in Israel can a Jew lead a fully normal life, and, indeed, he settled in Israel several years ago. Arguing for a "new Zionism," he insists, as did Herzl and Aḥad Ha-Am, that Zion must mean the regeneration of the spirit of the Jewish People. There must be a creative cultural exchange between Israel and world Jewry: "World Jewry without Eretz Yisrael is like a soul without a body; Eretz Yisrael without World Jewry is like a body without a soul."[68] While Kaplan approaches the Orthodox view that political Zionism is not enough and the mere building of a state is not the loftiest goal of Zionism, he is sharply critical of the Orthodox religious establishment in Israel. He and his colleagues have joined with Reformers and Conservatives in demanding an end to theocratic control over religious life in Israel and the recognition of non-Orthodox religious groups and clergy.

Reconstructionists have always sought to play down partisanship and to transcend party lines in cooperative efforts for a greater Jewry. Kaplan had hoped that his approach to Jewish life would unite all groups—religious and secular, Zionist and Orthodox. He has called for the creation of "organic communities," an updated version of the old Jewish kehillah or Cultusgemeinde based on voluntarism and democracy rather than coercion or compulsion. These organic communities or voluntary community councils would maintain vital statistics, induce Jews to join national Jewish organizations, budget the needs of Jewish life, activate ethical standards, coordinate Jewish education, foster religious and cultural life, help stamp out poverty, defend Jewish rights, and collaborate with non-Jewish groups for the common welfare.[69] Although his idea of "organic communities" has struck responsive chords, it has not been implemented as yet.

Reconstructionism has met with great approval in some quarters and severe denunciation in others. In the 1930s and 1940s, many Conservative and Reform rabbis identified with its ideology. A survey of Reform rabbis in 1967 showed that although its influence was waning, 24 percent considered themselves Reconstructionists, and 15 percent of Conservative rabbis listed themselves as sympathizers.[70] But with the changing philosophical *Zeitgeist*, Kaplan's philosophy lost out. As Dewey's pragmatism faded in popularity and Buber's existentialism replaced it, Kaplan's theories lost favor.

Naturally, the Orthodox were horrified by Kaplan's theories and activities. Why were they so incensed at Kaplan? Perhaps because he had emerged from their own ranks. Or, perhaps, because he had touched on the most sensitive nerves—God, revelation, Torah, and the chosen people. In any event, never was the clash of ideologies exposed in such tawdry nakedness as when Kaplan issued his Reconstructionist *Sabbath Prayer Book* in 1945. A group of ultra-Orthodox rabbis of the Agudat Ha-Rabbanim gathered at a New York hotel, excommunicated Kaplan, and burned a copy of the new *Siddur*. Even some of Kaplan's colleagues at the Jewish Theological Seminary turned on him. He was deeply hurt and considered those days the loneliest of his career. Many rallied to his side and he recouped his strength, but he never forgave the Orthodox for the sin of book-burning, and he and his Reconstructionist colleagues view the Orthodox as medieval fanatics and bigots whose vices outweigh their virtues.

Reconstructionism has profoundly influenced the other movements in Judaism in a measure that exceeds the small numbers formally affiliated with the movement. Charles Liebman has shown that the bulk of American Jews subscribe to Kaplan's views, if only unconsciously. They *do* view Judaism as a religious civilization. They *do* prefer his rationalistic approach to Torah, revelation, and *mizvot*. They *do* subscribe to his non-supernatural

God idea. They *do* accept his conception of Jewish peoplehood. They agree with his spiritual Zionism. And they accept his reinterpretation of Jewish values. Why, then, are there not several million partisans of Reconstructionism? Partly because Kaplan refused to form another movement until quite recently, and partly because his views are not as well known as they should be.[71]

Nevertheless, Reconstructionism has affected all movements in American Judaism. Most Reform and Conservative Jews define Judaism as a religious civilization. Kaplan's analysis of the problems of living in two civilizations simultaneously and of participating in Jewish life on a voluntaristic basis has elicited favorable responses in all quarters. His synagogue-center has become the norm for most American synagogues, including many Orthodox ones. His concept of peoplehood and "New Zionism" is widely accepted. His emancipation of women (including the Bat Mitzvah ceremony, female participation in ritual, ordination of women, women leaders, etc.) has been embraced even in some liberal Orthodox circles. In a word, Mordecai M. Kaplan and Reconstructionism have been vital leavening in the ferment that is American Jewish ideology.

VI

The nationalist response to Enlightenment and Emancipation was no less forceful than the religious. It followed varied courses. One was the *Galut* (Diaspora) nationalist school, which found its greatest ideologist in historian Simon Dubnow.[72] Dubnow was sharply critical of the religious movements as well as of the new Zionist groups. He believed that Judaism had progressed beyond the territorial stage of development, and that to revert to it now by returning to the Land of Israel would represent retrogression rather than progress. Accordingly, this school of thought championed the notion that Jews must have minority rights to develop their own culture, language, and institutions in whichever country they reside. This approach was not totally without success, as evidenced by the battle for minority rights at the Paris Peace Conference of 1919 and by the farcical Soviet plan to grant Jewish national rights and establish an "autonomous Jewish nation" in Birobidzhan. But all efforts were doomed to failure as minority rights were crushed beneath the heels of Nazis and Communists alike.[73]

These various secular ideologies were transported to America as well but with less success than in Europe. *Galut* nationalism, popularized here by Dr. Chaim Zhitlowsky (1865–1943), labor Bundism, Communism, anarchism, and trade unionism did have their impact on American Jewry. While *Galut* nationalism was unsuccessful here because American Jews, unlike Polish or Russian Jews, had full rights and saw no need to clamor for "minority rights," radicalism was popular with workers who were rejecting the world of their fathers as well as the old religion and mores. In their rush to become Americans, these young rebels cast off ancestral practices and flung themselves into a variety of radical causes, often with cruel and tramautic impact on the older generation.[74] Morris Raphael Cohen described the ideological-generational conflict in his autobiography:

> We called upon the old religion to justify itself on the basis of modern science and culture. But the old generation was not in a position to say how this could be done. . . . What ensued was a struggle between old and new ideals. Homes ceased to be places of peace and in the ensuing discord much of the proverbial strength of the Jewish family was lost.[75]

And Lincoln Steffens mused about the revolt of the young secularist Jews against their Orthodox fathers:

> It was a revolution. Their sons were rebels against the law of Moses; they were lost souls, lost to God, the family, and to Israel of old. . . . Two, three thousand years of continuous devotion, courage and suffering for a cause lost in a generation.[76]

But as American Jews settled into a middle-class affluence, the ideological clash engendered by secularist movements abated, and secularism has virtually disappeared as a viable philosophy.

The main nationalistic response to the challenge of the modern era, however, was not secularism or Bundism or Diaspora nationalism; rather, it was the Zionist movement. Zionism took several different shapes: It was a religious movement, a secular movement, a Socialist movement, a spiritual movement. Religious Zionism was fostered by Rabbis Samuel Mohilever, Jacob Reines, Meir Berlin (Bar-llan), Rav Kook, and the Mizrachi Party. Secular or political Zionism was the brainchild of Pinsker, Herzl, Nordau, and their successors. Socialist Zionism, which combined the ideals of a national renascence with Marxist-Leninist principles, was expounded by Ber Borochov, Nachman Syrkin, David Ben-Gurion, and others. Cultural or spiritual Zionist was first propounded by Moses Hess but was expounded in detail by Aḥad Ha-Am and, as we have seen, Mordecai M. Kaplan. Many within the Zionist movement share a profound pessimism in their conviction that Jewish life in *Galut* is impossible and that anti-Semitism is incurable, while at the same time they assert the optimistic hope that human beings can rebuild Erez Yisrael and that the Jews should not wait for the coming of the Messiah.[77]

Religious Zionism stemmed from the age-old yearning to return to Zion. Precursors such as Shabbetai Zvi and his disciple Abraham Cardozo had sought to implement a move to return to Zion, as had various groups of Hasidim and even some of the great Rebbes, such as the Baal Shem Tov and Naḥman of Bratslav. Religious Zionism, depressed by the growth of modern anti-Semitism and frustrated over the failure to receive civil rights in Eastern Europe, decided to "force God's hand," so to speak, and hasten the coming of the Messiah by human rather than supernatural means. Rabbis Yehudah Alkalai (1798–1878) and Zvi Hirsch Kalischer (1795–1874) joined with the Hibbat Zion movement, arguing that the Messiah will only come if Jews prove worthy by reviving their nationhood in Erez Yisrael. "The beginning of the redemption," wrote Kalischer, "will come about in a natural way through human initiative and the consent of the reigning powers to the ingathering of the dispersed Jews in the Holy Land."[78] The religious Zionists or Mizrachi (founded in 1902) followed this lead. They rejected secular-political Zionism and argued that a state is merely a means to an end, that Erez

Yisrael without Torah is like a body without a soul. "The Land of Israel for the People of Israel in accordance with the Torah of Israel" became their motto.

Secular-political Zionism followed a different approach. It was utterly convinced that anti-Semitism was an incurable, ineradicable illness and that Jewry in *Galut* is doomed to assimilate. Dr. Leon Pinsker (1821–1891) called on Jews to help themselves via "auto-emancipation" because Jews will forever be hated rivals of the gentiles. Emancipation was, in his words, but a broken reed which will pierce the hand of him who leans on it; as long as Jews are dispersed among the nations and a landless, ghostlike people, they will be hated and feared and ultimately persecuted. Pinsker argued for the normalization of the Jewish People in their own land, not necessarily in the Holy Land. He called for the convening of an international congress, the creation of a national fund, and a political campaign to gain international recognition for the project. Since Judeophobia is a psychic aberration, it is a hereditary disease that is incurable. The hope is to create a fatherland for Jewry.[79]

Theodor Herzl (1860–1904) took over where Pinkser left off but added his unique, charismatic personality in fathering modern political Zionism. His grandfather Simon Herzl had been a devotee of Alkalai, so it is possible that young Theodor had been unconsciously influenced by Zionist thought. The Dreyfus case of 1894–95 shocked him into reality. If in a free, democratic France citizens could shout, "Death to the Jews," then Emancipation was merely a mirage. Herzl wrote in his *Der Judenstaat* that "our enemies have made us one people without our consent."[80] Modern anti-Semitism differs from the older version because it is now a national question which can only be solved by making it a political-world question to be discussed and settled by civilized nations. No matter how loyal Jews are, wrote Herzl, anti-Semitism is bound to increase. The only hope is to create a home, secured by public rights, for Jews who either cannot or will not assimilate. Herzl was a practical, political person: he summoned the first Zionist Congress in Basle, Switzerland, in 1897. The Basle Platform was emphatically clear: "Zionism seeks to secure for the Jewish People a publicly recognized, legally secured home in Palestine for the Jewish People." Herzl was convinced that once Jews were in their own home, anti-Semitic enemies would probably disappear.

The Basle Congress provoked a storm of controversy on all sides. The ultra-pious denounced it as a secular, Godless attempt to force God's hand. Only the Messiah, they argued, could bring about the restoration of the People of Israel to its land. This group of implacable foes ultimately coalesced and formed Agudat Israel (1912), an international body of Orthodox Jews who were staunchly opposed to Zionism. Ultimately, Agudat Israel came to terms with the State of Israel.

On the other side of the spectrum were the more liberal and Reform rabbis, most of whom greeted the Basle Platform with derision and criticism. The Association of Rabbis in Germany declared on July 16, 1897,

> that the attempts of the Zionists to found a Jewish national state in Palestine are contrary to the messianic promises of Judaism as laid down in Holy Writ and in the later authorities; that Judaism demands of its adherents to serve the state in which they live and in every way to further its national interests; but no opposition thereto can be seen in the noble plan to colonize Palestine with Jewish agriculturalists, because that plan has no connection with the founding of a national state.[81]

The Central Conference of American Rabbis was even sharper in its attack on Herzl's program:

> Resolved, that we totally disapprove of any attempt for the establishment of a Jewish State. Such attempts show a misunderstanding of Israel's mission, which from the narrow political and national field has been expanded to the promotion among the whole human race of the broad and universalistic religion first proclaimed by the Jewish prophets. Such attempts do not benefit, but infinitely harm our Jewish brethren where they are still persecuted, by confirming the assertion of their enemies that the Jews are foreigners in the countries in which they are at home, and of which they are everwhere the most loyal and patriotic citizens.[82]

Additionally, Herzl had to contend with "fractions" (as the parties were called) within the superstructure of the Zionist movement. Among such "fractions" were the Socialist-Zionists, a party that fused the principles of Marx and Lenin with political Zionism. This group, known as Poalei Zion, led by Nachman Syrkin (1867–1924), Ber Borochov (1881–1917), and, in later years, by David Ben-Gurion (1886–1973), challenged many basic tenets of Herzl's Zionism. They criticized the political Zionists for bourgeois tendencies and for their failure to see that only by labor and Socialist principles could Israel be reborn in its own land.[83]

Herzl had to battle with other opponents as well. We must recall that there was a fundamental difference between the Western Zionists of the Herzl and Nordau type and the Eastern Zionists typified by Menahem Ussishkin, Aḥad Ha-Am, and the young Chaim Weizmann. The Western Zionists were urbane, somewhat assimilated, generally ignorant of Hebrew or Yiddish and Jewish sources, and convinced that political action and charters were the key to the reclamation of the Holy Land. The Eastern Zionists, on the other hand, were essentially unassimilated, were steeped in Hebrew and Yiddish and traditional religious learning and values, and were equally convinced that the only way to rebuild Zion was by practical action, such as settlements, immigration, agriculture projects, and population expansion in Israel. This fundamental rift became painfully apparent in the Uganda affair at the 1903 Zionist Congress.

For some time, Herzl had been exploring the possibility of a grant of land in East Africa from the British government in order to rescue the beleaguered Russian Jews from their oppressors. Since it was obvious that Palestine was not about to become the haven of refuge, he was prepared to accept a temporary substitute. In 1903, Lord Henry Landsdowne offered Herzl Uganda as the sought-after refuge. Herzl presented the plan to the sixth Congress and called for a vote. After a stormy session, he received 295 affirmative votes against 178 negative and 100 abstentions. Most of the negative votes were cast by the East European delegates, who stormed out of the Congress calling Herzl a traitor and affirming that for them it would be Zion or nothing. Herzl went to the delegates to soothe them. He found them weeping; some were seated on the floor as if in mourning.He had misjudged the depth of their loyalty to Ereẓ Yisrael. He assured them that he had not intended to betray the Basle Program; that Palestine was still his ultimate goal; that Uganda would merely be—in Nordau's words—a *Nachtasyl*, "a night shelter" for persecuted Russian Jews. He finally won them back to the Congress. But tensions ran high. A crazed young Russian Zionist attempted to assassinate Nordau over this issue. Ussishkin smarted and called a Russian Zionist Conference in Kharkov that year at which he warned Herzl that they would never be diverted from Ereẓ Yisrael. On the other side, Israel Zangwill and his followers were furious when Herzl dropped the Uganda proposal and similar alternative schemes. He and his group seceded from the Zionist Congress in 1905 and set up the Jewish Territorial Association to find other places of refuge for oppressed Jews. By 1925, however, the Association went out of existence.[84]

Herzl's political Zionism was sharply assailed from yet another ideological group—the spiritual or cultural Zionists. Spiritual Zionism differed from all the other versions in that it believed the others inadequate. Spiritual Zionism propounded the view that the land reborn was not an end in itself; that in any event, not all Jews would or could settle there; and that Zionism's primary goal must be the revival of the Jewish spirit and the renascence of Jewish culture. Moses Hess (1812-1875), former student of Karl Marx and Hegelian philosopher, was the first to expound this theme in his *Rome and Jerusalem* (1862). Hess wrote that the nationalism of his times vindicated the struggle of the Jew to regain his nationhood. But Jewish nationhood had no military ambitions; rather, it would help others achieve their own high destiny. Consequently, Hess argued that neither Enlightenment nor conversion nor Reform offered a solution to the Jewish problems. Only when the "holy spirit will again animate our people, when it awakens to a new life," will it create new things which we cannot at present imagine.[85] Hess agreed that the majority of Jews would not go to Erez Yisrael but held it could serve as a spiritual center for world Jewry in the tradition of similar centers that existed in the past.[86]

The great apostle of spiritual or cultural Zionism, and most trenchant critic of Herzl and political Zionism, was Aḥad Ha-Am (1859–1927). He was contemptuous of Western Zionists, whom he viewed as assimilated Jews, untutored in Hebrew sources. He disclaimed their political tactics; he insisted that diplomats would not win the Land of Israel back for the Jewish People. Aḥad Ha-Am viewed Zionism as the reconstruction of Judaism as a whole, the reviving of Jewish consciousness. He considered Zionism a cultural rather than a political phenomenon. A total ingathering of all Jews was impossible; but the creation of a "spiritual center" in Erez Yisrael was vital to pull together the atoms of Jewish communities. True love of Zion, he wrote, is "not merely a part of Judaism; nor is it something added on to Judaism; it is the whole of Judaism but with a different focal point. . . . It stands for a Judaism which shall have as its focal point the ideal of our nation's unity, its renascence, and its free development through the expression of universal human values in the terms of its own distinctive spirit."[87]

Aḥad Ha-Am criticized those who viewed a state as the end-all of Jewish life. He insisted that the Third Commonwealth must combine flesh and spirit and uplift the body by the spirit. He sharply attacked the Reform movement for failing to perceive that the Jewish religion is national, that in Judaism religion and nationalism are inseparable. He also assailed Dubnow's views on *Galut* nationalism because in *Galut* Jews cannot achieve the full play of creative faculties and education to imbue people with culture. His greatest fear was that Jews would live in slavery of mind and soul in the midst of political freedom, and that there was a very real danger that Jewish communities would fragmentize and take on the coloration of their surrounding culture:

> What Judaism has to fear is being split up into fragments. The manner in which the Jews work for the protection of their individuality depends everywhere on the character of that foreign spiritual

force which is at work in their surroundings and which arouses them to what we have called "competitive imitation." In the end, Israel will be no longer one people but a number of separate tribes, as at the beginning of history.[88]

Aḥad Ha-Am believed that only a turn eastward to the ancient spiritual center in Ereẓ Yisrael could unite the parts.

Somehow all of these diverse ideological interpretations of Zionism came together and have been subsumed under the World Zionist Organization. They work together, clash, debate, argue, feud. But they were able to pull together as one in creating the State of Israel. Each ideological trend has been imported into Israel and Israeli politics, and the division of the Knesset reflects these colorations.

Similarly, the Zionist movement took root in America. First, partisans of Hibbat Zion began to disseminate their ideas. With the arrival of Herzl's political Zionism, Zionist clubs and societies were formed in America under the leadership of Sabato Morais, Marcus Jastrow, Benjamin and Henrietta Szold, Gustav and Richard Gottheil, Judah Magnes, and Stephen S. Wise. The Federation of American Zionists was founded in 1898 and is today known as the Zionist Organization of America. Then came the Mizrachi in 1903 (currently called the Religious Zionists of America); then the Labor Zionist Alliance, the Revisionist Zionists of Vladimir Jabotinsky, Hadassah, and various women's groups. Today, the numerous Zionist groups are joined under a loosely structured umbrella known as the American Zionist Federation. They work together for the greater support of the State of Israel.

The anti-Zionists formed into two camps: The "classical" Reformers created the American Council for Judaism, which rejected Reform's new stress on Zionism and raised the old bugaboo about "dual loyalty." The second group consists of a small number of ultra-Orthodox Jews, many of them followers of the Satmar Rebbe, who refuse to recognize a secular State of Israel run by Godless heretics but prefer, instead, to wait for the Messiah. Clearly, there has been no lack of varied Zionist ideologies in

America, although American Jews never became as passionate about Zionist theory as did their European cousins.[89]

VII

Even from this brief survey of the clash of modern ideologies in Jewish life it is apparent that we are witnesses to a remarkably rich confluence of ideologies and theories. Perhaps never before in Jewish history since the days of the Second Commonwealth, when Pharisaism, Sadduceanism, Essenism, and other Jewish ideologies locked horns with each other and with a host of pagan schools of thought in the Graeco-Roman world, has Judaism been so variegated in its ideologies and practices, in America, as in Europe before, and in modern Israel as well. Naturally, these ideological differences have led to antagonisms and hostility; but they have also led to mutual influence and enrichment. Notwithstanding the hostility and even rancor, the varied religious, secular, and Zionist schools of thought have had an impact on each other and have altered each other's positions on basic issues.

This variegated pattern of ideology and action is perhaps the greatest legacy of Emancipation. Since Emancipation meant, above all, a free and open society in which a Jew is welcome, most Jews felt free to drink in the wine of freedom of ideas and action. Moreover, since Emancipation implied the end of Jewish self-government and quasi-independent communal rule, the monolithic and often repressively autocratic control over Jewish ideological and behavioral patterns was ended. Gone were the days when a Uriel da Costa or a Baruch Spinoza could be excommunicated for "heretical" ideas. With Emancipation, all options were open, dissent and freedom of thought and deed were possible, and pluralism of ideology became acceptable and even laudatory. Moreover, voluntarism replaced coercion, so that a Jew now had an option that had never existed before: to belong or not to belong to the Jewish community. As voluntarism replaced compulsion, freedom of ideology and practice has taken over where homogeneity and uniformity once held sway.

How has this freedom of thought and openness of ideology

affected American Jews? Are American Jews truly moved by ideological considerations?

In truth, Americans are more pragmatic then ideological. They are less inclined to theory and more to deeds. And this applies to American Jews as well. It is inconceivable that many American Jewish Zionists, for example, could be inflamed to the degree of the old Revisionists who challenged the Labor Zionists in pre-war Poland. Nor is it likely that any religious group, with the possible exception of the extremist Satmar Hasidim, would engage in violence against less Orthodox Jews, as occurred in Eastern Europe or as is seen in present-day Israel. To be sure, a survey of American Jewry indicates that 82 percent of heads of households identify with Judaism as a religion, although only a little more than half of that number actually belong to synagogues. Of those, 40.5 percent consider themselves Conservative, 30 percent Reform, and 11.4 percent Orthodox, with a fraction listing themselves as Reconstructionist and but 4.1 percent describing themselves as atheists or agnostics.[90] But how seriously do they take all of this? And is ideology meaningful in their lives? Does this merely amount to what Eugene Borowitz has described as "belonging without believing"?

It appears to many observers of Jewish life that Borowitz is right; that religious convictions are about as deep as the Jordan River; that people join synagogues for the most outlandish—and untheological—reasons; that Zionist affiliation is usually no criterion whatsoever of ideological commitment. Some prefer Conservative congregations to Reform because they insist on wearing caps at worship. Others go to Reform temples because they have lower requirements for religious-school education. Many join an Orthodox synagogue because it is nearer than the Reform. Still others join one synagogue in preference to another because it has a good gym and pool or is more prestigious. And many choose one synagogue over the next because after "shopping around" it turns out to be less expensive to join. The same phenomenon seems to be prevalent in Zionist life, and most Jews join one group rather than the next out of nostalgia or because of a personal idiosyncrasy. While the élite may take ideology seriously, the masses or folk seem to treat it disdainfully and indifferently. There is quite a gap between the "élite" and "folk" religions and between the leaders and rabbis and the masses of American Jews.[91]

Now there are advantages and disadvantages to this casual attitude toward ideology. The obvious advantage is that if ideology is really insignificant, passions are cooled, rivalries are toned down, factionalism and partisanship are lessened. And with the lessening of intergroup tensions and rivalries, greater cooperation is possible, greater unity of purpose and action feasible. American Jews have been able to accomplish great things, perhaps, because we have not been sundered by partisanship as were European Jewries.

On the other hand, the lack of ideological commitment is so glaring as to make a farce of much of our verbal commitments or organizational affiliations. There is, in other words, little passion in American Jewish life. And if there is little passion, then how can we expect to elicit the best from our people or arouse them to sacrifice for Judaism or Torah or the Jewish People or the Land of Israel? In the words of Eugene Borowitz:

> What other religious groups in America can boast of men who are zealously committed to interfaith activities, but who have no faith of their own, who worship in no church with any degree of regularity, and who observe no commandments but those that their organizational participation requires or common American decency decrees? What does it say of Jewish life in America when Reform Judaism appeals because it demands so little but confers so much status? When people blandly proclaim that they are non-observant Orthodox Jews? When Conservative Judaism makes a virtue out of not defining the center so that it may avoid alienating those disaffected on either side?[92]

American Jews are more concerned with the *act* of believing than the *content* of believing. Most join synagogues because of the "desire to remain separate," as Nathan Glazer and Daniel P. Moynihan suggest.[93] Even the Reform movement, which was founded on a carefully formulated theological program, has discovered that Reform theology is largely irrelevant as a shaper of values.[94]

Given the divisions that exist in American Jewry, is cooperation possible? Are there transcending principles that unite Jews despite ideological differences.?

On a pragmatic level, there has been a sense of *Kelal Yisrael*, of the common weal and the needs of the Jewish community here and abroad. And this transcending principle has pulled Jews and Jewish organizations together notwithstanding differences, partisanship, and institutional loyalties. The local boards of rabbis do work together harmoniously in a variety of areas, ranging from hospital and prison chaplaincies to radio and TV shows to lobbying for legislation vital to Jewish interests. Community groups, local federations of Jewish philanthropy, Jewish community councils, secular organizations (e.g., B'nai B'rith, the American Jewish Congress, the American Jewish Committee), Zionist organizations, and umbrella bodies, such as the Synagogue Council of America, the Council of Jewish Federations, and the Presidents' Conference of Major Jewish Organizations, do meet, do plan strategy, do transcend ideological borders, and do enormous work in philanthropy, legislation, and community affairs for *Kelal Yisrael*. These groups, although loosely federated, have raised huge sums for charity and for Israel, have battled anti-Semitism at home, have championed the cause of Soviet Jewry, and have united, if only on an *ad hoc* basis, all kinds of Jews.

Ideological cooperation is, however, a different matter. Since ideology tends to divide and fragmentize, there is little intergroup cooperation along ideological or philosophical grounds, whether in religious groups or secular organizations. Orthodox rabbis and laymen will work with the non-Orthodox in the Synagogue Council of America on practical problems of mutual interest but never on ideological issues. Likewise, Orthodox rabbis will unite with non-Orthodox colleagues in boards of rabbis on issues of community concern but never on a question of *Halakhah*. Reform and Conservative groups will join forces on a host of legislative problems but rarely on a matter of religious philosophy. And Zionist groups will all pull together for Israel's protection but will split up when it comes to theory.

Of course, there are a few exceptions. Rabbis and laymen of various movements do work together to foster certain religious ideals even if they are not congruent with their own views. For instance, Reform, Orthodox, and Conservative leaders have united in fighting for *kashrut* in hospitals and for the rights of Sabbath-observers in employment. It is not unusual to see rabbis of different persuasions or laymen from diverse religious trends pool their efforts at boards of rabbis or in the commissions on synagogue relations of various federations of Jewish philanthropies on behalf of a religious goal that they may not personally endorse. But this is the exception to the rule that when ideology is involved, the groups go their separate ways and cooperation is rare.

There are those who decry the cacophony and yearn for the good old days of monolithic, unified Jewish theology and practice. In truth, however, there never really was a unified *ideology* even if there was a basic unity of religious *behavior*. But it is impossible to turn back the clock, and nostalgic yearning will not undo the past two centuries. Most modern Jews would not like to still the voice of dissent and return to the age of repression or excommunication in preference to democracy and free expression. They find the variations of Jewish themes stimulating and exciting. And they believe that for all of our disharmony and dissents, our clashes and conflicts, we are the richer spiritually and intellectually.

NOTES

1. Jacob Katz, *Tradition and Crisis* (Glencoe, Ill., 1961), pp. 245 ff.
2. Cf. B. Spinoza, *Tractatus Theologico-Politicus* (London, 1909), chap. 3. Cf. Jacob Agus, *The Evolution of Jewish Thought* (New York, 1959), pp. 299–314.
3. See Arthur Hertzberg, *The French Enlightenment and the Jews* (New York, 1968), pp. 300 ff.
4. See Baron's essay, "The Modern Age," in *Great Ages and Ideas of the Jewish People*, ed. by Leo. W. Schwarz (New York, 1950), pp. 315 ff.
5. See H. Graetz, *History of the Jews* (Philadelphia, 1940), Vol. V, pp. 429 ff. Cf. Hertzberg, op. cit., pp. 328 and 345.
6. See Herbert Bloom's essay, "Felix Libertaté and the Emancipation of Dutch Jewry," in *Essays on Jewish Life and Thought*, ed. by J. Blau, P. Friedman, A. Hertzberg, and I. Mendelsohn (New York, 1959), pp. 105–122.

7. Cf. Robert Anchel, *Napoleon et les Juifs* (Paris, 1928), pp. 120 ff; Diogène Tama, *Transactions of the Parisian Sanhedrin* (London, 1807), pp. 105 ff; Graetz, op. cit., Vol. V, pp. 490 ff.

8. See Solomon Schechter's studies of Abraham Geiger and Leopold Zunz in his *Studies in Judaism, Third Series* (Philadelphia, 1945), pp. 47–142. Cf. Louis Ginzberg's essay, "Zechariah Frankel," in his *Students, Scholars and Saints* (Philadelphia, 1945), pp. 195–216. Ginzberg wrote that the science (*Wissenschaft*) of Judaism was "the most striking gift of the nineteenth century to Jews and Judaism" (p. 195). On Steinschneider see Alexander Marx, *Essays in Jewish Biography* (Philadelphia, 1948), pp. 112–184; Salo W. Baron, "Moritz Steinschneider's Contribution to Jewish Historiography," in the *Alexander Marx Jubilee Volume*, English section (New York, 1950), pp. 83–148.

9. Cf. Gershom Scholem, *Major Trends in Jewish Mysticism* (New York, 1954), p. 304; cf. his *The Messianic Idea in Judaism* (New York, 1974), pp. 140 f.

10. See David Philipson, *The Reform Movement in Judaism* (New York, 1967), pp. 51 ff; W. Gunther Plaut, *The Rise of Reform Judaism* (New York, 1963), pp. 20–62.

11. See Plaut, op. cit., pp. 62–70.

12. See Gilbert S. Rosenthal, *Four Parts to One God* (New York, 1973), pp. 88 ff.

13. See Sidney Ahlstrom, *A Religious History of the American People* (New Haven, 1972), pp. 4 ff., 583–614, 763–784. Cf. my *Four Paths to One God*, pp. 1–25, 89 ff., and passim; also cf. my essay, "Jewish Religion in America: A Study in Mutuality," *Judaism*, Vol. 25, No. 3 (Summer 1976), pp. 290–300.

14. See Philipson, op. cit., pp. 329–334, and Plaut, *The Growth of Reform Judaism* (New York, 1965), pp. 4–7.

15. See Philipson, op. cit., pp. 337 f., and Plaut, *Growth of Reform Judaism*, pp. 4–11.

16. See Kaufmann Kohler, *Jewish Theology* (Cincinnati, 1943), pp. viii f., 4, 8, 20, and 321.

17. Cf. Kohler, *Studies, Addresses, and Personal Papers* (New York, 1931), pp. 203, 212 f., 327–329, and passim.

18. See my *Four Paths to One God*, pp. 108–112.

19. For the full text, cf. Philipson, op. cit., pp. 355–357.

20. For the full text of the Columbus Platform, cf. Plaut, *The Growth of Reform Judaism*, pp. 96–98.

21. Cf. Solomon Freehof, *Recent Reform Responsa* (Cincinnati, 1963), pp. 7–12. Cf. his *Reform Responsa for Our Time* (Cincinnati, 1977), pp. 4 ff.

22. The complete text is in *Reform Judaism Today* by Eugene Borowitz (New York, 1978), Vol. I, pp. xix–xxv.

23. Cf. my *Four Paths to One God*, pp. 103–106.

24. Ibid., pp. 127 f. Cf. Plaut, "The Halacha of Reform," in *Contemporary Reform Jewish Thought*, ed. by Bernard Martin (Chicago, 1968), pp. 90–98.

25. Cf. my *Four Paths to One God*, pp. 130–134.

26. See Mordecai Waxman (ed.), *Tradition and Change* (New York, 1958), pp. 43–50.

27. For the early history of Conservatism, see Moshe Davis, *The Emergence of Conservative Judaism* (Philadelphia, 1968).

28. Cf. my *Four Paths to One God*, pp. 154 ff.

29. Ibid., pp. 154, 183, and passim. Actually, Kohut was the first to use the term "conservative" in this sense. Cf. Davis, *The Emergence of Conservative Judaism*, pp. 222–226, 239.

30. Cf. my *Four Paths to One God*, pp. 156 ff.

31. Ibid., p. 163.

32. Cf. Heschel, *God in Search of Man*, pp. 310, 320–332, 417 ff.

33. Cf. Kaplan, *Judaism as a Civilization* (New York, 1934), p. 47 and passim.

34. Cf. Heschel, op. cit., pp. 197, 282, and passim. Also cf. his *The Insecurity of Freedom* (Philadelphia, 1966), p. 205, and *The Sabbath* (New York, 1951), pp. 48 and passim.

35. See his *Studies in Judaism* (Philadelphia, 1896), Vol. I, pp. xviii f. and Vol. III, pp. 89–119. Cf. his *Some Aspects of Rabbinic Theology* (New York, 1936), pp. xvii f. and 117.

36. See Gordis's *Judaism for the Modern Age* (New York, 1955), pp. 127–152, 186–194; cf. his *A Faith for Moderns* (New York, 1971), pp. 281–283.

37. See my *Four Paths to One God*, pp. 190–192; cf. my essay, "Jewish Religion in America: A Study in Mutuality," cited in note 13, pp. 298–300.

38. For Schechter's views on Zion, see my *Four Paths to One God*, pp. 194–196.

39. Cf. Simon Dubnow, *History of the Jews in Russia and Poland* (Philadelphia, 1916), Vol. I, pp. 365 f.; Salo W. Baron, *The Russian Jews under Tsars and Soviets* (New York, 1964), pp. 27 f.

40. Cf. Charles Liebman, "Orthodoxy in American Jewish Life," *American Jewish Yearbook*, Vol. 66 (1965), pp. 21–97. Also cf. Jerome R. Mintz, "Ethnic Activism: The Hasidic Example," in *Judaism*, Vol. 28, No. 4 (Fall 1979), pp. 449–464.

41. The statement was reprinted in an ad in the *New York Times* of December 1, 1970, p. 39, in a scurrilous attack on the New York Board of Rabbis.

42. So wrote Soloveitchik in a letter to Rabbi Benjamin Lapidus published in *Conservative Judaism*, Vol. 11, No. 1 (Fall 1956), pp. 50–51.

43. Published in an ad in the *Jerusalem Post* of September 17, 1979.

44. Cf. S. R. Hirsch, *The Nineteen Letters on Judaism* (New York, 1960), pp. 107, 109, 161, etc.

45. Cf. Hirsch's *Horeb* (London, 1962), pp. 609 f.; *The Nineteen Letters on Judaism*, pp. 80–81; Noah Rosenbloom, *Tradition in an Age of Reform* (Philadelphia, 1976), pp. 68 ff., 82, 110–120, 422, etc. The phrase "Torah 'im derekh erez" is derived from Mishnah *Avot* 2:2.

46. On the history of Yeshiva University, see Gilbert Klaperman, *The Story of Yeshiva University* (New York, 1969).

47. See Davis, *The Emergence of Conservative Judaism*, pp. 315–322, 334, 351; cf. Charles Liebman in his article cited in note 40, pp. 54–56.

48. Cf. Liebman, ibid., pp. 32–34.

49. Cf. *Tradition*, Vol. 9, Nos. 1–2 (Spring–Summer 1967), pp. 14–69. Also cf. my *Four Paths to One God*, pp. 54 ff.

50. Cf. Eliezer Berkovits, "Authentic Judaism and Halakhah," *Judaism*, Vol. 19, No. 1 (Winter 1970), pp. 66–76, and more recently his volume *Crisis and Faith* (New York, 1976), pp. 84–128. Also cf. M. Lewittes, "The Nature and History of Jewish Law," in *Studies in Torah Judaism*, ed. by Leon D. Stitskin (New York, 1969), p. 303.

51. Cf. Emanuel Rackman, "Arrogance or Humility in Prayer," *Tradition*,

Vol. 1, No. 1 (Fall 1958), pp. 13–26. Also see my *Four Paths to One God*, pp. 74–77.

52. See Emanuel Rackman, *One Man's Judaism* (New York, 1970), p. 312.

53. Rabbi J. B. Soloveitchik has drawn up a theology of interreligious dialogue. See his article, "Confrontation," in *Tradition*, Vol. 6, No. 2 (Spring–Summer 1964), pp. 5–28.

54. Cf. my *Four Paths to One God*, pp. 77–81.

55. See Rackman, *One Man's Judaism*, pp. 3, 262–283. Cf. Ralph Pelcovitz, "Who Is the Orthodox Jew?" in *Jewish Life*, Vol. 32, No. 2 (November–December 1968), p. 16.

56. On the sources of Reconstructionism, see Ira Eisenstein, "Mordecai M. Kaplan and His Teachers," in *Mordecai M. Kaplan: An Evaluation*, ed. by Eugene Kohn and Ira Eisenstein (New York, 1952), pp. 15–25.

57. See Charles Liebman, "Reconstructionism in American Jewish Life," *American Jewish Yearbook*, Vol. 71 (1970), pp. 3–99. Cf. my *Four Paths to One God*, pp. 213–228.

58. Already in 1920 Kaplan had put forth these views. But when he issued his magnum opus, *Judaism as a Civilization*, in 1934, they were officially projected on the Jewish scene. See his *Judaism as a Civilization*, p. 47; cf. his *The Meaning of God in Modern Jewish Religion* (New York, 1937), p. 96, and *The Future of the American Jew* (New York, 1948), p. 221.

59. Cf. *Judaism as a Civilization*, pp. 384, 394. For a full statement of Kaplan's God concept, see *The Meaning of God in Modern Jewish Religion*.

60. Cf. Kaplan's *Judaism as a Civilization*, pp. 414 and 510; *The Greater Judaism in the Making* (New York, 1960), pp. 506–511; *Judaism Without Supernaturalism* (New York, 1958).

61. See his *Judaism as a Civilization*, pp. 91–169, and his *The Greater Judaism in the Making*, pp. 221–449.

62. See, for example, Eliezer Berkovits's critique of Kaplan's views in his essay, "Reconstructionist Theology," *Tradition*, Vol. 2, No. 1 (Fall 1959), pp. 20–66.

63. Cf. Kaplan's *The Greater Judaism in the Making*, pp. 508–511.

64. Cf. Kaplan's *Questions Jews Ask* (New York, 1956), p. 265. Cf. pp. 226–227.

65. Cf. my *Four Paths to One God*, pp. 243 ff.

66. Cf. Kaplan's *The Future of the American Jew*, pp. 211–230. Alone among Kaplan's disciples in challenging Kaplan's rejection of the chosen-people concept was Milton Steinberg. See his *Basic Judaism* (New York, 1947), p. 96.

67. Cf. Kaplan's *The Purpose and Meaning of Jewish Existence* (Philadelphia, 1964), pp. 290, 296, 312–318.

68. Cf. Kaplan's *A New Zionism* (New York, 1955), pp. 144, 149, 172.

69. Kaplan spelled out his notion of "organic communities" in his *The Future of the American Jew*, pp. 80 f., 114 f., and in his *A New Zionism*, p. 126.

70. Cf. Liebman's study cited in note 57, pp. 49–62.

71. Ibid., pp. 46 ff., 68–99. Cf. Milton Steinberg, *A Partisan Guide to the Jewish Problem* (New York, 1945), p. 185.

72. For Dubnow's views, see Koppel Pinson (ed.), *Nationalism and History* (Philadelphia, 1958), pp. 76 ff.

73. See Joseph Nedava, *Trotsky and the Jews* (Philadelphia, 1972), pp. 211–220.

Internationalist that he was, Trotsky bitterly opposed such nationalist schemes. But by 1937 he realized that European Jews were doomed, and he conceded the need to protect them in their own region although he described the Birobidzhan plan as "a bureaucratic farce."

74. Cf. Irving Howe, *The World of Our Fathers* (New York, 1976), pp. 15 ff., 70 ff., 101 f.; Milton Hindus, *The Old East Side* (Philadelphia, 1969), pp. 89 f. and passim; Moses Rischin, *The Promised City* (Cambridge, Mass., 1967).

75. Morris Raphael Cohen, *A Dreamer's Journey* (Boston, 1949), p. 98.

76. From *The Autobiography of Lincoln Steffens*, quoted in Hindus, op. cit., pp. 89 f.

77. Cf. Arthur Hertzberg, *The Zionist Idea* (Garden City, N.Y., 1959).

78. Ibid., pp. 109 f., quoted from a letter written in 1836 to the Berlin branch of the Rothschild family.

79. Cf. Pinsker, *Auto-Emancipation* (New York, 1944), pp. 76 f; 78 f., 82, 105, and passim.

80. Cf. Herzl, *The Jewish State* (New York, 1943), pp. 20 f., 42 f., 87, 92, 103 f., and passim.

81. Quoted in Richard Gottheil's *Zionism* (Philadelphia, 1914), pp. 103 f. Not all German Jews subscribed to this anti-Zionist platform. Max Bodenheimer and a small group of associates anticipated Herzl and founded the National-jüdische Vereinigung (July 11, 1897), later renamed the Zionistische Vereinigung für Deutschland. See Stephen M. Poppel, *Zionism in Germany 1897–1933* (Philadelphia, 1976), pp. 21 ff.

82. Cited in Plaut's *The Growth of Reform Judaism*, pp. 153 ff.

83. See Hertzberg, *The Zionist Idea*, pp. 331–366.

84. See Alex Bein, *Theodore Herzl* (Philadelphia, 1956), pp. 417 ff., 453–490; *The Diaries of Theodor Herzl*, ed. and translated by Marvin Lowenthal (New York, 1956), pp. 408 f.; Chaim Weizmann, *Trial and Error* (New York, 1949), pp. 83–88; Howard Sachar, *A History of Israel* (New York, 1976), pp. 3–77. It was the Uganda episode that convinced Herzl that the Jewish state would have to be Erez Yisrael and no other place. See his *Diary* entry for August 31, 1903, in Lowenthal's edition of his *Diary*, pp. 408 f.

85. Cf. Moses Hess, *Rome and Jerusalem* (New York, 1943), pp. 105, 143 f., etc.

86. Ibid., pp. 99 ff., 143 f., 162 ff., and passim.

87. See Aḥad Ha-Am's "Torah Sheba-Lev" in his *Complete Works* (Hebrew) (Tel Aviv, 1953), p. 53.

88. See Aḥad Ha-Am, *Complete Works*, pp. 28, 79–91, 130–181; *Collected Essays*, translated by Leon Simon (Philadelphia, 1912), pp. 121 ff., 181 ff., and passim.

89. Cf. Isidore Meyer (ed.), *Early History of Zionism in America* (New York, 1958); Israel Cohen, *The Zionist Movement* (New York, 1946), pp. 326–346; *Zionism*, ed. by the staff of the *Encyclopaedia Judaica* (Jerusalem, 1973), pp. 209–222.

90. These are the results of the survey by Dr. Fred Massarik for the Council of Jewish Federations. See my discussion thereof in my essay, "Jewish Religion in America: A Study in Mutuality," cited in note 13, pp. 290 f.

91. On the differences between "élite" and "folk" religion, cf. Charles Lieb-

man, *The Ambivalent American Jew* (Philadelphia, 1973), pp. 42–87. Cf. also my *Four Paths to One God*, pp. 271–276.

92. See Eugene Borowitz, *A New Jewish Theology in the Making* (Philadelphia, 1968), p. 46.

93. See their *Beyond the Melting Pot* (Cambridge, Mass., 1970), pp. 163, 180.

94. Cf. Leonard Fein et al., "Reform Is a Verb," in Marshall Sklare (ed.), *The Jewish Community in America* (New York, 1974), pp. 115–127.

SELECTED BIBLIOGRAPHY

Bleich, J. David. *Contemporary Halakhic Problems.* New York, 1977.

Davis, Moshe. *The Emergence of Conservative Judaism.* Philadelphia, 1968.

Freehof, Solomon B. *Reform Responsa for Our Time.* Cincinnati, 1977.

Gordis, Robert. *Understanding Conservative Judaism.* New York, 1978.

Goren, Arthur. *New York Jews and the Quest for Community.* New York, 1971.

Hertzberg, Arthur. *The French Enlightenment and the Jews.* New York, 1968.

———. *The Zionist Idea.* Garden City, N.Y., 1959.

Himmelfarb, Milton, ed. *The Condition of Jewish Belief.* New York, 1966.

Howe, Irving. *The World of Our Fathers.* New York, 1976.

Lamm, Norman, and Wurzburger, Walter S., eds. *A Treasury of Tradition.* New York, 1969.

Philipson, David. *The Reform Movement in Judaism,* New York, 1976.

Plaut, W. Gunther. *The Growth of Reform Judaism.* New York, 1965.

———. *The Rise of Reform Judaism.* New York, 1963.

Rosenbloom, Noah. *Tradition in an Age of Reform.* Philadelphia, 1976.

Rosenthal, Gilbert S. *Four Paths to One God.* New York, 1973.

Siegel, Seymour, ed. *Conservative Judaism and Jewish Law.* New York, 1977.

Waxman, Mordecai, ed. *Tradition and Change.* New York, 1958.

Contributors

STEVEN BAYME has taught at Yeshiva University, The Jewish Theological Seminary of America, and Hebrew Union College. He pursued his graduate and undergraduate education at Columbia University. Dr. Bayme's doctoral dissertation is entitled "Jewish Leadership and Anti-Semitism in Britain 1898–1918." His M.A. essay on "Conceptions of History in Zionist Thought" received an award from the Association for Jewish Studies.

SAMUEL H. DRESNER serves as Rabbi of the Moriah Congregation in Deerfield, Illinois. He received his Doctorate of Hebrew Letters from The Jewish Theological Seminary of America. He has served as editor of *Conservative Judaism*, and is the author of various works, including *Levi Yitzhak of Berditchev: Portrait of a Hasidic Master* and *The Zaddik*.

RAPHAEL JOSPE is Assistant Professor of Judaic Studies and Coordinator of the Center for Judaic Studies at the University of Denver. He pursued his undergraduate and graduate education at Brandeis University and the Hebrew University of Jerusalem, and received his Ph.D. in Medieval Jewish Philosophy from Brandeis. Co-editor of this volume and the author of several articles in Jewish philosophy and thought, he is also co-editor of *Go and Study: Essays and Studies in Honor of Alfred Jospe* and is preparing a book on the life and philosophy of Shem Tov ibn Falaquera.

DANIEL J. LASKER is Lecturer in Jewish Philosophy at the Ben Gurion University of the Negev, and previously taught at the University of Texas. He pursued his graduate and undergraduate education at Brandeis University and the Hebrew University of

255

Jerusalem, and received his Ph.D. from Brandeis. A specialist in medieval Jewish philosophy, Jewish-Christian relations, biblical commentaries, as well as Karaism, Dr. Lasker is the author of *Jewish Philosophical Polemics Against Christianity in the Middle Ages.*

GILBERT S. ROSENTHAL serves as Rabbi of Temple Beth El in Cedarhurst, New York. He received his Doctorate of Hebrew Letters from The Jewish Theological Seminary of America, and M.A. in History from Columbia University. He pursued his undergraduate training at Yeshiva University. Dr. Rosenthal's publications include *Four Paths to One God, Banking and Finance Among Jews in Renaissance Italy,* and *The American Rabbi.*

LAWRENCE H. SCHIFFMAN is Associate Professor of Hebrew and Director of Graduate Studies in the Department of Near Eastern Languages and Literatures of New York University. He pursued his graduate and undergraduate studies at Brandeis University, where he received his Ph.D. in Near Eastern and Judaic Studies. A specialist in the Dead Sea Scrolls, Dr. Schiffman's publications include *The Halakhah at Qumran.* He has also published articles on the use of computers in preparing critical editions of Rabbinic texts.

STANLEY M. WAGNER, co-editor of this volume, serves as Rabbi of the B.M.H. Congregation in Denver, Colorado, and is Director of the Center for Judaic Studies at the University of Denver. He pursued his undergraduate and graduate education at Yeshiva University, where he received his Doctorate of Hebrew Letters. Dr. Wagner is author of *A Piece of My Mind* and is editor of *Traditions of the American Jew* and co-editor of *Great Confrontations in Jewish History.*

Index

Index prepared by Ted Koppel, Penrose Library, University of Denver.